Designing with the Mind in Mind

Simple Guide to Understanding
User Interface Design Guidelines

Second Edition

Designing with the Mind in Mind

Simple Guide to Understanding
User Interface Design Guidelines

Second Edition

Jeff Johnson

AMSTERDAM • BOSTON • HEIDELBERG • LONDON
NEW YORK • OXFORD • PARIS • SAN DIEGO
SAN FRANCISCO • SINGAPORE • SYDNEY • TOKYO

Morgan Kaufmann is an imprint of Elsevier

Acquiring Editor: Meg Dunkerley
Editorial Project Manager: Heather Scherer
Project Manager: Priya Kumaraguruparan
Designer: Matthew Limbert

Morgan Kaufmann is an imprint of Elsevier
225 Wyman Street, Waltham, MA, 02451, USA

Notices
Knowledge and best practice in this field are constantly changing. As new research and experience
broaden our understanding, changes in research methods or professional practices, may become
necessary. Practitioners and researchers must always rely on their own experience and knowledge in
evaluating and using any information or methods described herein. In using such information or
methods they should be mindful of their own safety and the safety of others, including parties for
whom they have a professional responsibility. To the fullest extent of the law, neither the Publisher nor
the authors, contributors, or editors, assume any liability for any injury and/or damage to persons or
property as a matter of products liability,negligence or otherwise, or from any use or operation of any
methods, products, instructions, or ideas contained in the material herein.

Library of Congress Cataloging-in-Publication Data
Application submitted

British Library Cataloguing-in-Publication Data
A catalogue record for this book is available from the British Library

ISBN: 978-0-12-407914-4

For information on all Morgan Kaufmann publications,
visit our Web site at www.mkp.com

Working together
to grow libraries in
developing countries

www.elsevier.com • www.bookaid.org

Contents

Acknowledgments

I could not have written this book without a lot of help and the support of many people.

First are the students of the human–computer interaction course I taught as an Erskine Fellow at the University of Canterbury in New Zealand in 2006. It was for them that I developed a lecture providing a brief background in perceptual and cognitive psychology—just enough to enable them to understand and apply user-interface design guidelines. That lecture expanded into a professional development course, then into the first edition of this book. My need to prepare more comprehensive psychological background for an upper-level course in human–computer interaction that I taught at the University of Canterbury in 2013 provided motivation for expanding the topics covered and improving the explanations in this second edition.

Second, I thank my colleagues at the University of Canterbury who provided ideas, feedback on my ideas, and illustrations for the second edition's new chapter on Fitts' law: Professor Andy Cockburn, Dr. Sylvain Malacria, and Mathieu Nancel. I also thank my colleague and friend Professor Tim Bell for sharing user-interface examples and for other help while I was at the university working on the second edition.

Third, I thank the reviewers of the first edition—Susan Fowler, Robin Jeffries, Tim McCoy, and Jon Meads—and of the second edition—Susan Fowler, Robin Jeffries, and James Hartman. They made many helpful comments and suggestions that allowed me to greatly improve the book.

Fourth, I am grateful to four cognitive science researchers who directed me to important references, shared useful illustrations with me, or allowed me to bounce ideas off of them:

- Professor Edward Adelson, Department of Brain and Cognitive Sciences, Massachusetts Institute of Technology.

- Professor Dan Osherson, Department of Psychology, Princeton University.

- Dr. Dan Bullock, Department of Cognitive and Neural Systems, Boston University.

- Dr. Amy L. Milton, Department of Psychology and Downing College, University of Cambridge.

The book also was helped greatly by the care, oversight, logistical support, and nurturing provided by the staff at Elsevier, especially Meg Dunkerley, Heather Scherer, Lindsay Lawrence, and Priya Kumaraguruparan.

Last but not least, I thank my wife and friend Karen Ande for her love and support while I was researching and writing this book.

Foreword

It is gratifying to see this book go into a second edition because of the endorsement that implies for maturing the field of human–computer interaction beyond pure empirical methods.

Human–computer interaction (HCI) as a topic is basically simple. There is a person of some sort who wants to do some task like write an essay or pilot an airplane. What makes the activity HCI is inserting a mediating computer. In principle, our person could have done the task without the computer. She could have used a quill pen and ink, for example, or flown an airplane that uses hydraulic tubes to work the controls. These are not quite HCI. They do use intermediary tools or machines, and the process of their design and the facts of their use bear resemblance to those of HCI. In fact, they fit into HCI's uncle discipline of human factors. But it is the computer, and the process of contingent interaction the computer renders possible, that makes HCI distinctive.

The computer can transform a task's representation and needed skills. It can change the linear writing process into something more like sculpturing, the writer roughing out the whole, then adding or subtracting bits to refine the text. It can change the piloting process into a kind of supervision, letting the computer with inputs of speed, altitude, and location and outputs of throttle, flap, and rudder, do the actual flying. And if instead of one person we have a small group or a mass crowd, or if instead of a single computer we have a network of communicating mobile or embedded computers, or if instead of a simple task we have impinging cultural or coordination considerations, then we get the many variants of computer mediation that form the broad spectrum of HCI.

The components of a discipline of HCI would also seem simple. There is an artifact that must be engineered and implemented. There is the process of design for the interaction itself and the objects, virtual or physical, with which to interact. Then there are all the principles, abstractions, theories, facts, and phenomena surrounding HCI to know about. Let's call the first *interaction engineering* (e.g., using Harel statecharts to guide implementation), the second, *interaction design* (e.g., the design of the workflow for a smartphone to record diet), and the third, perhaps a little overly grandly, *interaction science* (e.g., the use of Fitts' law to design button sizes in an application). The hard bit for HCI is that fitting these three together is not easy. Beside work in HCI itself, each has its own literature not friendly to outsiders. The present book was written to bridge the gap between the relevant science that has been built up from the psychological literature and HCI design problems where the science could be of use.

Actually, the importance of linking engineering, design, and science together in HCI goes deeper. HCI is a technology. As Brian Arthur in his book *The Nature of*

Technology tells us, technologies largely derive from other technologies, not science. The flat panel displays now common are a substitute for CRT devices of yore, and these go back to modified radar screens on the Whirlwind computer. Furthermore, technologies are composed of parts that are themselves technologies. A laptop computer has a display for output and a key and a touchpad for input and several storage systems, and so on, each with its own technologies. But eventually all these technologies ground out in some phenomenon of nature that is not a technology, and here is a place where science plays a role. Some keyboard input devices use the natural phenomenon of electrical capacitance to sense keystrokes. Pressing a key brings two D-shaped pads close to a printed circuit board that is covered by an insulating film, thereby changing the pattern of capacitance. That is to say, this keyboard harnesses the natural phenomenon of capacitance in a reliable way that can be exploited to provide the HCI function of signaling an intended interaction to the computer.

Many natural phenomena are easy to understand and exploit by simple observation or modest tinkering. No science needed. But some, like capacitance, are much less obvious, and then you really need science to understand them. In some cases, the HCI system that is built generates its own phenomena, and you need science to understand the unexpected, emergent properties of seemingly obvious things. People sometimes believe that because they can intuitively understand the easy cases (e.g., with usability testing), they can understand all the cases. But this is not necessarily true. The natural phenomena to be exploited in HCI range from abstractions of computer science, such as the notion of the working set, to psychological theories of human cognition, perception, and movement, such as the nature of vision. Psychology, the area addressed by this book, is an area with an especially messy and at times contradictory literature, but it is also especially rich in phenomena that can be exploited for HCI technology.

I think it is underappreciated how important it is for the future development of HCI as a discipline that the field develops a supporting science base as illustrated by the current book for the field of psychology. It also involves HCI growing some of its own science bits.

Why is this important? There are at least three reasons. First, having some sort of theory enables *explanatory evaluation*. The use of A-B testing is limited if you don't know why there was a difference. On the other hand, if you have a theory that lets you interpret the difference, then you can fix it. You will never understand the problems of why a windows-based user interface can take excessive time to use by doing usability testing, for example, if you don't have the theoretical concept of the window working set. Second, it enables *generative design*. It allows a shift in representation of the design space. Once it is realized that a very important property of pointing devices is the bandwidth of the human motor group to which a transducer is going to be applied, then the problem gets reformulated to terms of how to connect those muscles and the consequence for the rest of the design. Third, it supports the *codification of knowledge*. Only by having theories and abstractions can we concisely cumulate our results and develop a field with sufficient power and depth.

Why isn't there wider use of science or theory in HCI? There are obvious reasons, like the fact that it isn't easy to get the relevant science linkages or results in the first place, that it's hard to make the connection with science in almost any engineering field, and that often the connection is made, but invisibly packaged, in a way that nonspecialists never need to see it. The poet tosses capacitance with his finger, but only knows he writes a poem. He thinks he writes with love, because someone understood electricity.

But, mainly, I think there isn't wider use of science or theory in HCI because it is difficult to put that knowledge into a form that is easily useful at the time of design need. Jeff Johnson in this book is careful to connect theory with design choice, and to do it in a practical way. He has accumulated grounded design rules that reach across the component parts of HCI, making it easier for designers as they design to keep them in mind.

Stuart K. Card

Introduction

USER-INTERFACE DESIGN RULES: WHERE DO THEY COME FROM AND HOW CAN THEY BE USED EFFECTIVELY?

For as long as people have been designing interactive computer systems, some have attempted to promote *good* design by publishing user-interface design guidelines (also called design rules). Early ones included:

- **Cheriton** (1976) proposed user-interface design guidelines for early interactive (time-shared) computer systems.

- **Norman** (1983a, 1983b) presented design rules for software user interfaces based on human cognition, including cognitive errors.

- **Smith and Mosier** (1986) wrote perhaps the most comprehensive set of user-interface design guidelines.

- **Shneiderman** (1987) included "Eight Golden Rules of Interface Design" in the first edition of his book *Designing the User Interface* and in all later editions.

- **Brown** (1988) wrote a book of design guidelines, appropriately titled *Human–Computer Interface Design Guidelines.*

- **Nielsen and Molich** (1990) offered a set of design rules for use in heuristic evaluation of user interfaces, and Nielsen and Mack (1994) updated them.

- **Marcus** (1992) presented guidelines for graphic design in online documents and user interfaces.

In the twenty-first century, additional user-interface design guidelines have been offered by Stone et al. (2005); Koyani et al. (2006); Johnson (2007); and Shneiderman and Plaisant (2009). Microsoft, Apple Computer, and Oracle publish guidelines for designing software for their platforms (Apple Computer, 2009; Microsoft Corporation, 2009; Oracle Corporation/Sun Microsystems, 2001).

How valuable are user-interface design guidelines? That depends on who applies them to design problems.

USER-INTERFACE DESIGN AND EVALUATION REQUIRES UNDERSTANDING AND EXPERIENCE

Following user-interface design guidelines is not as straightforward as following cooking recipes. Design rules often describe goals rather than actions. They are purposefully very general to make them broadly applicable, but that means that their exact meaning and applicability to specific design situations is open to interpretation.

Complicating matters further, more than one rule will often seem applicable to a given design situation. In such cases, the applicable design rules often conflict— that is, they suggest different designs. This requires designers to determine which competing design rule is more applicable to the given situation and should take precedence.

Design problems, even without competing design guidelines, often have multiple conflicting goals. For example:

* Bright screen *and* long battery life

* Lightweight *and* sturdy

* Multifunctional *and* easy to learn

* Powerful *and* simple

* High resolution *and* fast loading

* WYSIWYG (what you see is what you get) *and* usable by blind people

Satisfying all the design goals for a computer-based product or service usually requires tradeoffs—lots and lots of tradeoffs. Finding the right balance point between competing design rules requires further tradeoffs.

Given all of these complications, user-interface design rules and guidelines must be applied thoughtfully, not mindlessly, by people who are skilled in the art of user-interface design and/or evaluation. User-interface design rules and guidelines are more like *laws* than like *rote recipes*. Just as a set of laws is best applied and interpreted by lawyers and judges who are well versed in the laws, a set of user-interface design guidelines is best applied and interpreted by people who understand the basis for the guidelines and have learned from experience in applying them.

Unfortunately, with a few exceptions (e.g., Norman, 1983a), user-interface design guidelines are provided as simple lists of design edicts with little or no rationale or background.

Furthermore, although many early members of the user-interface design and usability profession had backgrounds in cognitive psychology, most newcomers to the field do not. That makes it difficult for them to apply user-interface design guidelines sensibly. Providing that rationale and background education is the focus of this book.

COMPARING USER-INTERFACE DESIGN GUIDELINES

Table I.1 places the two best-known user-interface guideline lists side by side to show the types of rules they contain and how they compare to each other (see the Appendix for additional guidelines lists). For example, both lists start with a rule calling for consistency in design. Both lists include a rule about preventing errors. The

Table I.1 Two Best-Known Lists of User-Interface Design Guidelines	
Shneiderman (1987); Shneiderman and Plaisant (2009)	**Nielsen and Molich (1990)**
Strive for consistency	Consistency and standards
Cater to universal usability	Visibility of system status
Offer informative feedback	Match between system and real world
Design task flows to yield closure	User control and freedom
Prevent errors	Error prevention
Permit easy reversal of actions	Recognition rather than recall
Make users feel they are in control	Flexibility and efficiency of use
Minimize short-term memory load	Aesthetic and minimalist design
	Help users recognize, diagnose, and recover from errors
	Provide online documentation and help

Nielsen-Molich rule to "help users recognize, diagnose, and recover from errors" corresponds closely to the Shneiderman-Plaisant rule to "permit easy reversal of actions." "User control and freedom" corresponds to "make users feel they are in control." There is a reason for this similarity, and it isn't just that later authors were influenced by earlier ones.

WHERE DO DESIGN GUIDELINES COME FROM?

For present purposes, the detailed design rules in each set of guidelines, such as those in Table I.1, are less important than what they have in common: their basis and origin. Where did these design rules come from? Were their authors—like clothing fashion designers—simply trying to impose their own personal design tastes on the computer and software industries?

If that were so, the different sets of design rules would be very different from each other, as the various authors sought to differentiate themselves from the others. In fact, all of these sets of user-interface design guidelines are quite similar if we ignore differences in wording, emphasis, and the state of computer technology when each set was written. Why?

The answer is that all of the design rules are based on human psychology: how people perceive, learn, reason, remember, and convert intentions into action. Many authors of design guidelines had at least some background in psychology that they applied to computer system design.

For example, Don Norman was a professor, researcher, and prolific author in the field of cognitive psychology long before he began writing about human-computer interaction. Norman's early human-computer design guidelines were based on research—his own and others'—on human cognition. He was especially interested in cognitive errors that people often make and how computer systems can be designed to lessen or eliminate the impact of those errors.

Similarly, other authors of user-interface design guidelines—for example, Brown, Shneiderman, Nielsen, and Molich—used knowledge of perceptual and cognitive psychology to try to improve the design of usable and useful interactive systems.

Bottom line: User-interface design guidelines are based on human psychology.

By reading this book, you will learn the most important aspects of the psychology underlying user-interface and usability design guidelines.

INTENDED AUDIENCE OF THIS BOOK

This book is intended mainly for software design and development professionals who have to apply user-interface and interaction design guidelines. This includes interaction designers, user-interface designers, user-experience designers, graphic designers, and hardware product designers. It also includes usability testers and evaluators, who often refer to design heuristics when reviewing software or analyzing observed usage problems.

A second intended audience is students of interaction design and human–computer interaction. A third intended audience is software development managers who want enough of a background in the psychological basis of user-interface design rules to understand and evaluate the work of the people they manage.

Our Perception is Biased

Our perception of the world around us is not a true depiction of what is actually there. Our perceptions are heavily biased by at least three factors:

- **The past:** our experience
- **The present:** the current context
- **The future:** our goals

PERCEPTION BIASED BY EXPERIENCE

Experience—your past perceptions—can bias your current perception in several different ways.

Perceptual priming

Imagine that you own a large insurance company. You are meeting with a real estate manager, discussing plans for a new campus of company buildings. The campus consists of a row of five buildings, the last two with T-shaped courtyards providing light for the cafeteria and fitness center. If the real estate manager showed you the map in Figure 1.1, you would see five black shapes representing the buildings.

Now imagine that instead of a real estate manager, you are meeting with an advertising manager. You are discussing a new billboard ad to be placed in certain markets around the country. The advertising manager shows you the same image, but in this scenario the image is a sketch of the ad, consisting of a single word: LIFE. In this scenario, you see a word, clearly and unambiguously.

When your perceptual system has been *primed* to see building shapes, you see building shapes, and the white areas between the buildings barely register in your perception. When your perceptual system has been primed to see text, you see text, and the black areas between the letters barely register.

FIGURE 1.1

Building map or word? What you see depends on what you were told to see.

FIGURE 1.2

Image showing the effect of mental priming of the visual system. What do you see?

A relatively famous example of how priming the mind can affect perception is an image, supposedly by R. C. James,[1] that initially looks to most people like a random splattering of paint (see Fig. 1.2) similar to the work of the painter Jackson Pollack. Before reading further, look at the image.

Only after you are told that it is a Dalmatian dog sniffing the ground near a tree can your visual system organize the image into a coherent picture. Moreover, once you've seen the dog, it is hard to go back to seeing just a random collection of spots.

---

[1] Published in Lindsay and Norman (1972), Figure 3-17, p. 146.

These priming examples are visual, but priming can also bias other types of perception, such as sentence comprehension. For example, the headline "New Vaccine Contains Rabies" would probably be understood differently by people who had recently heard stories about contaminated vaccines than by people who had recently heard stories about successful uses of vaccines to fight diseases.

Familiar perceptual patterns or frames

Much of our lives are spent in familiar situations: the rooms in our homes, our yards, our routes to and from school or work, our offices, neighborhood parks, stores, restaurants, etc. Repeated exposure to each type of situation builds a pattern in our minds of what to expect to see there. These *perceptual patterns*, which some researchers call *frames*, include the objects or events that are usually encountered in that situation.

For example, you know most rooms in your home well enough that you need not constantly scrutinize every detail. You know how they are laid out and where most objects are located. You can probably navigate much of your home in total darkness. But your experience with homes is broader than your specific home. In addition to having a pattern for your home, your brain has one for homes in general. It biases your perception of all homes, familiar and new. In a kitchen, you expect to see a stove and a sink. In a bathroom, you expect to see a toilet, a sink, and a shower or a bathtub (or both).

Mental frames for situations bias our perception to see the objects and events expected in each situation. They are a mental shortcut: by eliminating the need for us to constantly scrutinize every detail of our environment, they help us get around in our world. However, mental frames also make us see things that aren't really there.

For example, if you visit a house in which there is no stove in the kitchen, you might nonetheless later recall seeing one, because your mental frame for kitchens has a strong stove component. Similarly, part of the frame for eating at a restaurant is paying the bill, so you might recall paying for your dinner even if you absentmindedly walked out without paying. Your brain also has frames for back yards, schools, city streets, business offices, supermarkets, dentist visits, taxis, air travel, and other familiar situations.

Anyone who uses computers, websites, or smartphones has frames for the desktop and files, web browsers, websites, and various types of applications and online services. For example, when they visit a new Web site, experienced Web users expect to see a site name and logo, a navigation bar, some other links, and maybe a search box. When they book a flight online, they expect to specify trip details, examine search results, make a choice, and make a purchase.

Because of the perceptual frames users of computer software and websites have, they often click buttons or links without looking carefully at them. Their perception of the display is based more on what their frame for the situation leads them to expect than on what is actually on the screen. This sometimes confounds software designers, who expect users to see what is on the screen—but that isn't how human vision works.

FIGURE 1.3

The "Next" button is perceived to be in a consistent location, even when it isn't.

For example, if the positions of the "Next" and "Back" buttons on the last page of a multistep dialog box[2] switched, many people would not immediately notice the switch (see Fig. 1.3). Their visual system would have been lulled into inattention by the consistent placement of the buttons on the prior several pages. Even after unintentionally going backward a few times, they might continue to perceive the buttons

---

[2] Multistep dialog boxes are called *wizards* in user-interface designer jargon.

in their standard locations. This is why consistent placement of controls is a common user-interface guideline, to ensure that reality matches the user's frame for the situation.

Similarly, if we are trying to find something but it is in a different place or looks different from usual, we might miss it even though it is in plain view because our mental frames tune us to look for expected features in expected locations. For example, if the "Submit" button on one form in a Web site is shaped differently or is a different color from those on other forms on the site, users might not find it. This expectation-induced blindness is discussed more later in this chapter in the "Perception Biased by Goals" section.

Habituation

A third way in which experience biases perception is called *habituation*. Repeated exposure to the same (or highly similar) perceptions dulls our perceptual system's sensitivity to them. Habituation is a very low-level phenomenon of our nervous system: it occurs at a neuronal level. Even primitive animals like flatworms and amoeba, with very simple nervous systems, habituate to repeated stimuli (e.g., mild electric shocks or light-flashes). People, with our complex nervous systems, habituate to a range of events, from low-level ones like a continually beeping tone, to medium-level ones like a blinking ad on a Web site, to high-level ones like a person who tells the same jokes at every party or a politician giving a long, repetitious speech.

We experience habituation in computer usage when the same error messages or "Are you sure?" confirmation messages appear again and again. People initially notice them and perhaps respond, but eventually click them closed reflexively without bothering to read them.

Habituation is also a factor in a recent phenomenon variously labeled "social media burnout" (Nichols, 2013), "social media fatigue," or "Facebook vacations" (Rainie et al., 2013): newcomers to social media sites and tweeting are initially excited by the novelty of microblogging about their experiences, but sooner or later get tired of wasting time reading tweets about every little thing that their "friends" do or see—for example, "Man! Was that ever a great salmon salad I had for lunch today."

Attentional blink

Another low-level biasing of perception by past experience occurs just after we spot or hear something important. For a very brief period following the recognition—between 0.15 and 0.45 second—we are nearly deaf and blind to other visual stimuli, even though our ears and eyes stay functional. Researchers call this the *attentional blink* (Raymond et al., 1992, Stafford and Webb, 2005).[3] It is thought to be caused by the brain's perceptual and attention mechanisms being briefly fully occupied with processing the first recognition.

---

[3] Chapter 14 discusses the attentional blink interval in the context of other perceptual intervals.

A classic example: You are in a subway car as it enters a station, planning to meet two friends at that station. As the train arrives, your car passes one of your friends, and you spot him briefly through your window. In the next split second, your window passes your other friend, but you fail to notice her because her image hit your retina during the attentional blink that resulted from your recognition of your first friend.

When people use computer-based systems and online services, attentional blink can cause them to miss information or events if things appear in rapid succession. A popular modern technique for making documentary videos is to present a series of still photographs in rapid succession.[4] This technique is highly prone to attentional blink effects: if an image really captures your attention (e.g., it has a strong meaning for you), you will probably miss one or more of the immediately following images. In contrast, a captivating image in an auto-running slideshow (e.g., on a Web site or an information kiosk) is unlikely to cause attentional blink (i.e., missing the next image) because each image typically remains displayed for several seconds.

PERCEPTION BIASED BY CURRENT CONTEXT

When we try to understand how our visual perception works, it is tempting to think of it as a bottom-up process, combining basic features such as edges, lines, angles, curves, and patterns into figures and ultimately into meaningful objects. To take reading as an example, you might assume that our visual system first recognizes shapes as letters and then combines letters into words, words into sentences, and so on.

But visual perception—reading in particular—is not strictly a bottom-up process. It includes top-down influences too. For example, the word in which a character appears may affect how we identify the character (see Fig. 1.4).

Similarly, our overall comprehension of a sentence or a paragraph can even influence what words we see in it. For example, the same letter sequence can be read as different words depending on the meaning of the surrounding paragraph (see Fig. 1.5).

Contextual biasing of vision need not involve reading. The Müller–Lyer illusion is a famous example (see Fig. 1.6): the two horizontal lines are the same length, but the outward-pointing "fins" cause our visual system to see the top line as longer than the

THE CHT

FIGURE 1.4

The same character is perceived as H or A depending on the surrounding letters.

---

[4] For an example, search YouTube for "history of the world in two minutes."

Fold napkins. *Polish silverware.* Wash dishes.

French napkins. *Polish silverware.* German dishes.

FIGURE 1.5

The same phrase is perceived differently depending on the list it appears in.

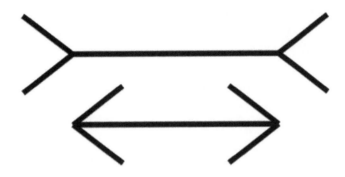

FIGURE 1.6

Müller–Lyer illusion: equal-length horizontal lines appear to have different lengths.

line with inward-pointing "fins." This and other optical illusions (see Fig. 1.7) trick us because our visual system does not use accurate, optimal methods to perceive the world. It developed through evolution, a semi-random process that layers jury-rigged—often incomplete and inaccurate—solutions on top of each other. It works fine most of the time, but it includes a lot of approximations, kludges, hacks, and outright "bugs" that cause it to fail in certain cases.

The examples in Figures 1.6 and 1.7 show vision being biased by *visual* context. However, biasing of perception by the current context works *between* different senses too. Perceptions in any of our five senses may affect simultaneous perceptions in any of our other senses. What we feel with our tactile sense can be biased by what we hear, see, or smell. What we see can be biased by what we hear, and what we hear can be biased by what we see. The following two examples of visual perception affect what we hear:

- ***McGurk effect.*** If you watch a video of someone saying "bah, bah, bah," then "dah, dah, dah," then "vah, vah, vah," but the audio is "bah, bah, bah" throughout, you will hear the syllable indicated by the speaker's lip movement rather than the syllable actually in the audio track.[5] Only by closing or averting your eyes do you hear the syllable as it really is. I'll bet you didn't know you could read lips, and in fact do so many times a day.

[5] Go to YouTube, search for "McGurk effect," and view (and hear) some of the resulting videos.

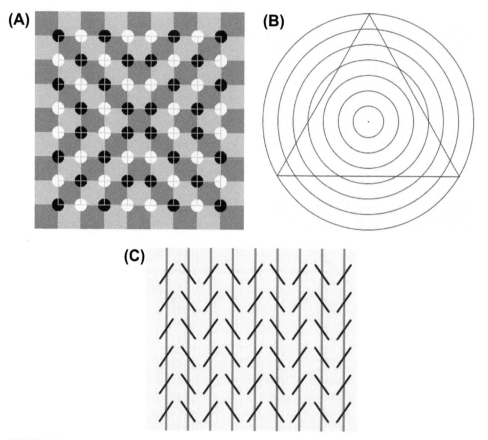

FIGURE 1.7

(A) The checkboard does *not* bulge in the middle; (B) the triangle sides are *not* bent; and (C) the red vertical lines are parallel.

- ***Ventriloquism.*** Ventriloquists don't throw their voice; they just learn to talk without moving their mouths much. Viewers' brains perceive the talking as coming from the nearest moving mouth: that of the ventriloquist's puppet (Eagleman, 2012).

An example of the opposite—hearing biasing vision—is the illusory flash effect. When a spot is flashed *once* briefly on a display but is accompanied by *two* quick beeps, it appears to flash twice. Similarly, the perceived rate of a blinking light can be adjusted by the frequency of a repeating click (Eagleman, 2012).

Later chapters explain how visual perception, reading, and recognition function in the human brain. For now, I will simply say that the pattern of neural activity that corresponds to recognizing a letter, a word, a face, or any object includes input from neural activity stimulated by the context. This context includes other nearby perceived objects and events, and even reactivated memories of previously perceived objects and events.

Context biases perception not only in people but also in lower animals. A friend of mine often brought her dog with her in her car when running errands. One day, as she drove into her driveway, a cat was in the front yard. The dog saw it and began barking. My friend opened the car door and the dog jumped out and ran after the cat, which turned and jumped through a bush to escape. The dog dove into the bush but missed the cat. The dog remained agitated for some time afterward.

Thereafter, for as long as my friend lived in that house, whenever she arrived at home with her dog in the car, he would get excited, bark, jump out of the car as soon as the door was opened, dash across the yard, and leap into the bush. There was no cat, but that didn't matter. Returning home in the car was enough to make the dog see one—perhaps even smell one. However, walking home, as the dog did after being taken for his daily walk, did not evoke the "cat mirage."

PERCEPTION BIASED BY GOALS

In addition to being biased by our past experience and the present context, our perception is influenced by our goals and plans for the future. Specifically, our goals:

- *Guide* our perceptual apparatus, so we sample what we need from the world around us.

- *Filter* our perceptions: things unrelated to our goals tend to be filtered out preconsciously, never registering in our conscious minds.

For example, when people navigate through software or a Web site, seeking information or a specific function, they don't read carefully. They scan screens quickly and superficially for items that seem related to their goal. They don't simply ignore items unrelated to their goals; they often don't even notice them.

To see this, glance at Figure 1.8 and look for scissors, and then immediately flip back to this page. Try it now.

Did you spot the scissors? Now, without looking back at the toolbox, can you say whether there is a screwdriver in the toolbox too?

Our goals filter our perceptions in other perceptual senses as well as in vision. A familiar example is the "cocktail party" effect. If you are conversing with someone at a crowded party, you can focus your attention to hear mainly what he or she is saying even though many other people are talking near you. The more interested you are in the conversation, the more strongly your brain filters out surrounding chatter. If you are bored by what your conversational partner is saying, you will probably hear much more of the conversations around you.

The effect was first documented in studies of air-traffic controllers, who were able to carry on a conversation with the pilots of their assigned aircraft even though

FIGURE 1.8

Toolbox: Are there scissors here?

many different conversations were occurring simultaneously on the same radio frequency, coming out of the same speaker in the control room (Arons, 1992). Research suggests that our ability to focus on one conversation among several simultaneous ones depends not only on our interest level in the conversation, but also on objective factors, such as the similarity of voices in the cacophony, the amount of general "noise" (e.g., clattering dishes or loud music), and the predictability of what your conversational partner is saying (Arons, 1992).

This filtering of perception by our goals is particularly true for adults, who tend to be more focused on goals than children are. Children are more stimulus-driven: their perception is less filtered by their goals. This characteristic makes them more distractible than adults, but it also makes them less biased as observers.

A parlor game demonstrates this age difference in perceptual filtering. It is similar to the Figure 1.8 exercise. Most households have a catch-all drawer for kitchen implements or tools. From your living room, send a visitor to the room where the catch-all drawer is, with instructions to fetch you a specific tool, such as measuring spoons or a pipe wrench. When the person returns with the tool, ask whether another specific tool was in the drawer. Most adults will not know what else was in the drawer. Children—if they can complete the task without being distracted by all the cool stuff in the drawer—will often be able to tell you more about what else was there.

Perceptual filtering can also be seen in how people navigate websites. Suppose I put you on the homepage of New Zealand's University of Canterbury (see Fig. 1.9) and asked you to find information about financial support for postgraduate students in the computer science department. You would scan the page and probably quickly click one of the links that share words with the goal that I gave you: Departments (top left), Scholarships (middle), then Postgraduate Students (bottom left) or Postgraduate (right). If you're a "search" person, you might instead go right to the Search box (top right), type words related to the goal, and click "Go."

Whether you browse or search, it is likely that you would leave the homepage without noticing that you were randomly chosen to win $100 (bottom right). Why? Because that was not related to your *goal*.

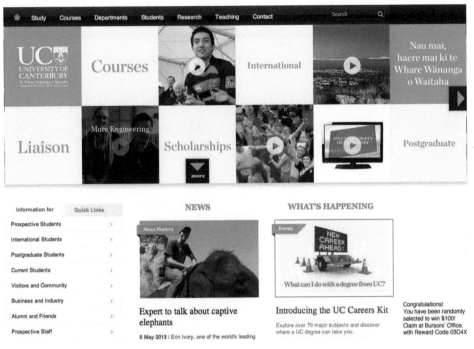

FIGURE 1.9

University of Canterbury Web site: navigating sites requires perceptual filtering.

What is the mechanism by which our current goals bias our perception? There are two:

- ***Influencing where we look.*** Perception is active, not passive. Think of your perceptual senses not as simply *filtering* what comes to you, but rather as *reaching out* into the world and *pulling in* what you need to perceive. Your hands, your primary touch sensors, literally do this, but the rest of your senses do it too. You constantly move your eyes, ears, hands, feet, body, and attention so as to sample exactly the things in your environment that are most relevant to what you are doing or about to do (Ware, 2008). If you are looking on a Web site for a campus map, your eyes and pointer-controlling hand are attracted to anything that might lead you to that goal. You more or less ignore anything unrelated to your goal.

- ***Sensitizing our perceptual system to certain features.*** When you are looking for something, your brain can prime your perception to be especially sensitive to features of what you are looking for (Ware, 2008). For example, when you are looking for a red car in a large parking lot, red cars will seem to pop out as you scan the lot, and cars of other colors will barely register in your consciousness, even though you do in some sense see them. Similarly, when you are trying to find your spouse in a dark, crowded room, your brain "programs" your auditory system to be especially sensitive to the combination of frequencies that make up his or her voice.

TAKING BIASED PERCEPTION INTO ACCOUNT WHEN DESIGNING

All these sources of perceptual bias of course have implications for user-interface design. Here are three.

Avoid ambiguity

Avoid ambiguous information displays, and test your design to verify that all users interpret the display in the same way. Where ambiguity is unavoidable, either rely on standards or conventions to resolve it, or prime users to resolve the ambiguity in the intended way.

For example, computer displays often shade buttons and text fields to make them look raised in relation to the background surface (see Fig. 1.10). This appearance relies on a convention, familiar to most experienced computer users, that the light source is at the top left of the screen. If an object were depicted as lit by a light source in a different location, users would not see the object as raised.

Be consistent

Place information and controls in consistent locations. Controls and data displays that serve the same function on different pages should be placed in the same position on each page on which they appear. They should also have the same color, text fonts, shading, and so on. This consistency allows users to spot and recognize them quickly.

Understand the goals

Users come to a system with goals they want to achieve. Designers should understand those goals. Realize that users' goals may vary, and that their goals strongly influence what they perceive. Ensure that at every point in an interaction, the information users need is available, prominent, and maps clearly to a possible user goal, so users will notice and use the information.

FIGURE 1.10

Buttons on computer screens are often shaded to make them look three dimensional, but the convention works only if the light source is assumed to be on the top left.

Our Vision is Optimized to See Structure

2

Early in the twentieth century, a group of German psychologists sought to explain how human visual perception works. They observed and catalogued many important visual phenomena. One of their basic findings was that human vision is holistic: our visual system automatically imposes structure on visual input and is wired to perceive whole shapes, figures, and objects rather than disconnected edges, lines, and areas. The German word for "shape" or "figure" is *Gestalt,* so these theories became known as the *Gestalt principles of visual perception*.

Today's perceptual and cognitive psychologists regard the Gestalt theory of perception as more of a *descriptive* framework than an *explanatory* and *predictive* theory. Today's theories of visual perception tend to be based heavily on the neurophysiology of the eyes, optic nerve, and brain (see Chapters 4-7).

Not surprisingly, the findings of neurophysiological researchers support the observations of the Gestalt psychologists. We really are—along with other animals—"wired" to perceive our surroundings in terms of whole objects (Stafford and Webb, 2005; Ware, 2008). Consequently, the Gestalt principles are still valid—if not as a fundamental explanation of visual perception, at least as a framework for describing it. They also provide a useful basis for guidelines for graphic design and user-interface design (Soegaard, 2007).

For present purposes, the most important Gestalt principles are Proximity, Similarity, Continuity, Closure, Symmetry, Figure/Ground, and Common Fate. The following sections describe each principle and provide examples from both static graphic design and user-interface design.

GESTALT PRINCIPLE: PROXIMITY

The Gestalt principle of *Proximity* is that the relative distance between objects in a display affects our perception of whether and how the objects are organized into

FIGURE 2.1

Proximity: items that are closer appear grouped as rows (A) and columns (B).

FIGURE 2.2

In Outlook's Distribution List Membership dialog box, list buttons are in a group box, separate from the control buttons.

subgroups. Objects that are near each other (relative to other objects) appear grouped, while those that are farther apart do not.

In Figure 2.1A, the stars are closer together horizontally than they are vertically, so we see three rows of stars, while the stars in Figure 2.1B are closer together vertically than they are horizontally, so we see three columns.

The Proximity principle has obvious relevance to the layout of control panels or data forms in software, Web sites, and electronic appliances. Designers often separate groups of on-screen controls and data displays by enclosing them in group boxes or by placing separator lines between groups (see Fig. 2.2).

However, according to the Proximity principle, items on a display can be visually grouped simply by spacing them closer to each other than to other controls, without group boxes or visible borders (see Fig. 2.3). Many graphic design experts recommend this approach to reduce visual clutter and code size in a user interface (Mullet and Sano, 1994).

FIGURE 2.3

In Mozilla Thunderbird's Subscribe Folders dialog box, controls are grouped using the Proximity principle.

FIGURE 2.4

In Discreet's Software Installer, poorly spaced radio buttons look grouped in vertical columns.

Conversely, if controls are poorly spaced (e.g., if connected controls are too far apart) people will have trouble perceiving them as related, making the software harder to learn and remember. For example, the Discreet Software Installer displays six horizontal pairs of radio buttons, each representing a two-way choice, but their spacing, due to the Proximity principle, makes them appear to be two vertical sets of radio buttons, each representing a six-way choice, at least until users try them and learn how they operate (see Fig. 2.4).

GESTALT PRINCIPLE: SIMILARITY

Another factor that affects our perception of grouping is expressed in the Gestalt principle of *Similarity*, where objects that look similar appear grouped, all other things being equal. In Figure 2.5, the slightly larger, "hollow" stars are perceived as a group.

The Page Setup dialog box in Mac OS applications uses the Similarity and Proximity principles to convey groupings (see Fig. 2.6). The three very similar and tightly spaced Orientation settings are clearly intended to appear grouped. The three menus are not so tightly spaced but look similar enough that they appear related even though that probably wasn't intended.

Similarly, the text fields in a form at book publisher Elsevier's Web site are organized into an upper group of eight for the name and address, a group of three split fields for phone numbers, and two single text fields. The four menus, in addition to being data fields, help separate the text field groups (see Fig. 2.7). By contrast, the labels are too far from their fields to seem connected to them.

FIGURE 2.5

Similarity: items appear grouped if they look more similar to each other than to other objects.

FIGURE 2.6

Mac OS Page Setup dialog box. The Similarity and Proximity principles are used to group the Orientation settings.

FIGURE 2.7

Similarity makes the text fields appear grouped in this online form at Elsevier.com.

GESTALT PRINCIPLE: CONTINUITY

In addition to the two Gestalt principles concerning our tendency to organize objects into groups, several Gestalt principles describe our visual system's tendency to resolve ambiguity or fill in missing data in such a way as to perceive whole objects. The first such principle, the principle of *Continuity,* states that our visual perception is biased to perceive continuous forms rather than disconnected segments.

For example, in Figure 2.8A, we automatically see two crossing lines—one blue and one orange. We don't see two separate orange segments and two separate blue ones, and we don't see a blue-and-orange V on top of an upside-down orange-and-blue V. In Figure 2.8B, we see a sea monster in water, not three pieces of one.

A well-known example of the use of the continuity principle in graphic design is the IBM® logo. It consists of disconnected blue patches, and yet it is not at all ambiguous; it is easily seen as three bold letters, perhaps viewed through something like venetian blinds (see Fig. 2.9).

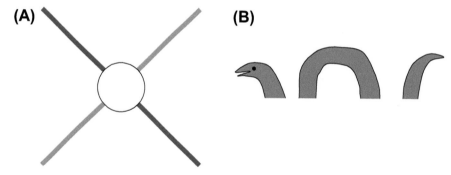

FIGURE 2.8

Continuity: Human vision is biased to see continuous forms, even adding missing data if necessary.

FIGURE 2.9

The IBM company logo uses the Continuity principle to form letters from disconnected patches.

FIGURE 2.10

Continuity: we see a slider as a single slot with a handle somewhere on it, not as two slots separated by a handle: (A) Mac OS and (B) ComponentOne.

Slider controls are a user-interface example of the Continuity principle. We see a slider as depicting a single range controlled by a handle that appears somewhere on the slider, not as two separate ranges separated by the handle (see Fig. 2.10A). Even displaying different colors on each side of a slider's handle doesn't completely "break" our perception of a slider as one continuous object, although ComponentOne's choice of strongly contrasting colors (gray vs. red) certainly strains that perception a bit (see Fig. 2.10B).

GESTALT PRINCIPLE: CLOSURE

Related to Continuity is the Gestalt principle of *Closure*, which states that our visual system automatically tries to close open figures so that they are perceived as whole objects rather than separate pieces. Thus, we perceive the disconnected arcs in Figure 2.11A as a circle.

Our visual system is so strongly biased to see objects that it can even interpret a totally blank area as an object. We see the combination of shapes in Figure 2.11B as a white triangle overlapping another triangle and three black circles, even though the figure really only contains three V shapes and three black pac-men.

The Closure principle is often applied in graphical user interfaces (GUIs). For example, GUIs often represent collections of objects (e.g., documents or messages) as *stacks* (see Fig. 2.12). Just showing one whole object and the edges of others "behind" it is enough to make users perceive a stack of objects, all whole.

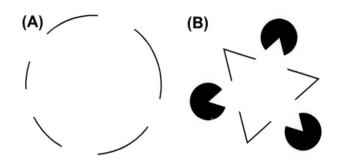

FIGURE 2.11

Closure: Human vision is biased to see whole objects, even when they are incomplete.

FIGURE 2.12

Icons depicting stacks of objects exhibit the Closure principle: partially visible objects are perceived as whole.

GESTALT PRINCIPLE: SYMMETRY

A third fact about our tendency to see objects is captured in the Gestalt principle of *Symmetry*. It states that we tend to parse complex scenes in a way that reduces the complexity. The data in our visual field usually has more than one possible interpretation, but our vision automatically organizes and interprets the data so as to simplify it and give it symmetry.

For example, we see the complex shape on the far left of Figure 2.13 as two overlapping diamonds, not as two touching corner bricks or a pinch-waist octahedron with a square in its center. A pair of overlapping diamonds is simpler than the other two interpretations shown on the right—it has fewer sides and more symmetry than the other two interpretations.

In printed graphics and on computer screens, our visual system's reliance on the symmetry principle can be exploited to represent three-dimensional objects on a two-dimensional display. This can be seen in a cover illustration for Paul Thagard's book *Coherence in Thought and Action* (Thagard, 2002; see Fig. 2.14) and in a three-dimensional depiction of a cityscape (see Fig. 2.15).

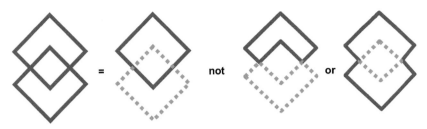

FIGURE 2.13

Symmetry: the human visual system tries to resolve complex scenes into combinations of simple, symmetrical shapes.

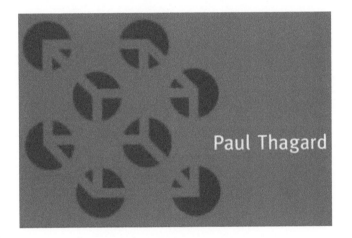

FIGURE 2.14

The cover of the book *Coherence in Thought and Action* (Thagard, 2002) uses the symmetry, Closure, and Continuity principles to depict a cube.

GESTALT PRINCIPLE: FIGURE/GROUND

The next Gestalt principle that describes how our visual system structures the data it receives is *Figure/Ground*. This principle states that our mind separates the visual field into the figure (the foreground) and ground (the background). The foreground consists of the elements of a scene that are the object of our primary attention, and the background is everything else.

The Figure/Ground principle also specifies that the visual system's parsing of scenes into figure and ground is influenced by characteristics of the scene. For example, when a small object or color patch overlaps a larger one, we tend to perceive the smaller object as the figure and the larger object as the ground (see Fig. 2.16).

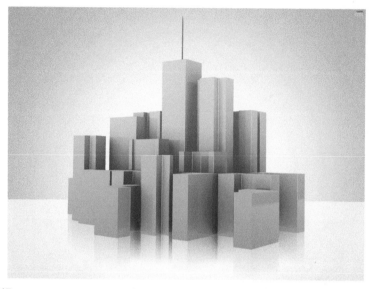

FIGURE 2.15

Symmetry: the human visual system parses very complex two-dimensional images into three-dimensional scenes.

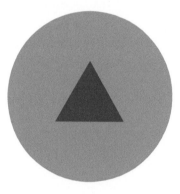

FIGURE 2.16

Figure/Ground: when objects overlap, we see the smaller as the figure and the larger as the ground.

However, our perception of figure versus ground is not completely determined by scene characteristics. It also depends on the viewer's focus of attention. Dutch artist M. C. Escher exploited this phenomenon to produce ambiguous images in which figure and ground switch roles as our attention shifts (see Fig. 2.17).

In user-interface and Web design, the Figure/Ground principle is often used to place an impression-inducing background "behind" the primary displayed content

FIGURE 2.17

M. C. Escher exploited figure/ground ambiguity in his art.

FIGURE 2.18

Figure/Ground is used at AndePhotos.com to display a thematic watermark "behind" the content.

(see Fig. 2.18). The background can convey information (e.g., the user's current location), or it can suggest a theme, brand, or mood for interpretation of the content.

Figure/Ground is also often used to pop up information over other content. Content that was formerly the figure—the focus of the users' attention—temporarily becomes the *background* for new information, which appears briefly as the new

FIGURE 2.19

Figure/Ground is used at PBS.org's mobile Web site to pop up a call-to-action "over" the page content.

figure (see Fig. 2.19). This approach is usually better than temporarily *replacing* the old information with the new information, because it provides context that helps keep people oriented regarding their place in the interaction.

GESTALT PRINCIPLE: COMMON FATE

The previous six Gestalt principles concerned perception of static (unmoving) figures and objects. One final Gestalt principle—Common Fate—concerns moving objects. The cCommon Fate principle is related to the Proximity and Similarity principles—like them, it affects whether we perceive objects as grouped. The Common Fate principle states that objects that move together are perceived as grouped or related.

For example, in a display showing dozens of pentagons, if seven of them wiggled in synchrony, people would see them as a related group, even if the wiggling pentagons were separated from each other and looked no different from all the other pentagons (see Fig. 2.20).

Common motion—implying common fates—is used in some animations to show relationships between entities. For example, Google's GapMinder graphs animate dots representing nations to show changes over time in various factors of economic development. Countries that move together share development histories (see Fig. 2.21).

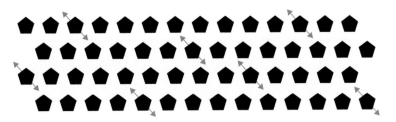

FIGURE 2.20

Common Fate: items appear grouped or related if they move together.

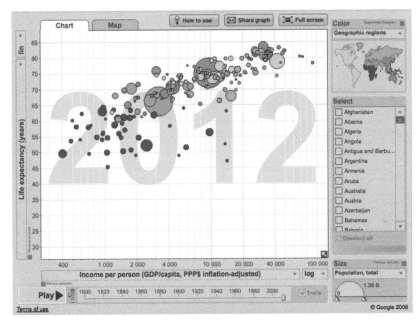

FIGURE 2.21

Common fate: GapMinder animates dots to show which nations have similar development histories (for details, animations, and videos, visit GapMinder.org).

GESTALT PRINCIPLES: COMBINED

Of course, in real-world visual scenes, the Gestalt principles work in concert, not in isolation. For example, a typical Mac OS desktop usually exemplifies six of the seven principles described here, excluding Common Fate): Proximity, Similarity, Continuity, Closure, Symmetry, and Figure/Ground (see Fig. 2.22). On a typical desktop, Common Fate is used (along with similarity) when a user selects several files or folders and drags them as a group to a new location (see Fig. 2.23).

FIGURE 2.22

All of the Gestalt principles except Common Fate play a role in this portion of a Mac OS desktop.

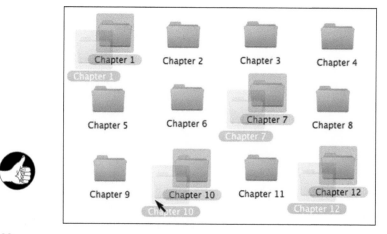

FIGURE 2.23

Similarity and Common Fate: when users drag folders that they have selected, common highlighting and motion make the selected folders appear grouped.

With all these Gestalt principles operating at once, *unintended* visual relationships can be implied by a design. A recommended practice, after designing a display, is to view it with each of the Gestalt principles in mind—Proximity, Similarity, Continuity, Closure, Symmetry, Figure/Ground, and Common Fate—to see if the design suggests any relationships between elements that you do *not* intend.

We Seek and Use Visual Structure

3

Chapter 2 used the Gestalt principles of visual perception to show how our visual system is optimized to perceive structure. Perceiving structure in our environment helps us make sense of objects and events quickly. Chapter 2 also mentioned that when people are navigating through software or Web sites, they don't scrutinize screens carefully and read every word. They scan quickly for relevant information. This chapter presents examples to show that when information is presented in a terse, structured way, it is easier for people to scan and understand.

Consider two presentations of the same information about an airline flight reservation. The first presentation is unstructured prose text; the second is structured text in outline form (see Fig. 3.1). The structured presentation of the reservation can be scanned and understood much more quickly than the prose presentation.

Unstructured:

You are booked on United flight 237, which departs from Auckland at 14:30 on Tuesday 15 Oct and arrives at San Francisco at 11:40 on Tuesday 15 Oct.

Structured:

Flight: **United 237, Auckland → San Francisco**
 Depart: **14:30   Tue 15 Oct**
 Arrive: **11:40   Tue 15 Oct**

FIGURE 3.1

Structured presentation of airline reservation information is easier to scan and understand.

The more structured and terse the presentation of information, the more quickly and easily people can scan and comprehend it. Look at the Contents page from the California Department of Motor Vehicles (see Fig. 3.2). The wordy, repetitive links slow users down and "bury" the important words they need to see.

Renewals, Duplicates, and Information Changes for Driver Licenses and/or ID Cards

- How to renew your driver license in person
- How to renew your driver license by mail
- How to renew your driver license by Internet
- How to renew your instruction permit
- How to apply for a duplicate driver license or identification (ID) card
- How to change your name on your driver license and/or identification (ID) card
- How to notify DMV of my change of address
- How to register for the organ donor gift of life program

FIGURE 3.2

Contents page at the California Department of Motor Vehicles (DMV) Web site buries the important information in repetitive prose.

Licenses & ID Cards:	Renewals, Duplicates, Changes		
• Renew license:	in person	by mail	by Internet
• Renew:	instruction permit		
• Apply for duplicate:	license	ID card	
• Change of:	name	address	
• Register as:	organ donor		

FIGURE 3.3

California DMV Web site Contents page with repetition eliminated and better visual structure.

Compare that with a terser, more structured hypothetical design that factors out needless repetition and marks as links only the words that represent options (see Fig. 3.3). All options presented in the actual Contents page are available in the revision, yet it consumes less screen space and is easier to scan.

Displaying search results is another situation in which structuring data and avoiding repetitive "noise" can improve people's ability to scan quickly and find what they seek. In 2006, search results at HP.com included so much repeated navigation data and metadata for each retrieved item that they were useless. By 2009, HP had eliminated the repetition and structured the results, making them easier to scan and more useful (see Fig. 3.4).

Of course, for information displays to be easy to scan, it is not enough merely to make them terse, structured, and nonrepetitious. They must also conform to the rules of graphic design, some of which were presented in Chapter 2.

For example, a prerelease version of a mortgage calculator on a real estate Web site presented its results in a table that violated at least two important rules of graphic design (see Fig. 3.5A). First, people usually read (online or offline) from top to bottom, but the labels for calculated amounts were *below* their corresponding values. Second, the labels were just as close to the value below as to their own

(A)

Search: color laser printer

Search results

» Buy HP **Color** LaserJet 1600 **Printer**(CB373A#ABA), HP **color laser printers**, HP LaserJets, HP **printers**, **Printers** direct from the ...
Buy HP **Color** LaserJet 1600 **Printer**(CB373A#ABA), HP **color laser printers**, HP LaserJets, HP **printers**, **Printers** direct from the HP Home & Home Office Store. On a budget but want ...
2006-12-05

» Buy HP **Color** LaserJet 4700dn **Printer**(Q7493A#ABA), HP **color laser printers**, HP LaserJets, HP **printers**, **Printers** direct from ..
Buy HP **Color** LaserJet 4700dn **Printer**(Q7493A#ABA), HP **color laser printers**, HP LaserJets, HP **printers**, **Printers** direct from the HP Home & Home Office Store. Get ready to deliver ...
2006-12-20

» Buy HP **Color** LaserJet 4700n **Printer**(Q7492A#ABA), HP **color laser printers**, HP LaserJets, HP **printers**, **Printers** direct from ..
Buy HP **Color** LaserJet 4700n **Printer**(Q7492A#ABA), HP **color laser printers**, HP LaserJets, HP **printers**, **Printers** direct from the HP Home & Home Office Store. Classy, brilliantly ...
2006-12-20

» Buy supplies for **Color laser** speciality paper, Paper for **laser printers**, Paper direct from the HP Home & Home Office Store
Buy supplies for **Color laser** speciality paper, Paper for **laser printers**, Paper direct from the HP Home & Home Office Store. Hewlett Packard computer and **printer** store. Shop for, ...
2006-12-09

» Buy supplies for **Color laser** speciality paper, Paper for **laser printers**, Paper, Printing supplies direct from the HP Home & ...
Buy supplies for **Color laser** speciality paper, Paper for **laser printers**, Paper, Printing supplies direct from the HP Home & Home Office Store. Hewlett Packard computer and **printer** ...
2006-12-06

(B)

Search: color laser printer

Search results

» HP® Official Store — Buy an HP Tri-fold **Color Laser** Glossy Brochure Paper (150 sheets, 8.5 x 11-inch) (Q6612A) from HP
Why outsource brochure printing when you can do it expertly on your own **laser printer**, in small batches tailored to your unique projects and clients? Ideal for use with HP **Color** ...

» **Color Laser Printers** At a glance - HP Small & Medium Business products
Summary of all HP **Color Laser Printers** currently available for purchase and recommended for Small & Medium Business. Includes links to compare products, obtain more information about a ...

» HP **Color** laserjets - **color laser printers** for large business - HP Large Enterprise Business
HP Large Enterprise Business - Find and compare **color laser printers**. Review the business features of HP **Color** LaserJets

» HP® Official Store — **Color** laser speciality paper, Paper for **laser** printers, Paper
Use these papers with your HP **Color** LaserJet **printer** for outsource-quality marketing materials and photos

» HP Press Release: Hewlett-Packard **Color** LaserJet 4550 Family Establishes New Generation of Internet-enabled **Color Laser** ...
Successor to the World's Best-selling **Color Laser Printer** Features Embedded Web Technologies Designed to Improve Ease of Use and Manageability.

» **Laser Printers**, Inkjet Printers, Photo Printers - HP
Choose from a wide variety of dependable HP **printers**, including **laser printers** and ink **printers**, all in one/multifunction **printers** and photo **printers**.

FIGURE 3.4

In 2006, HP.com's site search produced repetitious, "noisy" results (A), but by 2009 was improved (B).

(A)

Mortgage Summary

$1,840.59	**$662,611.22**
Monthly Payment	Total of 360 Payments
$318,861.22	**Sep, 2037**
Total Interest Paid	Pay-off Date
$93,750.00	**$0.00**
Total Tax Paid	Total PMI Paid

(B)

Mortgage Summary	
Monthly Payment	$ 1,840.59
Number of Payments	360
Total of Payments	$ 662,611.22
Interest Total	$ 318,861.22
Tax Total	$ 93,750.00
PMI Total	$ 0.00
Pay-off Date	Sep 2037

FIGURE 3.5

(A) Mortgage summary presented by a software mortgage calculator; (B) an improved design.

value, so proximity (see Chapter 2) could not be used to perceive that labels were grouped with their values. To understand this mortgage results table, users had to scrutinize it carefully and slowly figure out which labels went with which numbers.

The revised design, in contrast, allows users to perceive the correspondence between labels and values without conscious thought (see Fig. 3.5B).

STRUCTURE ENHANCES PEOPLE'S ABILITY TO SCAN LONG NUMBERS

Even small amounts of information can be made easier to scan if they are structured. Two examples are telephone numbers and credit card numbers (see Fig. 3.6). Traditionally, such numbers were broken into parts to make them easier to scan and remember.

A long number can be broken up in two ways: either the user interface breaks it up explicitly by providing a separate field for each part of the number, or the interface provides a single number field but lets users break the number into parts with spaces or punctuation (see Fig. 3.7A). However, many of today's computer presentations of phone and credit card numbers do not segment the numbers and do not

Easy:	(415) 123-4567
Hard:	4151234567
Easy:	1234 5678 9012 3456
Hard:	1234567890123456

FIGURE 3.6

Telephone and credit card numbers are easier to scan and understand when segmented.

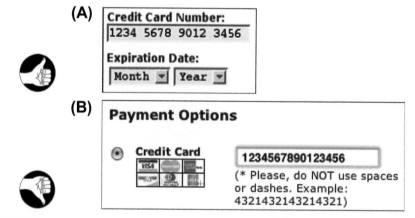

FIGURE 3.7

(A) At Democrats.org, credit card numbers can include spaces. (B) At StuffIt.com, they cannot, making them harder to scan and verify.

Date of Birth
You must be at least 18 years of age and either a United States citizen or a permanent resident of the U.S., or at least 21 years of age and a permanent resident of Puerto Rico.   ☐ / ☐ / ☐   *MM/DD/YYYY*

FIGURE 3.8

At BankOfAmerica.com, segmented data fields provide useful structure.

allow users to include spaces or other punctuation (see Fig. 3.7B). This limitation makes it harder for people to scan a number or verify that they typed it correctly, and so is considered a user-interface design blooper (Johnson, 2007). Forms presented in software and Web sites should accept credit card numbers, social security numbers, phone numbers, and so on in a variety of different formats and parse them into the internal format.

Segmenting data fields can provide useful visual structure even when the data to be entered is not, strictly speaking, a number. Dates are an example of a case in which segmented fields can improve readability and help prevent data entry errors, as shown by a date field at Bank of America's Web site (see Fig. 3.8).

DATA-SPECIFIC CONTROLS PROVIDE EVEN MORE STRUCTURE

A step up in structure from segmented data fields are data-specific controls. Instead of using simple text fields—whether segmented or not—designers can use controls that are designed specifically to display (and accept as input) a value of a specific type. For example, dates can be presented (and accepted) in the form of menus combined with pop-up calendar controls (see Fig. 3.9).

It is also possible to provide visual structure by mixing segmented text fields with data-specific controls, as demonstrated by an email address field at Southwest Airlines' Web site (see Fig. 3.10).

Depart
Oct ⬍ 21 ⬍ ▦
Morning ⬍

FIGURE 3.9

At NWA.com, dates are displayed and entered using a control that is specifically designed for dates.

FIGURE 3.10

At SWA.com email addresses are entered into fields structured to accept parts of the address.

VISUAL HIERARCHY LETS PEOPLE FOCUS ON THE RELEVANT INFORMATION

One of the most important goals in structuring information presentations is to provide a visual hierarchy—an arrangement that:

- Breaks the information into distinct sections, and breaks large sections into subsections.

- Labels each section and subsection prominently and in such a way as to clearly identify its content.

- Presents the sections and subsections as a hierarchy, with higher-level sections presented more strongly than lower-level ones.

A visual hierarchy allows people, when scanning information, to instantly separate what is relevant to their goals from what is irrelevant, and to focus their attention on the relevant information. They find what they are looking for more quickly because they can easily skip everything else.

Try it for yourself. Look at the two information displays in Figure 3.11 and find the information about prominence. How much longer does it take you to find it in the nonhierarchical presentation?

(A)

Create a Clear Visual Hierarchy

Organize and prioritize the contents of a page by using size, prominence, and content relationships. Let's look at these relationships more closely. The more important a headline is, the larger its font size should be. Big bold headlines help to grab the user's attention as they scan the Web page. The more important the headline or content, the higher up the page it should be placed. The most important or popular content should always be positioned prominently near the top of the page, so users can view it without having to scroll too far. Group similar content types by displaying the content in a similar visual style, or in a clearly defined area.

(B)

Create a Clear Visual Hierarchy

Organize and prioritize the contents of a page by using size, prominence, and content relationships.

Let's look at these relationships more closely:

- **Size.** The more important a headline is, the larger its font size should be. Big bold headlines help to grab the user's attention as they scan the Web page.

- **Prominence.** The more important the headline or content, the higher up the page it should be placed. The most important or popular content should always be positioned prominently near the top of the page, so users can view it without having to scroll too far.

- **Content Relationships.** Group similar content types by displaying the content in a similar visual style, or in a clearly defined area.

FIGURE 3.11

Find the advice about prominence in each of these displays. Prose text format (A) makes people read everything. Visual hierarchy (B) lets people ignore information irrelevant to their goals.

FIGURE 3.12

Visual hierarchy in interactive control panels and forms lets users find settings quickly: (A) Band-in-a-Box (bad) and (B) GarageBand (good).

The examples in Figure 3.11 show the value of visual hierarchy in a textual, read-only information display. Visual hierarchy is equally important in interactive control panels and forms—perhaps even more so. Compare dialog boxes from two different music software products (see Fig. 3.12). The Reharmonize dialog box of Band-in-a-Box has poor visual hierarchy, making it hard for users to find things quickly. In contrast, GarageBand's Audio/MIDI control panel has good visual hierarchy, so users can quickly find the settings they are interested in.

Used by permission, www.OK/Cancel.com.

Our Color Vision is Limited

4

Human color perception has both strengths and limitations, many of which are relevant to user-interface design. For example:

- Our vision is optimized to detect contrasts (edges), not absolute brightness.
- Our ability to distinguish colors depends on how colors are presented.
- Some people have color-blindness.
- The user's display and viewing conditions affect color perception.

To understand these qualities of human color vision, let's start with a brief description of how the human visual system processes color information from the environment.

HOW COLOR VISION WORKS

If you took introductory psychology or neurophysiology in college, you probably learned that the retina at the back of the human eye—the surface onto which the eye focuses images—has two types of light receptor cells: rods and cones. You probably also learned that the rods detect light levels but not colors, while the cones detect colors. Finally, you probably learned that there are three types of cones—sensitive to red, green, and blue light—suggesting that our color vision is similar to video cameras and computer displays, which detect or project a wide variety of colors through combinations of red, green, and blue pixels.

What you learned in college is only partly right. People with normal vision do in fact have rods and three types of cones[1] in their retinas. The rods are sensitive to overall brightness while the three types of cones are sensitive to different

---

[1] People with color-blindness may have fewer than three, and some women have four, cone types (Eagleman, 2012).

frequencies of light. But that is where the truth departs from what most people learned in college, until recently.

First, those of us who live in industrialized societies hardly use our rods at all. They function only at low levels of light. They are for getting around in poorly lighted environments—the environments our ancestors lived in until the nineteenth century. Today, we use our rods only when we are having dinner by candlelight, feeling our way around our dark house at night, camping outside after dark, etc. (see Chapter 5). In bright daylight and modern artificially lighted environments—where we spend most of our time—our rods are completely maxed out, providing no useful information. Most of the time, our vision is based entirely on input from our cones (Ware, 2008).

So how do our cones work? Are the three types of cones sensitive to red, green, and blue light, respectively? In fact, each type of cone is sensitive to a wider range of light frequencies than you might expect, and the sensitivity ranges of the three types overlap considerably. In addition, the overall sensitivity of the three types of cones differs greatly (see Fig. 4.1A):

- **Low frequency.** These cones are sensitive to light over almost the entire range of visible light, but are most sensitive to the middle (yellow) and low (red) frequencies.

- **Medium frequency.** These cones respond to light ranging from the high-frequency blues through the lower middle-frequency yellows and oranges. Overall, they are less sensitive than the low-frequency cones.

- **High frequency.** These cones are most sensitive to light at the upper end of the visible light spectrum—violets and blues—but they also respond weakly to middle frequencies, such as green. These cones are much less sensitive overall than the other two types of cones, and also less numerous. One result is that our eyes are much less sensitive to blues and violets than to other colors.

Compare a graph of the light sensitivity of our retinal cone cells (Fig. 4.1A) to what the graph might look like if electrical engineers had designed our retinas as a mosaic of receptors sensitive to red, green, and blue, like a camera (Fig. 4.1B).

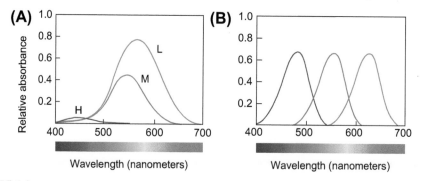

FIGURE 4.1

Sensitivity of the three types of retinal cones (A) versus artificial red, green, and blue receptors (B).

Given the odd relationships among the sensitivities of our three types of retinal cone cells, one might wonder how the brain combines the signals from the cones to allow us to see a broad range of colors.

The answer is by *subtraction*. Neurons in the visual cortex at the back of our brain subtract the signals coming over the optic nerves from the medium- and low-frequency cones, producing a red–green *difference* signal channel. Other neurons in the visual cortex subtract the signals from the high- and low-frequency cones, yielding a yellow–blue *difference* signal channel. A third group of neurons in the visual cortex *adds* the signals coming from the low- and medium-frequency cones to produce an overall luminance (or black–white) signal channel.[2] These three channels are called *color-opponent channels*.

The brain then applies additional subtractive processes to all three color-opponent channels: signals coming from a given area of the retina are effectively subtracted from similar signals coming from nearby areas of the retina.

VISION IS OPTIMIZED FOR CONTRAST, NOT BRIGHTNESS

All this subtraction makes our visual system much more sensitive to differences in color and brightness—that is, to contrasting colors and edges—than to absolute brightness levels.

To see this, look at the inner bar in Figure 4.2. The inner bar looks darker on the right, but in fact is one solid shade of gray. To our contrast-sensitive visual system, it looks lighter on the left and darker on the right because the outer rectangle is darker on the left and lighter on the right.

The sensitivity of our visual system to contrast rather than to absolute brightness is an advantage: it helped our distant ancestors recognize a leopard in the nearby bushes as the same dangerous animal whether they saw it in bright noon sunlight or in the early morning hours of a cloudy day. Similarly, being sensitive to color

FIGURE 4.2

The inner gray bar looks darker on the right, but in fact is all one shade of gray.

---

[2] The overall brightness sum omits the signal from the high-frequency (blue–violet) cones. Those cones are so insensitive that their contribution to the total would be negligible, so omitting them makes little difference.

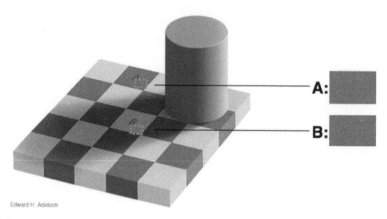

Edward H. Adelson

FIGURE 4.3

The squares marked A and B are the same gray. We see B as white because it is shaded from the cylinder's shadow.

contrasts rather than to absolute colors allows us to see a rose as the same red whether it is in the sun or the shade.

Brain researcher Edward H. Adelson at the Massachusetts Institute of Technology developed an outstanding illustration of our visual system's insensitivity to absolute brightness and its sensitivity to contrast (see Fig. 4.3). As difficult as it may be to believe, square A on the checkerboard is exactly the same shade as square B. Square B only appears white because it is depicted as being in the cylinder's shadow.

THE ABILITY TO DISCRIMINATE COLORS DEPENDS ON HOW COLORS ARE PRESENTED

Even our ability to detect differences between colors is limited. Because of how our visual system works, three presentation factors affect our ability to distinguish colors from each other:

- *Paleness.* The paler (less saturated) two colors are, the harder it is to tell them apart (see Fig. 4.4A).

- *Color patch size.* The smaller or thinner objects are, the harder it is to distinguish their colors (see Fig. 4.4B). Text is often thin, so the exact color of text is often hard to determine.

- *Separation.* The more separated color patches are, the more difficult it is to distinguish their colors, especially if the separation is great enough to require eye motion between patches (see Fig. 4.4C).

Several years ago, the online travel website ITN.net used two pale colors—white and pale yellow—to indicate which step of the reservation process the user was on (see Fig. 4.5). Some site visitors couldn't see which step they were on.

(A)   **(B)**   **(C)**

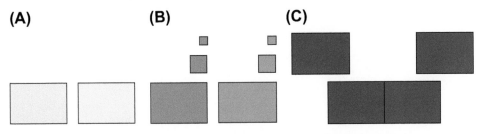

FIGURE 4.4

Factors affecting ability to distinguish colors: (A) paleness, (B) size, and (C) separation.

FIGURE 4.5

The pale color marking the current step makes it hard for users to see which step in the airline reservation process they are on in ITN.net's 2003 website.

FIGURE 4.6

Tiny color patches in this chart legend are hard to distinguish.

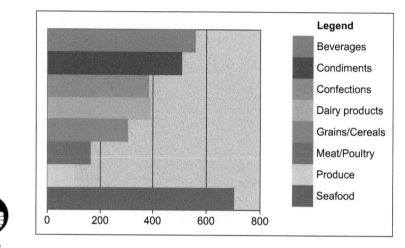

FIGURE 4.7

Large color patches make it easier to distinguish the colors.

- <u>Housing Units Authorized</u>, Percent Change October 2005 Year-to-Date Compared With a Year Earlier
- <u>Electricity Consumption per Capita, 2001</u>
- <u>Drinking and Wastewater Needs per Capita</u>, 2003 Dollars
- <u>Manufactured Homes as a Percent of Total Homes</u>, 2000
- <u>Percent of Occupied Housing Units That Are Owner Occupied</u>
- <u>Percent Change in Private Employment Due to Growth/Decline in Establishments, 2000-2001</u>
- <u>Labor-Force Participation Rate</u>, 2002
- <u>Number of Bank Offices per 10,000 People</u>, 2003
- <u>Total Foreign-Born</u>, 2000
- <u>Retail Gasoline Prices</u>, May 17, 2004
- <u>Total Manufactured Exports per Capita</u>, 2003
- <u>House Price Index,</u> Percent Change-Third Quarter 2002 to Third Quarter 2003
- <u>State and Local Government Per Capita General Fund Expenditure, 1977-2000</u>

FIGURE 4.8

The difference in color between visited and unvisited links is too subtle in MinneapolisFed.org's website.

Small color patches are often seen in data charts and plots. Many business graphics packages produce legends on charts and plots, but make the color patches in the legend very small (see Fig. 4.6). Color patches in chart legends should be large to help people distinguish the colors (see Fig. 4.7).

On websites, a common use of color is to distinguish unfollowed links from already followed ones. On some sites, the "followed" and "unfollowed" colors are too similar. The website of the Federal Reserve Bank of Minneapolis (see Fig. 4.8) has this problem. Furthermore, the two colors are shades of blue, the color range in which our eyes are least sensitive. Can you spot the two followed links?[3]

---

[3] Already followed links in Figure 4.8: Housing Units Authorized and House Price Index.

COLOR-BLINDNESS

A fourth factor of color presentation that affects design principles for interactive systems is whether the colors can be distinguished by people who have common types of color-blindness. Having color-blindness doesn't mean an inability to see colors. It just means that one or more of the color subtraction channels (see the "How Color Vision Works" section) don't function normally, making it difficult to distinguish certain pairs of colors. Approximately 8% of men and slightly under 0.5% of women have a color perception deficit: difficulty discriminating certain pairs of colors (Wolfmaier, 1999). The most common type of color-blindness is red–green; other types are much rarer. Figure 4.9 shows color pairs that people with red–green color-blindness have trouble distinguishing.

FIGURE 4.9

Red–green color-blind people can't distinguish (A) dark red from black, (B) blue from purple, and (C) light green from white.

FIGURE 4.10

MoneyDance's graph uses colors some users can't distinguish.

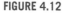

FIGURE 4.11

MoneyDance's graph rendered in grayscale.

FIGURE 4.12

Google logo: (A) normal and (B) after red–green color-blindness filter.

The home finance application MoneyDance provides a graphical breakdown of household expenses, using color to indicate the various expense categories (see Fig. 4.10). Unfortunately, many of the colors are hues that color-blind people cannot tell apart. For example, people with red–green color-blindness cannot distinguish the blue from the purple or the green from the khaki. If you are not color-blind, you can get an idea of which colors in an image will be hard to distinguish by converting the image to grayscale (see Fig. 4.11), but, as described in the "Guidelines for Using Color" section later in this chapter, it is best to run the image through a color-blindness filter or simulator (see Fig. 4.12).

EXTERNAL FACTORS THAT INFLUENCE THE ABILITY TO DISTINGUISH COLORS

Factors concerning the external environment also impact people's ability to distinguish colors. For example:

- ***Variation among color displays.*** Computer displays vary in how they display colors, depending on their technologies, driver software, or color settings.

Even monitors of the same model with the same settings may display colors slightly differently. Something that looks yellow on one display may look beige on another. Colors that are clearly different on one may look the same on another.

- *Grayscale displays.* Although most displays these days are color, there are devices, especially small handheld ones, with grayscale displays. For instance, Figure 4.11 shows that a grayscale display can make areas of different colors look the same.

- *Display angle.* Some computer displays, particularly LCD ones, work much better when viewed straight on than at an angle. When LCD displays are viewed at an angle, colors—and color differences—often are altered.

- *Ambient illumination.* Strong light on a display washes out colors before it washes out light and dark areas, reducing color displays to grayscale ones, as anyone who has tried to use a bank ATM in direct sunlight knows. In offices, glare and venetian blind shadows can mask color differences.

These four external factors are usually out of the software designer's control. Designers should, therefore, keep in mind that they don't have full control of users' color viewing experience. Colors that seem highly distinguishable in the development facility on the development team's computer displays and under normal office lighting conditions may not be as distinguishable in some of the environments where the software is used.

GUIDELINES FOR USING COLOR

In interactive software systems that rely on color to convey information, follow these five guidelines to assure that the users of the software receive the information:

1. *Distinguish colors by saturation and brightness, as well as hue.* Avoid subtle color differences. Make sure the contrast between colors is high (but see guideline 5). One way to test whether colors are different enough is to view them in grayscale. If you can't distinguish the colors when they are rendered in grays, they aren't different enough.

2. *Use distinctive colors.* Recall that our visual system combines the signals from retinal cone cells to produce three color-opponent channels: red–green, yellow–blue, and black–white (luminance). The colors that people can distinguish most easily are those that cause a strong signal (positive or negative) on one of the three color-perception channels, and neutral signals on the other two channels. Not surprisingly, those colors are red, green, yellow, blue, black, and white (see Fig. 4.13). All other colors cause signals on more than one color channel, and so our visual system cannot distinguish them from other colors as quickly and easily as it can distinguish those six colors (Ware, 2008).

FIGURE 4.13

The most distinctive colors: black, white, red, green, yellow, blue. Each color causes a strong signal on only one color-opponent channel.

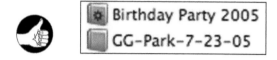

FIGURE 4.14

Apple's iPhoto uses color plus a symbol to distinguish two types of albums.

FIGURE 4.15

Opponent colors, placed on or directly next to each other, clash.

3. *Avoid color pairs that color-blind people cannot distinguish.* Such pairs include dark red versus black, dark red versus dark green, blue versus purple, light green versus white. Don't use dark reds, blues, or violets against any dark colors. Instead, use dark reds, blues, and violets against light yellows and greens. Use an online color-blindness simulator[4] to check web pages and images to see how people with various color-vision deficiencies would see them.

4. *Use color redundantly with other cues.* Don't rely on color alone. If you use color to mark something, mark it another way as well. Apple's iPhoto uses both color and a symbol to distinguish "smart" photo albums from regular albums (see Fig. 4.14).

5. *Separate strong opponent colors.* Placing opponent colors right next to or on top of each other causes a disturbing shimmering sensation, and so it should be avoided (see Fig. 4.15).

As shown in Figure 4.5, ITN.net used only pale yellow to mark customers' current step in making a reservation, which is too subtle. A simple way to strengthen the marking would be to make the current step bold and increase the saturation of the

---

[4] Search the Web for "color-blindness filter" or "color-blindness simulator."

(A)

Air, Car, & Hotel
Reservations

| Air Availability | 1 | Search | 2 | Availability | 3 | Itinerary Review | 4 | Final Confirmation |

(B)

FLIGHT RESERVATIONS

SEARCH — ▶ **SELECT** ▶ — REVIEW — PURCHASE — CONFIRM

FIGURE 4.16

ITN.net's current step is highlighted in two ways: with color and shape.

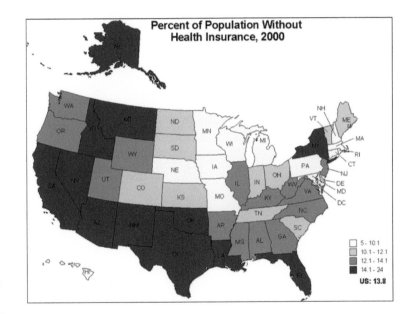

FIGURE 4.17

MinneapolisFed.org's graph uses shade differences visible to all sighted people, on any display.

yellow (see Fig. 4.16A). But ITN.net opted for a totally new design, which also uses color redundantly with shape (see Figure 4.16B).

A graph from the Federal Reserve Bank uses shades of gray (see Fig. 4.17). This is a well-designed graph. Any sighted person could read it.

Our Peripheral Vision is Poor

5

Chapter 4 explained that the human visual system differs from a digital camera in the way it detects and processes color. Our visual system also differs from a camera in its resolution. On a digital camera's photo sensor, photoreceptive elements are spread uniformly in a tight matrix, so the spatial resolution is constant across the entire image frame. The human visual system is not like that.

This chapter explains why

- Stationary items in muted colors presented in the periphery of people's visual field often will not be noticed.

- Motion in the periphery is usually noticed.

RESOLUTION OF THE FOVEA COMPARED TO THE PERIPHERY

The spatial resolution of the human visual field drops greatly from the center to the edges. There are three reasons for this:

- *Pixel density.* Each eye has 6 to 7 million retinal cone cells. They are packed much more tightly in the center of our visual field—a small region called the *fovea*—than they are at the edges of the retina (see Fig. 5.1). The fovea has about 158,000 cone cells in each square millimeter. The rest of the retina has only 9,000 cone cells per square millimeter.

- *Data compression.* Cone cells in the fovea connect 1:1 to the ganglial neuron cells that begin the processing and transmission of visual data, while elsewhere on the retina, multiple photoreceptor cells (cones and rods) connect to each ganglion cell. In technical terms, information from the visual periphery is compressed (with data loss) before transmission to the brain, while information from the fovea is not.

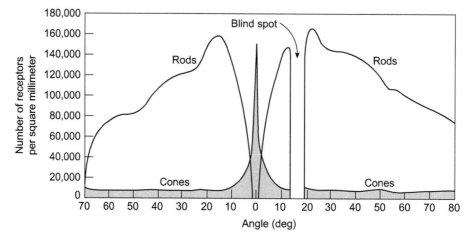

FIGURE 5.1

Distribution of photoreceptor cells (cones and rods) across the retina. *From Lindsay and Norman (1972).*

- ***Processing resources.*** The fovea is only about 1% of the retina, but the brain's visual cortex devotes about 50% of its area to input from the fovea. The other half of the visual cortex processes data from the remaining 99% of the retina.

The result is that our vision has much, much greater resolution in the center of our visual field than elsewhere (Lindsay and Norman, 1972; Waloszek, 2005). Said in developer jargon: in the center 1% of your visual field (i.e., the fovea), you have a high-resolution TIFF, and everywhere else, you have only a low-resolution JPEG. That is *nothing like* a digital camera.

To visualize how small the fovea is compared to your entire visual field, hold your arm straight out and look at your thumb. Your thumbnail, viewed at arm's length, corresponds approximately to the fovea (Ware, 2008). While you have your eyes focused on the thumbnail, everything else in your visual field falls outside of your fovea on your retina.

In the fovea, people with normal vision have very high resolution: they can resolve several thousand dots within that region—better resolution than many of today's pocket digital cameras. Just outside of the fovea, the resolution is already down to a few dozen dots per inch viewed at arm's length. At the edges of our vision, the "pixels" of our visual system are as large as a melon (or human head) at arm's length (see Fig. 5.2).

Even though our eyes have more rods than cones—125 million versus 6-7 million—peripheral vision has much lower resolution than foveal vision. This is because while most of our cone cells are densely packed in the fovea (1% of the retina's area), the rods are spread out over the rest of the retina (99% of the retina's area). In people with normal vision, peripheral vision is about 20/200, which in the United States is considered

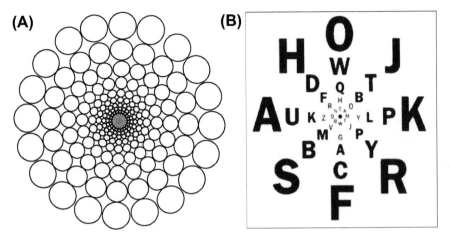

FIGURE 5.2

The resolution of our visual field is high in the center but much lower at the edges. *Right image from* Vision Research, *Vol. 14 (1974), Elsevier.*

legally blind. Think about that: in the periphery of your visual field, you are legally blind. Here is how brain researcher David Eagleman (2012; page 23) describes it:

> The resolution in your peripheral vision is roughly equivalent to looking through a frosted shower door, and yet you enjoy the illusion of seeing the periphery clearly. ... Wherever you cast your eyes appears to be in sharp focus, and therefore you assume the whole visual world is in focus.

If our peripheral vision has such low resolution, one might wonder why we don't see the world in a kind of tunnel vision where everything is out of focus except what we are directly looking at now. Instead, we seem to see our surroundings sharply and clearly all around us. We experience this illusion because our eyes move rapidly and constantly about three times per second even when we don't realize it, focusing our fovea on selected pieces of our environment. Our brain fills in the rest in a gross, impressionistic way based on what we know and expect.[1] Our brain does not have to maintain a high-resolution mental model of our environment because it can order the eyes to sample and resample details in the environment as needed (Clark, 1998).

For example, as you read this page, your eyes dart around, scanning and reading. No matter where on the page your eyes are focused, you have the impression of viewing a complete page of text, because, of course, you are.

---

[1] Our brains also fill in perceptual gaps that occur during rapid (saccadic) eye movements, when vision is suppressed (see Chapter 14).

@

FIGURE 5.3

To "see" the retinal gap, cover your left eye, hold this book near your face, and focus your right eye on the **+**. Move the book slowly away from you, staying focused on the **+**. The @ will disappear at some point.

But now, imagine that you are viewing this page on a computer screen, and the computer is tracking your eye movements and knows where your fovea is on the page. Imagine that wherever you look, the right text for that spot on the page is shown clearly in the small area corresponding to your fovea, but everywhere else on the page, the computer shows random, meaningless text. As your fovea flits around the page, the computer quickly updates each area where your fovea stops to show the correct text there, while the last position of your fovea returns to textual noise. Amazingly, experiments have shown that people *rarely notice* this: not only can they read, they believe that they are viewing a full page of meaningful text (Clark, 1998). However, it does slow people's reading, even if they don't realize it (Larson, 2004).

The fact that retinal cone cells are distributed tightly in and near the fovea, and sparsely in the periphery of the retina, affects not only spatial resolution but color resolution. We can discriminate colors better in the center of our visual field than at the edges.

Another interesting fact about our visual field is that it has a gap—a small area (blind spot) in which we see nothing. The gap corresponds to the spot on our retina where the optic nerve and blood vessels exit the back of the eye (see Fig. 5.1). There are no retinal rod or cone cells at that spot, so when the image of an object in our visual field happens to fall on that part of the retina, we don't see it. We usually don't notice this hole in our vision because our brain fills it in with the surrounding content, like a graphic artist using Photoshop to fill in a blemish on a photograph by copying nearby background pixels.

People sometimes experience the blind spot when they gaze at stars. As you look at one star, a nearby star may disappear briefly into the blind spot until you shift your gaze. You can also observe the gap by trying the exercise in Figure 5.3. Some people have other gaps resulting from imperfections on the retina, retinal damage, or brain strokes that affect the visual cortex,[2] but the optic nerve gap is an imperfection everyone shares.

IS THE VISUAL PERIPHERY GOOD FOR ANYTHING?

It seems that the fovea is better than the periphery at just about everything. One might wonder why we have peripheral vision. What is it good for? Our peripheral vision serves three important functions: it guides fovea, detects motion, and lets us see better in the dark.

[2] See VisionSimulations.com.

Function 1: Guides fovea

First, peripheral vision provides low-resolution cues to guide our eye movements so that our fovea visits all the interesting and crucial parts of our visual field. Our eyes don't scan our environment randomly. They move so as to focus our fovea on important things, the most important ones (usually) first. The fuzzy cues on the outskirts of our visual field provide the data that helps our brain plan where to move our eyes, and in what order.

For example, when we scan a medicine label for a "use by" date, a fuzzy blob in the periphery with the vague form of a date is enough to cause an eye movement that lands the fovea there to allow us to check it. If we are browsing a produce market looking for strawberries, a blurry reddish patch at the edge of our visual field draws our eyes and our attention, even though sometimes it may turn out to be radishes instead of strawberries. If we hear an animal growl nearby, a fuzzy animal-like shape in the corner of our eye will be enough to zip our eyes in that direction, especially if the shape is moving toward us (see Fig. 5.4).

How peripheral vision guides and augments central, foveal vision is discussed more in the "Visual Search Is Linear Unless Targets 'Pop' in the Periphery" section later in this chapter.

Function 2: Detects motion

A related guiding function of peripheral vision is that it is good at detecting motion. Anything that moves in our visual periphery, even slightly, is likely to draw our attention—and hence our fovea—toward it. The reason for this phenomenon is that our ancestors—including prehuman ones—were selected for their ability to spot food and avoid predators. As a result, even though we can move our eyes under conscious, intentional control, some of the mechanisms that control where they look are preconscious, involuntary, and very fast.

FIGURE 5.4

A moving shape at the edge of our vision draws our eye: it could be food, or it might consider us food.

What if we have no reason to expect that there might be anything interesting in a certain spot in the periphery,[3] and nothing in that spot attracts our attention? Our eyes may never move our fovea to that spot, so we may never see what is there.

Function 3: Lets us see better in the dark

A third function of peripheral vision is to allow us to see in low-light conditions—for example, on starlit nights, in caves, around campfires, etc. These were conditions under which vision evolved, and in which people—like the animals that preceded them on Earth—spent much of their time until the invention of the electric light bulb in the 1800s.

Just as the rods are overloaded in well-lighted conditions (see Chapter 5), the cones don't function very well in low light, so our rods take over. Low-light, rods-only vision is called *scotopic vision*. An interesting fact is that because there are no rods in the fovea, you can see objects better in low-light conditions (e.g., faint stars) if you don't look directly at them.

EXAMPLES FROM COMPUTER USER INTERFACES

The low acuity of our peripheral vision explains why software and website users fail to notice error messages in some applications and websites. When someone clicks a button or a link, that is usually where his or her fovea is positioned. Everything on the screen that is not within 1-2 centimeters of the click location (assuming normal computer viewing distance) is in peripheral vision, where resolution is low. If, after the click, an error message appears in the periphery, it should not be surprising that the person might not notice it.

For example, at InformaWorld.com, the online publications website of Informa Healthcare, if a user enters an incorrect username or password and clicks "Sign In," an error message appears in a "message bar" far away from where the user's eyes are most likely focused (see Fig. 5.5). The red word "Error" might appear in the user's peripheral vision as a small reddish blob, which would help draw the eyes in that direction. However, the red blob could fall into a gap in the viewer's visual field, and so not be noticed at all.

Consider the sequence of events from a user's point of view. The user enters a username and password and then clicks "Sign In." The page redisplays with blank fields. The user thinks "Huh? I gave it my login information and hit 'Sign In,' didn't I? Did I hit the wrong button?" The user reenters the username and password, and clicks "Sign In" again. The page redisplays with empty fields again. Now the user is really confused. The user sighs (or curses), sits back in his chair and lets his eyes scan the screen. Suddenly noticing the error message, the user says "A-ha! Has that error message been there all along?"

---

[3] See Chapter 1 on how expectations bias our perceptions.

FIGURE 5.5

This error message for a faulty sign-in appears in peripheral vision, where it will probably be missed.

Even when an error message is placed nearer to the center of the viewer's visual field than in the preceding example, other factors can diminish its visibility. For example, until recently the website of Airborne.com signaled a login failure by displaying an error message in red just above the Login ID field (see Fig. 5.6). This error message is entirely in red and fairly near the "Login" button where the user's eyes are probably focused. Nonetheless, some users would not notice this error message when it first appeared. Can you think of any reasons people might not initially see this error message?

One reason is that even though the error message is much closer to where users will be looking when they click the "Login" button, it is still in the periphery, not in the fovea. The fovea is small: just a centimeter or two on a computer screen, assuming the user is the usual distance from the screen.

A second reason is that the error message is not the only thing near the top of the page that is red. The page title is also red. Resolution in the periphery is low, so when the error message appears, the user's visual system may not register any change: there was something red up there before, and there still is (see Fig. 5.7).

If the page title were black or any other color besides red, the red error message would be more likely to be noticed, even though it appears in the periphery of the users' visual field.

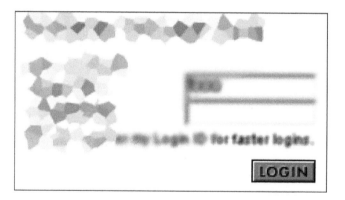

FIGURE 5.6

This error message for a faulty login is missed by some users even though it is not far from the "Login" button.

FIGURE 5.7

Simulation of a user's visual field while the fovea is fixed on the "Login" button.

COMMON METHODS OF MAKING MESSAGES VISIBLE

There are several common and well-known methods of ensuring that an error message will be seen:

- ***Put it where users are looking.*** People focus in predictable places when interacting with graphical user interfaces (GUIs). In Western societies, people tend to traverse forms and control panels from upper left to lower right. While moving the screen pointer, people usually look either at where it is or where they are moving it to. When people click a button or link, they can usually be assumed to be looking directly at it, at least for a few moments afterward. Designers can use this predictability to position error messages near where they expect users to be looking.

FIGURE 5.8

This error message for faulty sign-in is displayed more prominently, near where users will be looking.

- **Mark the error.** Somehow mark the error prominently to indicate clearly that something is wrong. Often this can be done by simply placing the error message near what it refers to, unless that would place the message too far from where users are likely to be looking.

- **Use an error symbol.** Make errors or error messages more visible by marking them with an error symbol, such as ⚠, ⚠, ⓘ, or ✖.

- **Reserve red for errors.** By convention, in interactive computer systems the color red connotes *alert, danger, problem, error*, etc. Using red for any other information on a computer display invites misinterpretation. But suppose you are designing a website for Stanford University, which has red as its school color. Or suppose you are designing for a Chinese market, where red is considered an auspicious, positive color. What do you do? Use another color for errors, mark them with error symbols, or use stronger methods (see the next section).

An improved version of the InformaWorld sign-in error screen uses several of these techniques (see Fig. 5.8).

At America Online's website, the form for registering for a new email account follows the guidelines pretty well (see Fig. 5.9). Data fields with errors are marked with red error symbols. Error messages are displayed in red and are near the error. Furthermore, most of the error messages appear as soon as an erroneous entry is made, when

FIGURE 5.9

New member registration at AOL.com displays error messages prominently, near each error.

the user is still focused on that part of the form, rather than only after the user submits the form. It is unlikely that AOL users will miss seeing these error messages.

HEAVY ARTILLERY FOR MAKING USERS NOTICE MESSAGES

If the common, conventional methods of making users notice messages are not enough, three stronger methods are available to user-interface designers: pop-up message in error dialog box, use of sound (e.g., beep), and wiggle or blink briefly. However, these methods, while very effective, have significant negative effects, so they should be used sparingly and with great care.

Method 1: Pop-up message in error dialog box

Displaying an error message in a dialog box sticks it right in the user's face, making it hard to miss. Error dialog boxes interrupt the user's work and demand immediate attention. That is good if the error message signals a critical condition, but it can annoy people if such an approach is used for a minor message, such as confirming the execution of a user-requested action.

The annoyance of pop-up messages rises with the degree of modality. *Nonmodal* pop-ups allow users to ignore them and continue working. *Application-modal* pop-ups block any further work in the application that displayed the error, but allow users to interact with other software on their computer. *System-modal* pop-ups block any user action until the dialog has been dismissed.

Application-modal pop-ups should be used sparingly—for example, only when application data may be lost if the user doesn't attend to the error. System-modal

FIGURE 5.10

REI's pop-up dialog box signals required data that was omitted. It is hard to miss, but perhaps overkill.

pop-ups should be used extremely rarely—basically only when the system is about to crash and take hours of work with it, or if people will die if the user misses the error message.

On the Web, an additional reason to avoid pop-up error dialog boxes is that some people set their browsers to block *all* pop-up windows. If your website relies on pop-up error messages, some users may never see them.

REI.com has an example of a pop-up dialog being used to display an error message. The message is displayed when someone who is registering as a new customer omits required fields in the form (see Fig. 5.10). Is this an appropriate use of a pop-up dialog? AOL.com (see Fig. 5.9) shows that missing data errors can be signaled quite well without pop-up dialogs, so REI.com's use of them seems a bit heavy-handed.

Examples of more appropriate use of error dialog boxes come from Microsoft Excel (see Fig. 5.11A) and Adobe InDesign (see Fig. 5.11B). In both cases, loss of data is at stake.

Method 2: Use sound (e.g., beep)

When a computer beeps, that tells its user something has happened that requires attention. The person's eyes reflexively begin scanning the screen for whatever caused the beep. This can allow the user to notice an error message that is someplace other than where the user was just looking, such as in a standard error message box on the display. That is the value of beeping.

However, imagine many people in a cubicle work environment or a classroom, all using an application that signals all errors and warnings by beeping. Such a workplace would be very annoying, to say the least. Worse, people wouldn't be able to tell whether their own computer or someone else's was beeping.

FIGURE 5.11

Appropriate pop-up error dialogs: (A) Microsoft Excel and (B) Adobe InDesign.

The opposite situation is noisy work environments (e.g., factories or computer server rooms), where auditory signals emitted by an application might be masked by ambient noise. Even in non-noisy environments, some computer users simply prefer quiet, and mute the sound on their computers or turn it way down.

For these reasons, signaling errors and other conditions with sound are remedies that can be used only in very special, controlled situations.

Computer games often use sound to signal events and conditions. In games, sound isn't annoying; it is expected. Its use in games is widespread, even in game arcades, where dozens of machines are all banging, roaring, buzzing, clanging, beeping, and playing music at once. (Well, it is annoying to parents who have to go into the arcades and endure all the screeching and booming to retrieve their kids, but the games aren't designed for parents.)

Method 3: Wiggle or blink briefly

As described earlier in this chapter, our peripheral vision is good at detecting motion, and motion in the periphery causes reflexive eye movements that bring the motion into the fovea. User-interface designers can make use of this by wiggling or flashing messages briefly when they want to ensure that users see them. It doesn't take much motion to trigger eye movement toward the motion. Just a tiny bit of motion is enough to make a viewer's eyes zip over in that direction. Millions of years of evolution have had quite an effect.

As an example of using motion to attract users' eye attention, Apple's iCloud online service briefly shakes the entire dialog box horizontally when a user enters an invalid username or password (see Fig. 5.12). In addition to clearly indicating "No" (like a person shaking his head), this attracts the users' eyeballs, guaranteed. (Because, after all, the motion in the corner of your eye might be a leopard.)

The most common use of blinking in computer user interfaces (other than advertisements) is in menu bars. When an action (e.g., Edit or Copy) is selected from a

FIGURE 5.12

Apple's iCloud shakes the dialog box briefly on login errors to attract a user's fovea toward it.

menu, it usually blinks once before the menu closes to confirm that the system "got" the command—that is, that the user didn't miss the menu item. This use of blinking is very common. It is so quick that most computer users aren't even aware of it, but if menu items didn't blink once, we would have less confidence that we actually selected them.

Motion and blinking, like pop-up dialog boxes and beeping, must be used sparingly. Most experienced computer users consider wiggling, blinking objects on screen to be annoying. Most of us have learned to ignore displays that blink because many such displays are advertisements. Conversely, a few computer users have attentional impairments that make it difficult for them to ignore something that is blinking or wiggling.

Therefore, if wiggling or blinking is used, it should be brief—it should last about a quarter- to a half-second, no longer. Otherwise, it quickly goes from an unconscious attention-grabber to a conscious annoyance.

Use heavy-artillery methods sparingly to avoid habituating your users

There is one final reason to use the preceding heavy-artillery methods sparingly (i.e., only for critical messages): to avoid *habituating* your users. When pop-ups, sound, motion, and blinking are used too often to attract users' attention, a psychological phenomenon called *habituation* sets in (see Chapter 1). Our brain pays less and less attention to any stimulus that occurs frequently.

It is like the old fable of the boy who cried "Wolf!" too often: eventually, the villagers learned to ignore his cries, so when a wolf actually did come, his cries went unheeded. Overuse of strong attention-getting methods can cause important messages to be blocked by habituation.

VISUAL SEARCH IS LINEAR UNLESS TARGETS "POP" IN THE PERIPHERY

As explained earlier, one function of peripheral vision is to drive our eyes to focus the fovea on important things—things we are seeking or that might be a threat. Objects moving in our peripheral vision fairly reliably "yank" our eyes in that direction.

When we are looking for an object, our entire visual system, including the periphery, primes itself to detect that object. In fact, the periphery is a *crucial* component in visual search, despite its low spatial and color resolution. However, just how helpful the periphery is in aiding visual search depends strongly on what we are looking for.

Look quickly at Figure 5.13 and find the Z.

To find the Z, you had to scan carefully through the characters until your fovea landed on it. In the lingo of vision researchers, the time to find the Z is *linear*: it depends approximately linearly on the number of distracting characters and the position of the Z among them.

Now look quickly at Figure 5.14 and find the bold character.

That was much easier (i.e., faster), wasn't it? You didn't have to scan your fovea carefully through the distracting characters. Your periphery quickly detected the boldness and determined its location, and because that is what you were seeking,

```
L Q R B  T J P L F  BM R W  S
F R  N Q  S P D  C H K  U T
 G T H U  J L U 9 J  V Y I  A
E  X C F T Y N  H T D  O L L8
G V  N  G R Y J  G Z S  T 6 S
3 L C  T V B H U S E M U K
W Q E L  F G  H  U Y I K D 9
```

FIGURE 5.13

Finding the Z requires scanning carefully through the characters.

```
G T H U  J L U 9 J  V Y I  A
L Q R B  T J P L F  BM R W  S
3 L C  T V B H U S E M U K
F R  N Q  S P D  C H K  U T
W Q E L  F G  H  B Y I K D 9
G V  N  **G** R Y J  G Z S  T 6 S
E  X C F T Y N  H T D  O L L8
```

FIGURE 5.14

Finding the bold letter does **not** require scanning through everything.

```
L Q R B T J P L F BM R W S
F R N Q  S P D  C H K  U T
 G T H U  J L U 9 J  V Y I  A
E  X C F T Y N H T D  O L L8
3 L C  T V B H U S E M  U K
G V  N  G R Y J G Z  S T 6 S
W Q E L  F G  H  U Y I K D 9
```

FIGURE 5.15

Counting L's is hard; character shape doesn't "pop" among characters.

```
W Q E L  F G H  U Y I K D 9
F  R N Q  S P D  C H K  U T
3 L C  T V B H U S E M  U K
 G T H U  J L U 9 J  V Y I  A
L Q R B  T J P L F  BM R W S
E  X C F T  Y N H T D  O L L8
G V  N  G R Y J G Z S T 6 S
```

FIGURE 5.16

Counting blue characters is easy because color "pops."

your visual system moved your fovea there. Your periphery could not determine exactly *what* was bold—that is beyond its resolution and abilities—but it did locate the boldness. In vision-researcher lingo, the periphery was primed to look for boldness in parallel over its entire area, and boldness is a distinctive feature of the target, so searching for a bold target is nonlinear. In designer lingo, we simply say that boldness "pops out" ("pops" for short) in the periphery, assuming that only the target is bold.

Color "pops" even more strongly. Compare counting the L's in Figure 5.15 with counting the blue characters in Figure 5.16.

What else makes things "pop" in the periphery? As described earlier, the periphery easily detects motion, so motion "pops." Generalizing from *boldness*, we also can say that font *weight* "pops," because if all but one of the characters on a display were bold, the *non*bold character would stand out. Basically, a visual target will pop out in your periphery if it differs from surrounding objects in features the periphery can detect. The more distinctive features of the target, the more it "pops," assuming the periphery can detect those features.

Using peripheral "pop" in design

Designers use peripheral "pop" to focus the attention of a product's users, as well as to allow users to find information faster. Chapter 3 described how visual hierarchy—titles, headings, boldness, bullets, and indenting—can make it easier for users to spot

FIGURE 5.17

Google Maps uses color to show traffic conditions. Red indicates traffic jams.

and extract from text the information they need. Glance back at Figure 3.11 in Chapter 3 and see how the headings and bullets make the topics and subtopics "pop" so readers can go right to them.

Many interactive systems use color to indicate status, usually reserving red for problems. Online maps and some vehicle GPS devices mark traffic jams with red so they stand out (see Fig. 5.17). Systems for controlling air traffic mark potential collisions in red (see Fig. 5.18). Applications for monitoring servers and networks use color to show the health status of assets or groups of them (see Fig. 5.19).

These are all uses of peripheral "pop" to make important information stand out and visual search nonlinear.

When there are many possible targets

Sometimes in displays of many items, *any* of them could be what the user wants. Examples include command menus (see Fig. 5.20A) and object pallets (see Fig. 5.20B). Let's assume that the application cannot anticipate which item or items a user is likely to want, and highlight those. That is a fair assumption for today's applications.[4] Are users doomed to have to search linearly through such displays for the item they want?

That depends. Designers can try to make each item so distinctive that when a specific one is the user's target, the user's peripheral vision will be able to spot it among

---

[4] But in the not-too-distant future it might not be.

FIGURE 5.18

Air traffic control systems often use red to make potential collisions stand out.

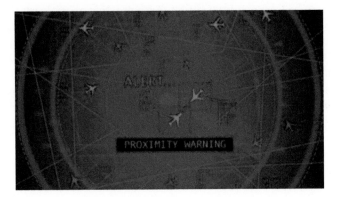

FIGURE 5.19

Paessler's monitoring tool uses color to show the health of network components.

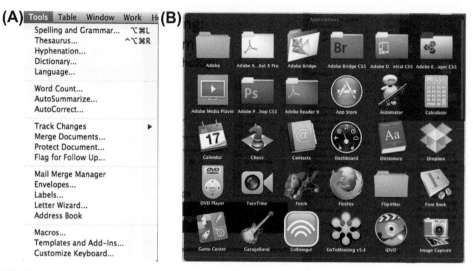

FIGURE 5.20

(A) Microsoft Word Tools menu, and (B) MacOS application pallet.

all the other items. Designing distinctive sets of icons is hard—especially when the set is large—but it can be done (see Johnson et. al, 1989). Designing sets of icons that are so distinctive that they can be distinguished in peripheral vision is *very* hard, but not impossible. For example, if a user goes to the Mac OS application pallet to open his or her calendar, a white rectangular blob in the periphery with something black in the middle is more likely to attract the user's eye than a blue circular blob (see Fig. 5.20B). The trick is not to get too fancy and detailed with the icons—give each one a distinctive color and gross shape.

On the other hand, if the potential targets are all words, as in command menus (see Fig. 20A), visual distinctiveness is not an option. In textual menus and lists, visual search *will* be linear, at least at first. With practice, users learn the positions of frequently used items in menus, lists, and pallets, so searching for particular items is no longer linear.

That is why applications should *never* move items around in menus, lists, or pallets. Doing that prevents users from learning item positions, thereby dooming them to search linearly forever. Therefore, "dynamic menus" is considered a major user-interface design blooper (Johnson, 2007).

Reading is Unnatural

6

Most people in industrialized nations grow up in households and school districts that promote education and reading. They learn to read as young children and become good readers by adolescence. As adults, most of our activities during a normal day involve reading. The process of reading—deciphering words into their meaning—is for most educated adults automatic, leaving our conscious minds free to ponder the meaning and implications of what we are reading. Because of this background, it is common for good readers to consider reading to be as "natural" a human activity as speaking is.

WE'RE WIRED FOR LANGUAGE, BUT NOT FOR READING

Speaking and understanding spoken language *is* a natural human ability, but reading is *not*. Over hundreds of thousands—perhaps millions—of years, the human brain evolved the neural structures necessary to support spoken language. As a result, normal humans are born with an innate ability to learn as toddlers, with no systematic training, whatever language they are exposed to. After early childhood, this ability decreases significantly. By adolescence, learning a new language is the same as learning any other skill: it requires instruction and practice, and the learning and processing are handled by different brain areas from those that handled it in early childhood (Sousa, 2005).

In contrast, *writing* and *reading* did not exist until a few thousand years BCE and did not become *common* until only four or five centuries ago—*long* after the human brain had evolved into its modern state. At no time during childhood do our brains show any special innate ability to learn to read. Instead, reading is an artificial skill that we learn by systematic instruction and practice, like playing a violin, juggling, or reading music (Sousa, 2005).

Many people never learn to read well, or at all

Because people are not innately "wired" to learn to read, children who either lack caregivers who read to them or who receive inadequate reading instruction in

(A)

አዲስ አበባ ሰኔ 15/93/ኢዜአ/ -- ኢጣሊያ ለኢትዮጵያ የ375 ሚሊዮን ዶላር ዕዳ ስርዝ ለማገረረግ መወሰኗን አዲስ አበባ የሚገኘው የአገሪቱ ኤምባሲ

(B)

དགེ་འདུན་དམ་པ་ཆོས་ལྡན་བློས་བའི་བགྲ་ཤེས་རྒྱག ཨི་དང་ལྐ་དང་ལྐ་མ་ཨིན་གྱི་མཆོང་བའི་གནས༎

ཆོགས་གྱི་མཆོག་རབ་དོ་ཚ་ཤེས་དང་དཔལ་གྱི་གཤི། དེ་ནི་འདིག་ཏེན་དགེ་བའི་བགྲ་ཤེས་གཟུམ་པ་ཨིན༎ ༎

FIGURE 6.1

To see how it feels to be illiterate, look at text printed in a foreign script: (A) Amharic and (B) Tibetan.

school may never learn to read. There are a great many such people, especially in the developing world. By comparison, very few people never learn a spoken language.

For a variety of reasons, some people who learn to read never become good at it. Perhaps their parents did not value and promote reading. Perhaps they attended substandard schools or didn't attend school at all. Perhaps they learned a second language but never learned to read well in that language. People who have cognitive or perceptual impairments such as dyslexia may never read easily.

A person's ability to read is specific to a language and a script (a system of writing). To see what text looks like to someone who cannot read, just look at a paragraph printed in a language and script that you do not know (see Fig. 6.1).

Alternatively, you can approximate the feeling of illiteracy by taking a page written in a familiar script and language—such as a page of this book—and turning it upside down. Turn this book upside down and try reading the next few paragraphs. This exercise only approximates the feeling of illiteracy. You will discover that the inverted text appears foreign and illegible at first, but after a minute you will be able to read it, albeit slowly and laboriously.

Learning to read = training our visual system

Learning to read involves training our visual system to recognize patterns—the patterns exhibited by text. These patterns run a gamut from low level to high level:

- Lines, contours, and shapes are basic visual features that our brain recognizes innately. We don't have to learn to recognize them.

- Basic features combine to form patterns that we learn to identify as characters—letters, numeric digits, and other standard symbols. In ideographic scripts, such as Chinese, symbols represent entire words or concepts.

- In alphabetic scripts, patterns of characters form morphemes, which we learn to recognize as packets of meaning—for example, "farm," "tax," "-ed," and "-ing" are morphemes in English.

- Morphemes combine to form patterns that we recognize as words—for example, "farm," "tax," "-ed," and "-ing" can be combined to form the words "farm," "farmed," "farming," "tax," "taxed," and "taxing." Even ideographic scripts include symbols that serve as morphemes or modifiers of meaning rather than as words or concepts.

- Words combine to form patterns that we learn to recognize as phrases, idiomatic expressions, and sentences.

- Sentences combine to form paragraphs.

Actually, only part of our visual system is trained to recognize textual patterns involved in reading: the fovea and a small area immediately surrounding it (known as the *perifovea*), and the downstream neural networks running through the optic nerve to the visual cortex and into various parts of our brain. The neural networks starting elsewhere in our retinas do not get trained to read. More about this is explained later in the chapter.

Learning to read also involves training the brain's systems that control eye movement to move our eyes in a specific way over text. The main direction of eye movement depends on the direction in which the language we are reading is written: European language scripts are read left to right, many middle Eastern language scripts are read right to left, and some language scripts are read top to bottom. Beyond that, the precise eye movements differ depending on whether we are reading, skimming for overall meaning, or scanning for specific words.

How we read

Assuming our visual system and brain have successfully been trained, reading becomes semi-automatic or fully automatic—both the eye movement and the processing.

As explained earlier, the center of our visual field—the fovea and perifovea—is the only part of our visual field that is trained to read. All text that we read enters our visual system after being scanned by the central area, which means that reading requires a lot of eye movement.

As explained in Chapter 5 on the discussion of peripheral vision, our eyes constantly jump around, several times a second. Each of these movements, called *saccades*, lasts about 0.1 second. Saccades are ballistic, like firing a shell from a cannon: their endpoint is determined when they are triggered, and once triggered, they always execute to completion. As described in earlier chapters, the destinations of saccadic eye movements are programmed by the brain from a combination of our goals, events in the visual periphery, events detected and localized by other perceptual senses, and past history including training.

When we read, we may feel that our eyes scan smoothly across the lines of text, but that feeling is incorrect. In reality, our eyes continue with saccades during reading, but the movements generally follow the line of text. They fix our fovea on a word, pause there for a fraction of a second to allow basic patterns to be captured and transmitted to the brain for further analysis, then jump to the next important word (Larson, 2004). Eye fixations while reading always land on words, usually near the center, never on word boundaries (see Fig. 6.2). Very common small connector and function words like "a," "and," "the," "or," "is," and "but" are usually skipped over, their presence either detected in perifoveal vision or simply assumed. Most of the saccades during reading are in the text's normal reading direction, but a few—about 10%—jump backwards to previous words. At the end of each line of text, our eyes jump to where our brain guesses the next line begins.[1]

How much can we take in during each eye fixation during reading? For reading European-language scripts at normal reading distances and text-font sizes, the fovea clearly sees 3–4 characters on either side of the fixation point. The perifovea sees out about 15–20 characters from the fixation point, but not very clearly (see Fig. 6.3). According to reading researcher Kevin Larson (2004), the reading area in and around the fovea consists of three distinct zones (for European-language scripts):

Closest to the fixation point is where word recognition takes place. This zone is usually large enough to capture the word being fixated, and often includes smaller function words directly to the right of the fixated word. The next zone extends a few letters past the word recognition zone, and readers gather preliminary information about the next letters in this zone. The final zone extends out to 15 letters past the fixation point. Information gathered out this far is used to identify the length of upcoming words and to identify the best location for the next fixation point.

FIGURE 6.2

Saccadic eye movements during reading jump between important words.

FIGURE 6.3

Visibility of words in a line of text, with fovea fixed on the word "years."

[1] Later we will see that centered text disrupts the brain's guess about where the next line starts.

Because our visual system has been trained to read, perception around the fixation point is asymmetrical: it is more sensitive to characters in the reading direction than in the other direction. For European-language scripts, this is toward the right. That makes sense because characters to the left of the fixation point have usually already been read.

IS READING FEATURE-DRIVEN OR CONTEXT-DRIVEN?

As explained earlier, reading involves recognizing features and patterns. Pattern recognition, and therefore reading, can be either a bottom-up, feature-driven process, or a top-down, context-driven process.

In feature-driven reading, the visual system starts by identifying simple features—line segments in a certain orientation or curves of a certain radius—on a page or display, and then combines them into more complex features, such as angles, multiple curves, shapes, and patterns. Then the brain recognizes certain shapes as characters or symbols representing letters, numbers, or, for ideographic scripts, words. In alphabetic scripts, groups of letters are perceived as morphemes and words. In all types of scripts, sequences of words are parsed into phrases, sentences, and paragraphs that have meaning.

Feature-driven reading is sometimes referred to as "bottom-up" or "context-free." The brain's ability to recognize basic features—lines, edges, angles, etc.—is built in and therefore automatic from birth. In contrast, recognition of morphemes, words, and phrases has to be learned. It starts out as a nonautomatic, conscious process requiring conscious analysis of letters, morphemes, and words, but with enough practice it becomes automatic (Sousa, 2005). Obviously, the more common a morpheme, word, or phrase, the more likely that recognition of it will become automatic. With ideographic scripts such as Chinese, which have many times more symbols than alphabetic scripts do, people typically take many years longer to become skilled readers.

Context-driven or top-down reading operates in parallel with feature-driven reading but it works the opposite way: from whole sentences or the gist of a paragraph *down* to the words and characters. The visual system starts by recognizing high-level patterns like words, phrases, and sentences, or by knowing the text's meaning in advance. It then uses that knowledge to figure out—or guess—what the components of the high-level pattern must be (Boulton, 2009). Context-driven reading is less likely to become fully automatic because most phrase-level and sentence-level patterns and contexts don't occur frequently enough to allow their recognition to become burned into neural firing patterns. But there are exceptions, such as idiomatic expressions.

To experience context-driven reading, glance quickly at Figure 6.4, then immediately direct your eyes back here and finish reading this paragraph. Try it now. What did the text say?

Now look at the same sentence again more carefully. Do you read it the same way now?

> # The rain in Spain falls manly in the the plain

FIGURE 6.4

Top-down recognition of the expression can inhibit seeing the actual text.

Also, based on what we have already read and our knowledge of the world, our brains can sometimes predict text that the fovea has not yet read (or its meaning), allowing us to skip reading it. For example, if at the end of a page we read "It was a dark and stormy," we would expect the first word on the next page to be "night." We would be surprised if it was some other word (e.g., "cow").

Feature-driven, bottom-up reading dominates; context assists

It has been known for decades that reading involves both feature-driven (bottom-up) processing and context-driven (top-down) processing. In addition to being able to figure out the meaning of a sentence by analyzing the letters and words in it, people can determine the words of a sentence by knowing the meaning of the sentence, or the letters in a word by knowing what word it is (see Fig. 6.5). The question is: Is skilled reading primarily bottom-up or top-down, or is neither mode dominant?

Early scientific studies of reading—from the late 1800s through about 1980—seemed to show that people recognize words first and from that determine what letters are present. The theory of reading that emerged from those findings was that our visual system recognizes words primarily from their overall *shape*. This theory failed to account for certain experimental results and so was controversial among reading researchers, but it nonetheless gained wide acceptance among nonresearchers, especially in the graphic design field (Larson, 2004; Herrmann, 2011).

(A) | Mray had a ltilte lmab, its feclee was withe as sown. And ervey wehre taht Mray wnet, the lmab was srue to go.

(B) | Twinkle twinkle little star how I wonder what you are

FIGURE 6.5

Top-down reading: most readers, especially those who know the songs from which these text passages are taken, can read these passages even though the words (A) have all but their first and last letters scrambled and (B) are mostly obscured.

Similarly, educational researchers in the 1970s applied information theory to reading, and assumed that because of redundancies in written language, top-down, context-driven reading would be faster than bottom-up, feature-driven reading. This assumption led them to hypothesize that reading for highly skilled (fast) readers would be dominated by context-driven (top-down) processing. This theory was probably responsible for many speed-reading methods of the 1970s and 1980s, which supposedly trained people to read fast by taking in whole phrases and sentences at a time.

However, empirical studies of readers conducted since then have demonstrated conclusively that those early theories were false. Summing up the research are statements from reading researchers Kevin Larson (2004) and Keith Stanovich (Bolton, 2009), respectively:

Word shape is no longer a viable model of word recognition. The bulk of scientific evidence says that we recognize a word's component letters, then use that visual information to recognize a word.

Context [is] important, but it's a more important aid for the poorer reader who doesn't have automatic context-free recognition instantiated.

In other words, reading consists mainly of context-free, bottom-up, feature-driven processes. In skilled readers, these processes are well learned to the point of being automatic. Context-driven reading today is considered mainly a backup method that, although it operates in parallel with feature-based reading, is only relevant when feature-driven reading is difficult or insufficiently automatic.

Skilled readers may resort to context-based reading when feature-based reading is disrupted by poor presentation of information (see examples later in this chapter). Also, in the race between context-based and feature-based reading to decipher the text we see, contextual cues sometimes win out over features. As an example of context-based reading, Americans visiting England sometimes misread "to let" signs as "toilet," because in the United States they see the word "toilet" often, but they almost never see the phrase "to let"—Americans use "for rent" instead.

In less skilled readers, feature-based reading is not automatic; it is conscious and laborious. Therefore, more of their reading is context-based. Their involuntary use of context-based reading and nonautomatic feature-based reading consumes short-term cognitive capacity, leaving little for comprehension.[2] They have to focus on

---

[2] Chapter 10 describes the differences between automatic and controlled cognitive processing. Here, we will simply say that controlled processes burden working memory, while automatic processes do not.

deciphering the stream of words, leaving no capacity for constructing the meaning of sentences and paragraphs. That is why poor readers can read a passage aloud but afterward have no idea what they just read.

Why is context-free (bottom-up) reading not automatic in some adults? Some people didn't get enough experience reading as young children for the feature-driven recognition processes to become automatic. As they grow up, they find reading mentally laborious and taxing, so they avoid reading, which perpetuates and compounds their deficit (Boulton, 2009).

SKILLED AND UNSKILLED READING USE DIFFERENT PARTS OF THE BRAIN

Before the 1980s, researchers who wanted to understand which parts of the brain are involved in language and reading were limited mainly to studying people who had suffered brain injuries. For example, in the mid-19th century, doctors found that people with brain damage near the left temple—an area now called *Broca's area* after the doctor who discovered it—can understand speech but have trouble speaking, and that people with brain damage near the left ear—now called *Wernicke's area*— cannot understand speech (Sousa, 2005) (see Fig. 6.6).

In recent decades, new methods of observing the operation of functioning brains in living people have been developed: electroencephalography (EEG), functional magnetic resonance imaging (fMRI), and functional magnetic resonance spectroscopy (fMRS). These methods allow researchers to watch the response in different areas of a person's brain—including the sequence in which they respond—as the person perceives various stimuli or performs specific tasks (Minnery and Fine, 2009).

FIGURE 6.6

The human brain, showing Broca's area and Wernicke's area.

Using these methods, researchers have discovered that the neural pathways involved in reading differ for novice versus skilled readers. Of course, the first area to respond during reading is the occipital (or visual) cortex at the back of the brain. That is the same regardless of a person's reading skill. After that, the pathways diverge (Sousa, 2005):

- *Novice*. First an area of the brain just above and behind Wernicke's area becomes active. Researchers have come to view this as the area where, at least with alphabetic scripts such as English and German, words are "sounded out" and assembled—that is, letters are analyzed and matched with their corresponding sounds. The word-analysis area then communicates with Broca's area and the frontal lobe, where morphemes and words—units of meaning—are recognized and overall meaning is extracted. For ideographic languages, where symbols represent whole words and often have a graphical correspondence to their meaning, sounding out of words is not part of reading.

- *Advanced.* The word-analysis area is skipped. Instead the occipitotemporal area (behind the ear, not far from the visual cortex) becomes active. The prevailing view is that this area recognizes words as a whole without sounding them out, and then that activity activates pathways toward the front of the brain that correspond to the word's meaning and mental image. Broca's area is only slightly involved.

Findings from brain scan methods of course don't indicate exactly what processes are being used, but they support the theory that advanced readers use different processes from those novice readers use.

POOR INFORMATION DESIGN CAN DISRUPT READING

Careless writing or presentation of text can reduce skilled readers' automatic, context-free reading to conscious, context-based reading, burdening working memory, thereby decreasing speed and comprehension. In unskilled readers, poor text presentation can block reading altogether.

Uncommon or unfamiliar vocabulary

One way software often disrupts reading is by using unfamiliar vocabulary—words the intended readers don't know very well or at all.

One type of unfamiliar terminology is computer jargon, sometimes known as "geek speak." For example, an intranet application displayed the following error message if a user tried to use the application after more than 15 minutes of letting it sit idle:

Your session has expired. Please reauthenticate.

The application was for finding resources—rooms, equipment, etc.—within the company. Its users included receptionists, accountants, and managers, as well as engineers. Most nontechnical users would not understand the word "reauthenticate," so they would drop out of automatic reading mode into conscious wondering about the message's meaning. To avoid disrupting reading, the application's developers could have used the more familiar instruction, "Login again." For a discussion of how "geek speak" in computer-based systems affects learning, see Chapter 11.

Reading can also be disrupted by uncommon terms even if they are not computer technology terms. Here are some rare English words, including many that appear mainly in contracts, privacy statements, or other legal documents:

- *Aforementioned:* mentioned previously
- *Bailiwick:* the region in which a sheriff has legal powers; more generally: domain of control
- *Disclaim:* renounce any claim to or connection with; disown; repudiate
- *Heretofore:* up to the present time; before now
- *Jurisprudence:* the principles and theories on which a legal system is based
- *Obfuscate:* make something difficult to perceive or understand
- *Penultimate:* next to the last, as in "the next to the last chapter of a book"

When readers—even skilled ones—encounter such a word, their automatic reading processes probably won't recognize it. Instead, their brain uses less automatic processes, such as sounding out the word's parts and using them to figure out its meaning, figuring out the meaning from the context in which the word appears, or looking the word up in a dictionary.

Difficult scripts and typefaces

Even when the vocabulary is familiar, reading can be disrupted by typefaces with unfamiliar or hard-to-distinguish shapes. Context-free, automatic reading is based on recognizing letters and words bottom-up from their lower-level visual features. Our visual system is quite literally a neural network that must be *trained* to recognize certain combinations of shapes as characters. Therefore, a typeface with difficult-to-recognize features and shapes will be hard to read. For example, try to read Abraham Lincoln's Gettysburg Address in an outline typeface in ALL CAPS (see Fig. 6.7).

Comparison studies show that skilled readers read uppercase text 10–15% more slowly than lowercase text. Current-day researchers attribute that difference mainly to a lack of practice reading uppercase text, not to an inherent lower recognizability of uppercase text (Larson, 2004). Nonetheless, it is important for designers to be aware of the practice effect (Herrmann, 2011).

ABRAHAM LINCOLN'S GETTYSBURG ADDRESS

FOUR SCORE AND SEVEN YEARS AGO OUR FATHERS BROUGHT FORTH ON THIS CONTINENT, A NEW NATION, CONCEIVED IN LIBERTY, AND DEDICATED TO THE PROPOSITION THAT ALL MEN ARE CREATED EQUAL.
NOW WE ARE ENGAGED IN A GREAT CIVIL WAR, TESTING WHETHER THAT NATION, OR ANY NATION SO CONCEIVED AND SO DEDICATED, CAN LONG ENDURE. WE ARE MET ON A GREAT BATTLE-FIELD OF THAT WAR. WE HAVE COME TO DEDICATE A PORTION OF THAT FIELD, AS A FINAL RESTING PLACE FOR THOSE WHO HERE GAVE THEIR LIVES THAT THAT NATION MIGHT LIVE. IT IS ALTOGETHER FITTING AND PROPER THAT WE SHOULD DO THIS.
BUT, IN A LARGER SENSE, WE CAN NOT DEDICATE -- WE CAN NOT CONSECRATE -- WE CAN NOT HALLOW -- THIS GROUND. THE BRAVE MEN, LIVING AND DEAD, WHO STRUGGLED HERE, HAVE CONSECRATED IT, FAR ABOVE OUR POOR POWER TO ADD OR DETRACT. THE WORLD WILL LITTLE NOTE, NOR LONG REMEMBER WHAT WE SAY HERE, BUT IT CAN NEVER FORGET WHAT THEY DID HERE. IT IS FOR US THE LIVING, RATHER, TO BE DEDICATED HERE TO THE UNFINISHED WORK WHICH THEY WHO FOUGHT HERE HAVE THUS FAR SO NOBLY ADVANCED. IT IS RATHER FOR US TO BE HERE DEDICATED TO THE GREAT TASK REMAINING BEFORE US -- THAT FROM THESE HONORED DEAD WE TAKE INCREASED DEVOTION TO THAT CAUSE FOR WHICH THEY GAVE THE LAST FULL MEASURE OF DEVOTION -- THAT WE HERE HIGHLY RESOLVE THAT THESE DEAD SHALL NOT HAVE DIED IN VAIN -- THAT THIS NATION, UNDER GOD, SHALL HAVE A NEW BIRTH OF FREEDOM -- AND THAT GOVERNMENT OF THE PEOPLE, BY THE PEOPLE, FOR THE PEOPLE, SHALL NOT PERISH FROM THE EARTH.

FIGURE 6.7

Text in ALL CAPS is harder to read because we are not practiced at doing it. Outline typefaces complicate feature recognition. This example demonstrates both.

Tiny fonts

Another way to make text hard to read in software applications, websites, and electronic appliances is to use fonts that are too small for their intended readers' visual system to resolve. For example, try to read the first paragraph of the U.S. Constitution in a seven-point font (see Fig. 6.8).

We the people of the United States, in Order to form a more perfect Union, establish Justice, insure domestic Tranquility, provide for the common defense, promote the general Welfare, and secure the Blessings of Liberty to ourselves and our Posterity, do ordain and establish this Constitution for the United States of America.

FIGURE 6.8

The opening paragraph of the U.S. Constitution, presented in a seven-point font.

Developers sometimes use tiny fonts because they have a lot of text to display in a small amount of space. But if the intended users of the system cannot read the text, or can read it only laboriously, the text might as well not be there.

Text on noisy background

Visual noise in and around text can disrupt recognition of features, characters, and words, and therefore drop reading out of automatic feature-based mode into a more conscious and context-based mode. In software user interfaces and websites, visual noise often results from designers' placing text over a patterned background or displaying text in colors that contrast poorly with the background, as an example from Arvanitakis.com shows (see Fig. 6.9).

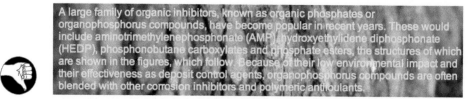

FIGURE 6.9

Arvanitakis.com uses text on a noisy background and poor color contrast.

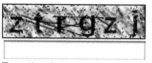

Type the characters you see in the picture above.

FIGURE 6.10

Text that is intentionally displayed with noise so that Web-crawling software cannot read it is called a captcha.

There are situations in which designers *intend* to make text hard to read. For example, a common security measure on the Web is to ask site users to identify distorted words, as proof that they are a live human beings and not an Internet "'bot." This relies on the fact that most people can read text that Internet 'bots cannot currently read. Text displayed as a challenge to test a registrant's humanity is called a *captcha*[3] (see Fig. 6.10).

Of course, *most* text displayed in a user interface should be *easy* to read. A patterned background need not be especially strong to disrupt people's ability to read text placed over it. For example, the Federal Reserve Bank's collection of websites formerly provided a mortgage calculator that was decorated with a repeating pastel background with a home and neighborhood theme. Although well-intentioned, the decorated background made the calculator hard to read (see Fig. 6.11).

Information buried in repetition

Visual noise can also come from the text itself. If successive lines of text contain a lot of repetition, readers receive poor feedback about what line they are focused on, plus it is hard to pick out the important information. For example, recall the example from the California Department of Motor Vehicles web site in Chapter 3 (see Fig. 3.2).

---

[3] The term originally comes from the word "capture," but it is also said to be an acronym for "Completely Automated Public Turing test to tell Computers and Humans Apart."

FIGURE 6.11

The Federal Reserve Bank's online mortgage calculator displayed text on a patterned background.

FIGURE 6.12

Apple.com's "Buy Computer" page lists options in which the important information (keyboard language compatibility) is buried in repetition.

Another example of repetition that creates noise is the computer store on Apple.com. The pages for ordering a laptop computer list different keyboard options for a computer in a very repetitive way, making it hard to see that the essential difference between the keyboards is the language that they support (see Fig. 6.12).

Centered text

One aspect of reading that is highly automatic in most skilled readers is eye movement. In automatic (fast) reading, our eyes are trained to go back to the same horizontal position and down one line. If text is centered or right-aligned, each line of text starts in a different horizontal position. Automatic eye movements, therefore, take our eyes back to the wrong place, so we must consciously adjust our gaze to the *actual* start of each line. This drops us out of automatic mode and slows us down greatly. With poetry and wedding invitations, that is probably okay, but with any

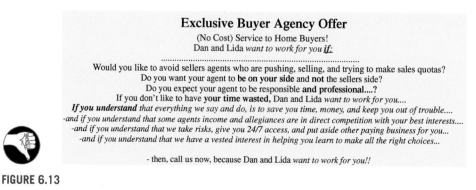

FIGURE 6.13

FargoHomes.com centers text, thwarting automatic eye movement patterns.

other type of text, it is a disadvantage. An example of centered prose text is provided by the web site of FargoHomes, a real estate company (see Fig. 6.13). Try reading the text quickly to demonstrate to yourself how your eyes move.

The same site also centers numbered lists, *really* messing up readers' automatic eye movement (see Fig. 6.14). Try scanning the list quickly.

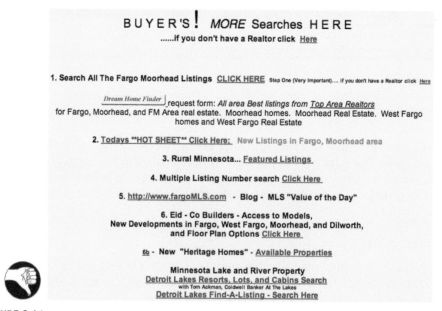

FIGURE 6.14

FargoHomes.com centers numbered items, really thwarting automatic eye movement patterns.

Design implications: Don't disrupt reading; support it!

Obviously, a designer's goal should be to support reading, not disrupt it. Skilled (fast) reading is mostly automatic and mostly based on feature, character, and word recognition. The easier the recognition, the easier and faster the reading. Less skilled reading, by contrast, is greatly assisted by *contextual* cues.

Designers of interactive systems can support both reading methods by following these guidelines:

1) Ensure that text in user interfaces allows the feature-based automatic processes to function effectively by avoiding the disruptive flaws described earlier: difficult or tiny fonts, patterned backgrounds, centering, etc.

2) Use restricted, highly consistent vocabularies—sometimes referred to in the industry as *plain language*[4] or *simplified language* (Redish, 2007).

3) Format text to create a visual hierarchy (see Chapter 3) to facilitate easy scanning: use headings, bulleted lists, tables, and visually emphasized words (see Fig. 6.15).

Experienced information architects, content editors, and graphic designers can be very useful in ensuring that text is presented to support easy scanning and reading.

FIGURE 6.15
Microsoft Word's "Help" homepage is easy to scan and read.

[4]For more information on plain language, see the U.S. government website, www.plainlanguage.gov.

FIGURE 6.16

SmartDraw's "Text Entry Properties" dialog box displays too much text for its simple functionality.

MUCH OF THE READING REQUIRED BY SOFTWARE IS UNNECESSARY

In addition to committing design mistakes that disrupt reading, many software user interfaces simply present *too much* text, requiring users to read more than is necessary. Consider how much unnecessary text there is in a dialog box for setting text entry properties in the SmartDraw application (see Fig. 6.16).

Software designers often justify lengthy instructions by arguing: "We need all that text to explain clearly to users what to do." However, instructions can often be shortened with no loss of clarity. Let's examine how the Jeep company, between 2002 and 2007, shortened its instructions for finding a local Jeep dealer (see Fig. 6.17):

4) *2002:* The "Find a Dealer" page displayed a large paragraph of prose text, with numbered instructions buried in it, and a form asking for more information than needed to find a dealer near the user.

Jeep

FIND A DEALER

It's easy to locate a dealer. 1. Click and hold box number 1 to select your search by Zip Code, City, Dealership Name or State. 2. Enter the Zip Code, City, or Dealership Name in the box marked number 2. 3. If searching by State only, select the state from the pull-down menu in box number 3. **If choosing to search by city or state, type the city in box 2 then select a state in the box marked number 3 to make your search complete. 4. Once finished, simply click the "Search" button.

Search by:
① Zip Code ⬍

Enter Zip Code,City, or Dealership name:
②

Select a State:
③ Choose One ⬍

④ ⊡ SEARCH FOR A DEALER

If you are a member of the U.S. Military, an executive, or a diplomat living outside the U.S., click here for special options.

2002

Jeep

FIND A DEALER

It's easy to locate a Jeep Dealer near you.

- Select Zipcode, City or Dealership Name
  (If you choose to search by city, you will be prompted to provide the state.)
- Provide the Zip Code, City or Dealership Name
- Click on Search

Search by:
① Zip Code ▾

Enter Zip Code,City, or Dealership name:
②

③ ⊡ SEARCH FOR A DEALER

2003

FIND A DEALER ▾

Enter Zip   GO

2007

FIGURE 6.17

Between 2002 and 2007, Jeep.com drastically reduced the reading required by "Find a Dealer."

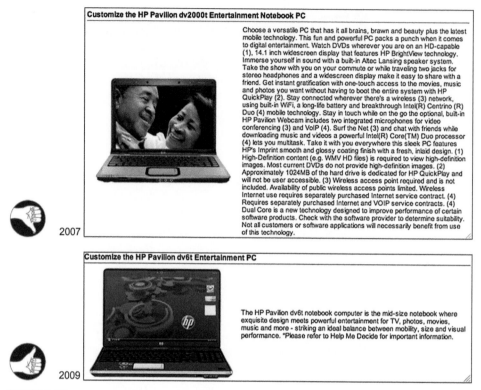

FIGURE 6.18

Between 2007 and 2009, Costco.com drastically reduced the text in product descriptions.

5) *2003:* The instructions on the "Find a Dealer" page had been boiled down to three bullet points, and the form required less information.

6) *2007:* "Find a Dealer" had been cut to one field (zip code) and a "Go" button on the homepage.

Even when text describes products rather than explaining instructions, it is counterproductive to put all a vendor wants to say about a product into a lengthy prose description that people have to read from start to end. Most potential customers cannot or will not read it. Compare Costco.com's descriptions of laptop computers in 2007 with those in 2009 (see Fig. 6.18).

Design implications: Minimize the need for reading

Too much text in a user interface loses poor readers, who unfortunately are a significant percentage of the population. Too much text even alienates *good* readers: it turns using an interactive system into an intimidating amount of *work*.

Minimize the amount of prose text in a user interface; don't present users with long blocks of prose text to read. In instructions, use the *least* amount of text that gets most users to their intended goals. In a product description, provide a brief overview of the product and let users request more detail if they want it. Technical writers and content editors can assist greatly in doing this. For additional advice on how to eliminate unnecessary text, see Krug (2005) and Redish (2007).

TEST ON REAL USERS

Finally, designers should test their designs on the intended user population to be confident that users can read all essential text quickly and effortlessly. Some testing can be done early, using prototypes and partial implementations, but it should also be done just before release. Fortunately, last-minute changes to text font sizes and formats are usually easy to make.

Our Attention is Limited; Our Memory is Imperfect

7

Just as the human visual system has strengths and weaknesses, so do human attention and memory. This chapter describes some of those strengths and weaknesses as background for understanding how we can design interactive systems to support and augment attention and memory rather than burdening or confusing them. We will start with an overview of how memory works, and how it is related to attention.

SHORT- VERSUS LONG-TERM MEMORY

Psychologists historically have distinguished *short-term* memory from *long-term* memory. Short-term memory covers situations in which information is retained for intervals ranging from a fraction of a second to a few minutes. Long-term memory covers situations in which information is retained over longer periods (e.g., hours, days, years, even lifetimes).

It is tempting to think of short- and long-term memory as separate memory stores. Indeed, some theories of memory have considered them separate. After all, in a digital computer, the short-term memory stores (central processing unit [CPU] data registers) are separate from the long-term memory stores (random access memory [RAM], hard disk, flash memory, CD-ROM, etc.). More direct evidence comes from findings that damage to certain parts of the human brain results in short-term memory deficits but not long-term ones, or vice versa. Finally, the speed with which information or plans can disappear from our immediate awareness contrasts sharply with the seeming permanence of our memory of important events in our lives, faces of significant people, activities we have practiced, and information we have studied. These phenomena led many researchers to theorize that short-term memory is a separate store in the brain where information is held temporarily after entering through our perceptual senses (e.g., visual or auditory), or after being retrieved from long-term memory (see Fig. 7.1).

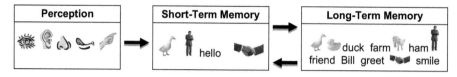

FIGURE 7.1

Traditional (antiquated) view of short-term versus long-term memory.

A MODERN VIEW OF MEMORY

Recent research on memory and brain function indicates that short- and long-term memory are functions of a single memory system—one that is more closely linked with perception than previously thought (Jonides et al., 2008).

Long-term memory

Perceptions enter through the visual, auditory, olfactory, gustatory, or tactile sensory systems and trigger responses starting in areas of the brain dedicated to each sense (e.g., visual cortex, auditory cortex), then spread into other areas of the brain that are *not* specific to any particular sensory modality. The sensory modality–specific areas of the brain detect only simple features of the data, such as a dark–light edge, diagonal line, high-pitched tone, sour taste, red color, or rightward motion. Downstream areas of the brain combine low-level features to detect higher-level features of the input, such as animal, the word "duck," Uncle Kevin, minor key, threat, or fairness.

As described in Chapter 1, the set of neurons activated by a perceived stimulus depends on both the features and context of the stimulus. The context is as important as the features of the stimulus in determining what neural patterns are activated. For example, a dog barking near you when you are walking in your neighborhood activates a different pattern of neural activity in your brain than the same sound heard when you are safely inside your car. The more similar two perceptual stimuli are—that is, the more features and contextual elements they share—the more overlap there is between the sets of neurons that fire in response to them.

The initial strength of a perception depends on how much it is amplified or dampened by other brain activity. All perceptions create some kind of trace, but some are so weak that they can be considered as not registered: the pattern was activated once but never again.

Memory formation consists of changes in the neurons involved in a neural activity pattern, which make the pattern easier to reactivate in the future.[1] Some such changes result from chemicals released near neural endings that boost or inhibit their sensitivity to stimulation. These changes last only until the chemicals dissipate

---

[1] There is evidence that the long-term neural changes associated with learning occur mainly during sleep, suggesting that separating learning sessions by periods of sleep may facilitate learning (Stafford and Webb, 2005).

or are neutralized by other chemicals. More permanent changes occur when neurons grow and branch, forming new connections with others.

Activating a memory consists of reactivating the same pattern of neural activity that occurred when the memory was formed. Somehow the brain distinguishes initial activations of neural patterns from *reactivations*—perhaps by measuring the relative ease with which the pattern was reactivated. New perceptions very similar to the original ones reactivate the same patterns of neurons, resulting in *recognition* if the reactivated perception reaches awareness. In the absence of a similar perception, stimulation from activity in other parts of the brain can also reactivate a pattern of neural activity, which if it reaches awareness results in *recall*.

The more often a neural memory pattern is reactivated, the stronger it becomes—that is, the easier it is to reactivate—which in turn means that the perception it corresponds to is easier to recognize and recall. Neural memory patterns can also be strengthened or weakened by excitatory or inhibitory signals from other parts of the brain.

A particular memory is not located in any specific spot in the brain. The neural activity pattern comprising a memory involves a network of millions of neurons extending over a wide area. Activity patterns for different memories overlap, depending on which features they share. Removing, damaging, or inhibiting neurons in a particular part of the brain typically does not completely wipe out memories that involve those neurons, but rather just reduces the detail or accuracy of the memory by deleting features.[2] However, some areas in a neural activity pattern may be critical pathways, so that removing, damaging, or inhibiting them may prevent most of the pattern from activating, thereby effectively eliminating the corresponding memory.

For example, researchers have long known that the hippocampus, twin seahorse-shaped neural clusters near the base of the brain, plays an important role in storing long-term memories. The modern view is that the hippocampus is a controlling mechanism that directs neural rewiring so as to "burn" memories into the brain's wiring. The amygdala, two jellybean-shaped clusters on the frontal tips of the hippocampus, has a similar role, but it specializes in storing memories of emotionally intense, threatening situations (Eagleman, 2012).

Cognitive psychologists view human long-term memory as consisting of several distinct functions:

- *Semantic* long-term memory stores *facts and relationships.*

- *Episodic* long-term memory records *past events.*

- *Procedural* long-term memory remembers *action sequences.*

These distinctions, while important and interesting, are beyond the scope of this book.

---

[2] This is similar to the effect of cutting pieces out of a holographic image: it reduces the overall resolution of the image, rather than removing areas of it, as with an ordinary photograph.

Short-term memory

The processes just discussed are about long-term memory. What about short-term memory? What psychologists call short-term memory is actually a *combination* of phenomena involving perception, attention, and retrieval from long-term memory.

One component of short-term memory is perceptual. Each of our perceptual senses has its own very brief short-term "memory" that is the result of residual neural activity after a perceptual stimulus ceases, like a bell that rings briefly after it is struck. Until they fade away, these residual perceptions are available as possible input to our brain's attention and memory-storage mechanisms, which integrate input from our various perceptual systems, focus our awareness on some of that input, and store some of it in long-term memory. These sensory-specific residual perceptions together comprise a minor component of short-term memory. Here, we are only interested in them as potential inputs to working memory.

Also available as potential input to working memory are long-term memories reactivated through recognition or recall. As explained earlier, each long-term memory corresponds to a specific pattern of neural activity distributed across our brain. While activated, a memory pattern is a candidate for our attention and therefore potential input for working memory.

The human brain has multiple attention mechanisms, some voluntary and some involuntary. They focus our awareness on a very small subset of the perceptions and activated long-term memories while ignoring everything else. That tiny subset of all the available information from our perceptual systems and our long-term memories that we are aware of *right now* is the main component of our short-term memory, the part that cognitive scientists often call *working memory*. It integrates information from all of our sensory modalities and our long-term memory. Henceforth, we will restrict our discussion of short-term memory to working memory.

So what is working memory? First, here is what it is *not*: it is not a *store*—it is not a *place* in the brain where memories and perceptions *go* to be worked on. And it is nothing like accumulators or fast random-access memory in digital computers.

Instead, working memory is our combined focus of attention: everything that we are conscious of at a given time. More precisely, it is a few perceptions and long-term memories that are activated enough that we remain aware of them over a short period. Psychologists also view working memory as including an executive function—based mainly in the frontal cerebral cortex—that manipulates items we are attending to and, if needed, refreshes their activation so they remain in our awareness (Baddeley, 2012).

A useful—if oversimplified—analogy for memory is a huge, dark, musty warehouse. The warehouse is full of long-term memories, piled haphazardly (not stacked neatly), intermingled and tangled, and mostly covered with dust and cobwebs. Doors along the walls represent our perceptual senses: sight, hearing, smell, taste, touch. They open briefly to let perceptions in. As perceptions enter, they are briefly illuminated by light coming in from outside, but they quickly are pushed (by more entering perceptions) into the dark tangled piles of old memories.

In the ceiling of the warehouse are a small fixed number of searchlights, controlled by the attention mechanism's executive function (Baddeley, 2012). They swing around and focus on items in the memory piles, illuminating them for a while until they swing away to focus elsewhere. Sometimes one or two searchlights focus on new items after they enter through the doors. When a searchlight moves to focus on something new, whatever it had been focusing on is plunged into darkness.

The small fixed number of searchlights represents the limited capacity of working memory. What is illuminated by them (and briefly through the open doors) represents the contents of working memory: out of the vast warehouse's entire contents, the few items we are attending to at any moment. See Figure 7.2 for a visual.

The warehouse analogy is too simple and should not be taken too seriously. As Chapter 1 explained, our senses are *not* just passive doorways into our brains, through which our environment "pushes" perceptions. Rather, our brain actively and continually *seeks out* important events and features in our environment and "pulls" perceptions in as needed (Ware, 2008). Furthermore, the brain is buzzing with activity most of the time and its internal activity is only modulated—not determined—by sensory input (Eagleman, 2012). Also, as described earlier, memories are embodied as networks of neurons distributed around the brain, not as objects in a specific location. Finally, activating a memory in the brain can activate related ones; our warehouse-with-searchlights analogy doesn't represent that.

Nonetheless, the analogy—especially the part about the searchlights—illustrates that working memory is a *combination* of several *foci of attention*—the currently

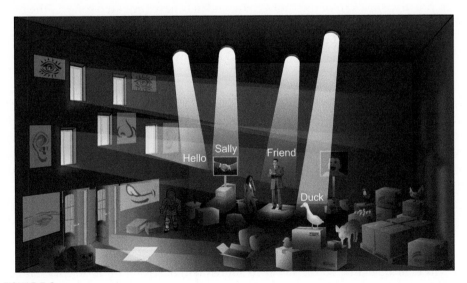

FIGURE 7.2

Modern view of memory: a dark warehouse full of stuff (long-term memory), with searchlights focused on a few items (short-term memory).

activated neural patterns of which we are aware—and that the capacity of working memory is extremely limited, and the content at any given moment is very volatile.

What about the earlier finding that damage to some parts of the brain causes short-term memory deficits, while other types of brain damage cause long-term memory deficits? The current interpretation is that some types of damage decrease or eliminate the brain's ability to focus attention on specific objects and events, while other types of damage harm the brain's ability to store or retrieve long-term memories.

CHARACTERISTICS OF ATTENTION AND WORKING MEMORY

As noted, working memory is equal to the focus of our attention. Whatever is in that focus is what we are conscious of at any moment. But what determines what we attend to and how much we can attend to at any given time?

Attention is highly focused and selective

Most of what is going on around you at this moment you are unaware of. Your perceptual system and brain sample very selectively from your surroundings, because they don't have the capacity to process everything.

Right now you are conscious of the last few words and ideas you've read, but probably not the color of the wall in front of you. But now that I've shifted your attention, you *are* conscious of the wall's color, and may have forgotten some of the ideas you read on the previous page.

Chapter 1 described how our perception is filtered and biased by our goals. For example, if you are looking for your friend in a crowded shopping mall, your visual system "primes" itself to notice people who look like your friend (including how he or she is dressed), and barely notice everything else. Simultaneously, your auditory system primes itself to notice voices that sound like your friend's voice, and even footsteps that sound like those of your friend. Human-shaped blobs in your peripheral vision and sounds localized by your auditory system that match your friend snap your eyes and head toward them. While you look, anyone looking or sounding similar to your friend attracts your attention, and you won't notice other people or events that would normally have interested you.

Besides focusing on objects and events related to our current goals, our attention is drawn to:

- *Movement, especially movement near or toward us.* For example, something jumps at you while you walk on a street, or something swings toward your head in a haunted house ride at an amusement park, or a car in an adjacent lane suddenly swerves toward your lane (see the discussion of the *flinch reflex* in Chapter 14).

- *Threats.* Anything that signals or portends danger to us or people in our care.

- *Faces of other people.* We are primed from birth to notice faces more than other objects in our environment.

- *Sex and food.* Even if we are happily married and well fed, these things attract our attention. Even the mere words probably quickly got your attention.

These things, along with our current goals, draw our attention involuntarily. We don't become aware of something in our environment and then orient ourselves toward it. It's the other way around: our perceptual system detects something attention-worthy and orients us toward it preconsciously, and only afterwards do we become aware of it.[3]

Capacity of attention (a.k.a. working memory)

The primary characteristics of working memory are its low capacity and volatility. But what is the capacity? In terms of the warehouse analogy presented earlier, what is *the small fixed number* of searchlights?

Many college-educated people have read about "the magical number seven, plus or minus two," proposed by cognitive psychologist George Miller in 1956 as the limit on the number of simultaneous unrelated items in human working memory (Miller, 1956).

Miller's characterization of the working memory limit naturally raises several questions:

- *What are the items in working memory?* They are current perceptions and retrieved memories. They are goals, numbers, words, names, sounds, images, odors—anything one can be aware of. In the brain, they are patterns of neural activity.

- *Why must items be unrelated?* Because if two items are related, they correspond to one big neural activity pattern—one set of features—and hence one item, not two.

- *Why the fudge-factor of plus or minus two?* Because researchers cannot measure with perfect accuracy how much people can keep track of, and because of differences between individuals in working memory capacity.

Later research in the 1960s and 1970s found Miller's estimate to be too high. In the experiments Miller considered, some of the items presented to people to remember could be "chunked" (i.e., considered related), making it appear that people's working memory was holding more items than it actually was. Furthermore, all the subjects in Miller's experiments were college students. Working memory capacity varies in the general population. When the experiments were revised to disallow unintended chunking and include noncollege students as subjects, the average capacity of working memory was shown to be more like four plus or minus one—that is, three to five items (Broadbent, 1975; Mastin, 2010). Thus, in our warehouse analogy, there would be only four searchlights.

---

[3] Exactly how long afterwards is discussed in Chapter 14.

More recent research has cast doubt on the idea that the capacity of working memory should be measured in whole items or "chunks." It turns out that in early working memory experiments, people were asked to briefly remember items (e.g., words or images) that were quite different from each other—that is, they had very few features in common. In such a situation, people don't have to remember every feature of an item to recall it a few seconds later; remembering some of its features is enough. So people appeared to recall items as a whole, and therefore working memory capacity seemed measurable in whole items.

Recent experiments have given people items to remember that are similar—that is, they share many features. In that situation, to recall an item and not confuse it with other items, people must remember more of its features. In these experiments, researchers found that people remember more details (i.e., features) of some items than of others, and the items they remember in greater detail are the ones they paid more attention to (Bays and Husain, 2008). This suggests that the unit of attention—and therefore the capacity of working memory—is best measured in item features rather than whole items or "chunks" (Cowan et al., 2004). This jibes with the modern view of the brain as a feature-recognition device, but it is controversial among memory researchers, some of whom argue that the basic capacity of human working memory is three to five whole items, but that is reduced if people attend to a large number of details (i.e., features) of the items (Alvarez and Cavanagh, 2004).

Bottom line: The true capacity of human working memory is still a research topic.

The second important characteristic of working memory is how volatile it is. Cognitive psychologists used to say that new items arriving in working memory often bump old ones out, but that way of describing the volatility is based on the view of working memory as a temporary storage place for information. The modern view of working memory as the current focus of attention makes it even clearer: focusing attention on new information turns it away from some of what it was focusing on. That is why the searchlight analogy is useful.

However we describe it, information can easily be lost from working memory. If items in working memory don't get combined or rehearsed, they are at risk of having the focus shifted away from them. This volatility applies to goals as well as to the details of objects. Losing items from working memory corresponds to forgetting or losing track of something you were doing. We have all had such experiences, for example:

- Going to another room for something, but once there we can't remember why we came.

- Taking a phone call, and afterward not remembering what we were doing before the call.

- Something yanks our attention away from a conversation, and then we can't remember what we were talking about.

- In the middle of adding a long list of numbers, something distracts us, so we have to start over.

WORKING MEMORY TEST

To test your working memory, get a pen or pencil and two blank sheets of paper and follow these instructions:

1. Place one blank sheet of paper after this page in the book and use it to cover the next page.

2. Flip to the next page for three seconds, pull the paper cover down and read the **black numbers** at the top, and flip back to this page. Don't peek at other numbers on that page unless you want to ruin the test.

3. Say your phone number backward, out loud.

4. Now write down the black numbers from memory. … Did you get all of them?

5. Flip back to the next page for three seconds, read the red numbers (under the black ones), and flip back.

6. Write down the numbers from memory. These would be easier to recall than the first ones if you noticed that they are the first seven digits of π (3.141592), because then they would be only one number, not seven.

7. Flip back to the next page for 3 seconds, read the **green numbers**, and flip back.

8. Write down the numbers from memory. If you noticed that they are odd numbers from 1 to 13, they would be easier to recall, because they would be three chunks ("odd, 1, 13" or "odd, seven from 1"), not seven.

9. Flip back to the next page for three seconds, read the orange words, and flip back.

10. Write down the words from memory. … Could you recall them all?

11. Flip back to the next page for three seconds, read the **blue words**, and flip back.

12. Write down the words from memory. … It was certainly a lot easier to recall them all because they form a sentence, so they could be memorized as one sentence rather than seven words.

3 8 4 7 5 3 9

3 1 4 1 5 9 2

1 3 5 7 9 11 13

town river corn string car shovel

what is the meaning of life

IMPLICATIONS OF WORKING MEMORY CHARACTERISTICS FOR USER-INTERFACE DESIGN

The capacity and volatility of working memory have many implications for the design of interactive computer systems. The basic implication is that user interfaces should help people remember essential information from one moment to the next. Don't require people to remember system status or what they have done, because their attention is focused on their primary goal and progress toward it. Specific examples follow.

Modes

The limited capacity and volatility of working memory is one reason why user-interface design guidelines often say to either avoid designs that have *modes* or provide adequate mode feedback. In a moded user interface, some user actions have different effects depending on what mode the system is in. For example:

- In a car, pressing the accelerator pedal can move the car either forwards, backwards, or not at all, depending on whether the transmission is in drive, reverse, or neutral. The transmission sets a mode in the car's user interface.

- In many digital cameras, pressing the shutter button can either snap a photo or start a video recording, depending on which mode is selected.

- In a drawing program, clicking and dragging normally selects one or more graphic objects on the drawing, but when the software is in "draw rectangle" mode, clicking and dragging adds a rectangle to the drawing and stretches it to the desired size.

Moded user interfaces have advantages; that is why many interactive systems have them. Modes allow a device to have more functions than controls: the same control provides different functions in different modes. Modes allow an interactive system to assign different meanings to the same gestures to reduce the number of gestures users must learn.

However, one well-known *dis*advantage of modes is that people often make *mode errors*: they forget what mode the system is in and do the wrong thing by mistake (Johnson, 1990). This is especially true in systems that give poor feedback about what the current mode is. Because of the problem of mode errors, many user-interface design guidelines say to either avoid modes or provide strong feedback about which mode the system is in. Human working memory is too unreliable for designers to assume that users can, without clear, continuous feedback, keep track of what mode the system is in, even when the users are the ones changing the system from one mode to another.

Search results

When people use a search function on a computer to find information, they enter the search terms, start the search, and then review the results. Evaluating the results often requires knowing what the search terms were. If working memory were less limited, people would always remember, when browsing the results, what they had entered as search terms just a few seconds earlier. But as we have seen, working memory is very limited. When the results appear, a person's attention naturally turns away from what he or she entered and toward the results. Therefore, it should be no surprise that people viewing search results often do not remember the search terms they just typed.

Unfortunately, some designers of online search functions don't understand that. Search results sometimes don't show the search terms that generated the results. For example, in 2006, the search results page at Slate.com provided search fields so users could search again, but didn't show what a user had searched for (see Fig. 7.3A). A recent version of the site shows the user's search terms (see Fig. 7.3B), reducing the burden on users' working memory.

Calls to action

A well-known "netiquette" guideline for writing email messages, especially messages that require responses or ask the recipients to do something, is to restrict each message to one topic. If a message contains multiple topics or requests, its recipients may focus on one of them (usually the first one), get engrossed in responding to that, and forget to respond to the rest of the email. The guideline to put different topics or requests into separate emails is a direct result of the limited capacity of human attention.

(A)

Search for:

[   ] 🔍 Search

Advanced Search Options

Topics [   ]

Departments [   ]

Authors [   ]

Publication Date

from [   ]

to [   ]

🔍 Search

Found 968 matches.   `<< 1 - 25 of 968 >>`

Ranks	Headline	Author	Published	Department
****	**Defendant DeLay? Part 2** Who blurted out, "$100,000"? A hypothesis.	Timothy Noah	Oct 06, 2004	Chatterbox
****	**The Tom DeLay Scandals** A scorecard.	Nicholas Thompson	Apr 07, 2005	Gist, The
****	**The Wall Street Journal vs. Tom DeLay** Has the editorial page gotten ... nice?	Timothy Noah	Dec 12, 2001	Chatterbox
****	**Defendant DeLay?** Nick Smith's bribery accusations	Timothy Noah	Oct 01, 2004	Chatterbox

(B)

HOME / SEARCH

Search Results

[iwatch   ] [Search]

What Do We Know About Apple's "iWatch"? (VIDEO)
Slate V Staff | TRENDING NEWS CHANNEL | Monday, Feb. 11, 2013, at 4:33 PM

💬 Comment   👍 Like   🐦 Tweet

Is Apple Working on a Smart Watch?
Daniel Politi | THE SLATEST | Sunday, Feb. 10, 2013, at 3:48 PM

💬 Comment   👍 Like   🐦 Tweet

FIGURE 7.3

Slate.com search results: (A) in 2007, users' search terms were not shown, but (B) in 2013, search terms are shown.

Web designers are familiar with a similar guideline: Avoid putting competing calls to action on a page. Each page should have only *one* dominant call to action— or one for each possible user goal—to not overwhelm users' attention capacity and cause them go down paths that don't achieve their (or the site owner's) goals.

A related guideline: Once users have specified their goal, don't distract them from accomplishing it by displaying extraneous links and calls to action. Instead, guide them to the goal by using a design pattern called the *process funnel* (van Duyne et al., 2002; see also Johnson, 2007).

Instructions

If you asked a friend for a recipe or for directions to her home, and she gave you a long sequence of steps, you probably would not try to remember it all. You would know that you could not reliably keep all of the instructions in your working memory, so you would write them down or ask your friend to send them to you by email. Later, while following the instructions, you would put them where you could refer to them until you reached the goal.

Similarly, interactive systems that display instructions for multistep operations should allow people to refer to the instructions while executing them until completing all the steps. Most interactive systems do this (see Fig. 7.4), but some do not (see Fig. 7.5).

Navigation depth

Using a software product, digital device, phone menu system, or Web site often involves navigating to the user's desired information or goal. It is well established that navigation hierarchies that are broad and shallow are easier for most people— especially those who are nontechnical—to find their way around in than narrow, deep hierarchies (Cooper, 1999). This applies to hierarchies of application windows and dialog boxes, as well as to menu hierarchies (Johnson, 2007).

FIGURE 7.4

Instructions in Windows Help files remain displayed while users follow them.

FIGURE 7.5

Instructions for Windows XP wireless setup start by telling users to close the instructions.

A related guideline: In hierarchies deeper than two levels, provide navigation "breadcrumb" paths to constantly remind users where they are (Nielsen, 1999; van Duyne et al., 2002).

These guidelines, like the others mentioned earlier, are based on the limited capacity of human working memory. Requiring a user to drill down through eight levels of dialog boxes, web pages, menus, or tables—especially with no visible reminders of their location—will probably exceed the user's working memory capacity, thereby causing him or her to forget where he or she came from or what his or her overall goals were.

CHARACTERISTICS OF LONG-TERM MEMORY

Long-term memory differs from working memory in many respects. Unlike working memory, it actually *is* a memory store.

However, specific memories are not stored in any one neuron or location in the brain. As described earlier, memories, like perceptions, consist of patterns of activation of large sets of neurons. Related memories correspond to overlapping patterns of activated neurons. This means that every memory is stored in a distributed fashion, spread among many parts of the brain. In this way, long-term memory in the brain is similar to holographic light images.

Long-term memory evolved to serve our ancestors and us very well in getting around in our world. However, it has many weaknesses: it is error-prone, impressionist, free-associative, idiosyncratic, retroactively alterable, and easily biased by a variety of factors at the time of recording or retrieval. Let's examine some of these weaknesses.

Error-prone

Nearly everything we've ever experienced is stored in our long-term memory. Unlike working memory, the capacity of human long-term memory seems almost unlimited. Adult human brains each contain about 86 billion neurons (Herculano-Houzel, 2009). As described earlier, individual neurons do not store memories; memories are encoded by networks of neurons acting together. Even if only some of the brain's neurons are involved in memory, the large number of neurons allows for a great many different combinations of them, each capable of representing a different memory. Still, no one has yet measured or even estimated the maximum information capacity of the human brain.[4] Whatever the capacity is, it's a lot.

However, what is in long-term memory is not an accurate, high-resolution recording of our experiences. In terms familiar to computer engineers, one could characterize long-term memory as using heavy compression methods that drop a great deal of information. Images, concepts, events, sensations, actions—all are reduced to combinations of abstract features. Different memories are stored at different levels of detail—that is, with more or fewer features.

For example, the face of a man you met briefly who is not important to you might be stored simply as an average Caucasian male face with a beard, with no other details—a whole face reduced to three features. If you were asked later to describe the man in his absence, the most you could honestly say was that he was a "white guy with a beard." You would not be able to pick him out of a police lineup of other Caucasian men with beards. In contrast, your memory of your best friend's face includes many more features, allowing you to give a more detailed description and pick your friend out of any police lineup. Nonetheless, it is still a set of features, not anything like a bitmap image.

As another example, I have a vivid childhood memory of being run over by a plow and badly cut, but my father says it happened to my brother. One of us is wrong.

In the realm of human–computer interaction, a Microsoft Word user may remember that there is a command to insert a page number, but may not remember which *menu* the command is in. That specific feature may not have been recorded when the user learned how to insert page numbers. Alternatively, perhaps the menu-location feature *was* recorded, but just does not reactivate with the rest of the memory pattern when the user tries to recall how to insert a page number.

Weighted by emotions

Chapter 1 described a dog that remembered seeing a cat in his front yard every time he returned home in the family car. The dog was excited when he first saw the cat, so his memory of it was strong and vivid.

A comparable human example would be an adult could easily have strong memories of her first day at nursery school, but probably not of her tenth. On the first day, she was probably upset about being left at the school by her parents, whereas by the tenth day, being left there was nothing unusual.

Retroactively alterable

Suppose that while you are on an ocean cruise with your family, you see a whale-shark. Years later, when you and your family are discussing the trip, you might remember

---

[4] The closest researchers have come is Landauer's (1986) use of the average human learning rate to calculate the amount of information a person can learn in a lifetime: 10^9 bits, or a few hundred megabytes.

A LONG-TERM MEMORY TEST

Test your long-term memory by answering the following questions:

1. Was there a roll of tape in the toolbox in Chapter 1?
2. What was your *previous* phone number?
3. Which of these words were *not* in the list presented in the working memory test earlier in this chapter: city, stream, corn, auto, twine, spade?
4. What was your first-grade teacher's name? Second grade? Third grade? …
5. What Web site was presented earlier that does not show search terms when it displays search results?

Regarding question 3: When words are memorized, often what is retained is the *concept*, rather than the exact word that was presented. For example, one could hear the word "town" and later recall it as "city."

seeing a whale, and one of your relatives might recall seeing a shark. For both of you, some details in long-term memory were dropped because they did not fit a common concept.

A true example comes from 1983, when the late President Ronald Reagan was speaking with Jewish leaders during his first term as president. He spoke about being in Europe during World War II and helping to liberate Jews from the Nazi concentration camps. The trouble was, he was never in Europe during World War II. When he was an actor, he was in a *movie* about World War II, made entirely in Hollywood. That important detail was missing from his memory.

IMPLICATIONS OF LONG-TERM MEMORY CHARACTERISTICS FOR USER-INTERFACE DESIGN

The main thing that the characteristics of long-term memory imply is that people need tools to augment it. Since prehistoric times, people have invented technologies to help them remember things over long periods: notched sticks, knotted ropes, mnemonics, verbal stories and histories retold around campfires, writing, scrolls, books, number systems, shopping lists, checklists, phone directories, datebooks, accounting ledgers, oven timers, computers, portable digital assistants (PDAs), online shared calendars, etc.

Given that humankind has a need for technologies that *augment* memory, it seems clear that software designers should try to provide software that fulfills that need. At the very least, designers should avoid developing systems that *burden* long-term memory. Yet that is exactly what many interactive systems do.

Authentication is one functional area in which many software systems place burdensome demands on users' long-term memory. For example, a web application developed a few years ago told users to change their personal identification number (PIN) "to a number that is easy to remember," but then imposed restrictions that made it impossible to do so (see Fig. 7.6). Whoever wrote those instructions seems to have realized that the PIN requirements were unreasonable, because the instructions end by advising users to write down their PIN! Nevermind that writing a PIN down creates a security risk and adds yet *another* memory task: users must remember where they hid their written-down PIN.

A contrasting example of burdening people's long-term memory for the sake of security comes from Intuit.com. To purchase software, visitors must register. The site requires users to select a security question from a menu (see Fig. 7.7). What if you can't answer *any* of the questions? What if you don't recall your first pet's name, your high school mascot, or any of the answers to the other questions?

But that isn't where the memory burden ends. Some questions could have several possible answers. Many people had several elementary schools, childhood friends, or heroes. To register, they must choose a question and then *remember* which answer they gave to Intuit.com. How? Probably by writing it down somewhere. Then, when Intuit.com asks them the security question, they have to *remember* where they put the answer. Why burden people's memory, when it would be easy to let users make up a security question for which they can easily recall the one possible answer?

Such unreasonable demands on people's long-term memory counteract the security and productivity that computer-based applications supposedly provide (Schrage, 2005), as users:

- Place sticky notes on or near computers or "hide" them in desk drawers.

- Contact customer support to recover passwords they cannot recall.

Instruction:

Change your PIN to a number that is easy for you to remember. A PIN can be 6-10 digits and cannot start with 0.
Your PIN must be numeric.

New PIN:

Confirm New PIN:

Remember: Please write down your PIN.

FIGURE 7.6

Instructions tell users to create an easy-to-remember PIN, but the restrictions make that impossible.

FIGURE 7.7

Intuit.com's registration burdens long-term memory: users may have no unique, memorable answer for any of the questions.

FIGURE 7.8

NetworkSolutions.com lets users create a security question if none on the menu works for them.

- Use passwords that are easy for others to guess.
- Set up systems with no login requirements at all, or with one shared login and password.

The registration form at NetworkSolutions.com represents a small step toward more usable security. Like Intuit.com, it offers a choice of security questions, but it also allows users to create their own security question—one for which they can more easily remember the answer (see Fig. 7.8).

Another implication of long-term memory characteristics for interactive systems is that learning and long-term retention are enhanced by user-interface consistency.

The more consistent the operation of different functions, or the more consistent the actions on different types of objects, the less users have to learn. User interfaces that have many exceptions and little consistency from one function or object to another require users to store in their long-term memory many features about each function or object and its correct usage context. The need to encode more features makes such user interfaces harder to learn. It also makes it more likely that a user's memory will drop essential features during storage or retrieval, increasing the chances that the user will fail to remember, misremember, or make other memory errors.

Even though some have criticized the concept of consistency as ill-defined and easy to apply badly (Grudin, 1989), the fact is that consistency in a user interface greatly reduces the burden on users' long-term memory. Mark Twain once wrote: "If you tell the truth, you never have to remember anything." One could also say, "If everything worked the same way, you would not have to remember much." We will return to the issue of user-interface consistency in Chapter 11.

Limits on Attention Shape Our Thought and Action

8

When people interact purposefully with the world around them, including computer systems, some aspects of their behavior follow predictable patterns, some of which result from the limited capacity of attention and short-term memory. When interactive systems are designed to recognize and support those patterns, they fit better with the way people operate. Some user-interface design rules, then, are based directly on the patterns and thus indirectly on the limits of short-term memory and attention. This chapter describes seven important patterns.

WE FOCUS ON OUR GOALS AND PAY LITTLE ATTENTION TO OUR TOOLS

As Chapter 7 explained, our attention has very limited capacity. When people are doing a task—trying to accomplish a goal—most of their attention is focused on the goals and data related to that task. Normally, people devote very little attention to the tools they are using to perform a task, whether they are using computer applications, online services, or interactive appliances. Instead, people think about their tools only superficially, and then only when necessary.

We are, of course, *capable* of attending to our tools. However, attention (i.e., short-term memory) is limited in capacity. When people refocus their attention on their tools, it is pulled away from the details of the task. This shift increases the chances of users losing track of what they were doing or exactly where they were in doing it.

For example, if your lawn mower stops running while you are mowing your lawn, you will immediately stop and focus on the mower. Restarting the mower becomes your primary task, with the mower itself as the focus. You pay scant attention to any tools you use to restart the mower, just as you paid scant attention to the mower when your primary focus was the lawn. After you restart the mower and resume mowing the lawn, you probably wouldn't remember where you were in mowing the lawn, except that the lawn itself shows you.

Other tasks—for example, reading a document, measuring a table, counting gold-fish in a fish tank—might not provide such a clear reminder of your interrupted task and your position in it. You might have to start over from the beginning. You might even forget what you were doing altogether and go off to do something else.

That is why most software design guidelines state that software applications and most Web sites should not call attention to themselves; they should fade into the background and allow users to focus on their own goals. That design guideline is even the title of a popular web design book: *Don't Make Me Think* (Krug, 2005). That is, if your software or Web site makes me think about *it*, rather than what I am trying to do, you've lost me.

WE NOTICE THINGS MORE WHEN THEY ARE RELATED TO OUR GOALS

Chapter 1 described how our immediate goals filter and bias our perception. Chapter 7 discussed the connections between attention and memory. This chapter provides examples showing that perceptual filtering and biasing, attention, and memory are all closely related.

Our environment is full of perceptual details and events. Obviously, we cannot notice and keep track of everything that happens around us. Nonetheless, it is surprising to most people how little we notice of what goes on around us. Because of our extremely limited short-term memory and attention, we don't waste those resources. When an event happens, the few details about it that we notice and remember later are usually those that were important for our goals at the time of the event. This is demonstrated by two related psychological phenomena: *inattentional blindness* and *change blindness*.

Inattentional blindness

When our mind is intensely occupied with a task, goal, or emotion, we sometimes fail to notice objects and events in our environment that we otherwise would have noticed and remembered. This phenomenon has been heavily studied by psychologists and labeled *inattentional blindness* (Simons and Chabris, 1999; Simons, 2007).

A clear demonstration of inattentional blindness is an experiment in which human subjects watched a video of two basketball teams passing a ball from one player to another. Subjects were told to count the number of times the white-suited team passed the ball. While they watched the video and counted the ball-passes, a person in a gorilla suit sauntered onto the basketball court, thumped his chest, then walked out of view (see Fig. 8.1). Afterwards, subjects were asked what they remembered from the video. Surprisingly, about half of them did not notice the gorilla. Their attention was fully occupied with the task (Simons and Chabris, 1999).

FIGURE 8.1

Scene from video used in "invisible gorilla" study. *Figure provided by Daniel Simons.* For more information about the study and to see the video, go to www.dansimons.com or www.theinvisiblegorilla.com.

Change blindness

Another way researchers have shown that our goals strongly focus our attention and memory is through the following: show people a picture, then show them a second version of the same picture and ask them how the two pictures differ. Surprisingly, the second picture can differ from the first in many ways without people noticing. To explore further, researchers gave people questions to answer about the first picture, affecting their goals in looking at it, and therefore what features of the picture they paid attention to. The result was people don't notice differences in features other than those their goals made them pay attention to. This is called *change blindness* (Angier, 2008).

A particularly striking example of how our goals focus our attention and affect what we remember comes from experiments in which experimenters holding city maps posed as lost tourists and asked local people walking by for directions. When the local person focused on the tourist's map to figure out the best route, two workmen—actually, more experimenters—walked between the tourist and the advice-giver carrying a large door, and in that moment the tourist was replaced by another experimenter-tourist. Astoundingly, after the door passed, over half of the local people continued helping the tourist without noticing any change, even when the two tourists differed in hair color or in whether they had a beard (Simons and Levin, 1998).[1] Some people even failed to notice changes in gender. In summary,

---

[1] For demonstrations of change blindness, search YouTube for those words, or for "door study" and "person swap."

people focus on the tourist only long enough to determine if he or she is a threat or worth helping, record only that the person is a tourist who needs help, and then focus on the map and the task of giving directions.

When people interact with software, electronic appliances, or online services, it is not uncommon for them to fail to notice important changes in what is displayed. For example, in a study of seniors using travel websites, changes in price resulting from user actions were often not obvious. Even after spotting the price information, participants were prone to change blindness: when they changed trip options (e.g., departure city, additional excursions, cabin class), they often would not notice that the price changed (Finn and Johnson, 2013). The study only used older adults, so we don't know whether younger participants would have had the same trouble noticing price changes.

The user-interface design guideline that follows from such findings is to make changes obvious—that is, highly salient—and take steps to draw users' attention to the change. For example, a way to draw users' attention to a new error message is to vibrate it briefly when it first appears (see Chapter 6), or highlight it briefly before it reverts to a "normal" appearance.

What happens in our brains

Using functional magnetic resonance imagery (fMRI) and electrical encephalography (EEG), researchers have studied the effect of attention on how our brains respond to objects displayed on a computer screen.

When people passively watch a computer display with objects appearing, moving around, and disappearing, the visual cortex of their brains registers a certain activity level. When people are told to look for (i.e., pay attention to) certain objects, the activity level of their visual cortex increases significantly. When they are told to ignore certain objects, the neural activity level in their visual cortex actually drops when those objects appear. Later, their memory for which objects they saw and didn't see corresponds to the degree of attention they paid to them and to the level of brain activity (Gazzaley, 2009).

WE USE EXTERNAL AIDS TO KEEP TRACK OF WHAT WE ARE DOING

Because our short-term memory and attention are so limited, we learn not to rely on them. Instead, we mark up our environment to show us where we are in a task. Examples include:

- *Counting objects.* If possible, we move already counted objects into a different pile to indicate which objects have already been counted. If we cannot move an object, we point to the last object counted. To keep track of the number we are on, we count on our fingers, draw marks, or write numbers.

- **Reading books.** When we stop reading, we insert bookmarks to show what page we were on.

- **Arithmetic.** We learn methods of doing arithmetic on paper, or we use a calculator.

- **Checklists.** We use checklists to aid both our long- and short-term memory. In critical or rarely performed tasks, checklists help us remember everything that needs to be done. In that way, they augment our faulty long-term memory. While doing the task, we check off items as we complete them. That is a short-term memory aid. A checklist that we can't mark up is hard to use, so we copy it and mark the copy.

- **Editing documents.** People often keep to-be-edited documents, documents that are currently being edited, and already edited documents in separate folders.

One implication of this pattern is that interactive systems should indicate what users have done versus what they have not yet done. Most email applications do this by marking already-read versus unread messages, most Web sites do it by marking visited versus unvisited links, and many applications do it by marking completed steps of a multipart task (see Fig. 8.2).

A second design implication is that interactive systems should allow users to mark or move objects to indicate which ones they have worked on versus which ones they have not worked on. Mac OS lets users assign colors to files. Like moving files between folders, this technique can be used to keep track of where one is in a task (see Fig. 8.3).

	Software Update		
Install	**Name**	**Version**	**Size**
☐	Backup	3.1	6.0 MB
☐	iTunes Phone Driver	1.0	380 KB
☐	Backup	3.1.2	7.1 MB
✓ ☐	iTunes	7.6	44.7 MB
⟳ ☑	QuickTime	7.4	53.3 MB

QuickTime
Installing: Installing QuickTime 7

⬛⬛⬛⬛⬛⬛⬛⬛⬛⬛   (Stop)   (Install 2 Items)

FIGURE 8.2

The Mac OS Software Update shows which updates are done (green check) versus which are in progress (rotating circle).

▶ 🗀 Can't Edit Prev Entered Data	1/2/07
▶ 🗀 Cancel doesn't cancel	12/29/06
▶ 🗀 Missing options	1/13/09
▶ 🗀 Moving controls	9/14/09
▶ 🗀 Trapping User	9/14/09

FIGURE 8.3

Mac OS lets users assign colors to files or folders; users can use the colors to track their work.

Used by permission, www.OK/Cancel.com.

WE FOLLOW THE INFORMATION "SCENT" TOWARD OUR GOAL

Focusing our attention on our goals makes us interpret what we see on a display or hear in a telephone menu in a very *literal* way. People don't think deeply about instructions, command names, option labels, icons, navigation bar items, or any other aspect of the user interface of computer-based tools. If the goal in their head is to make a flight reservation, their attention will be attracted by anything displaying the words "buy," "flight," "ticket," or "reservation." Other items that a designer or marketer might think will attract customers, such as "bargain hotels," will not attract the attention of people who are trying to book a flight, although they might be noticed by people who are looking for bargains.

This tendency of people to notice only things on a computer display that match their goal, and the literal thinking that they exhibit when performing a task on a computer, has been called "following the *scent* of information toward the goal" (Chi

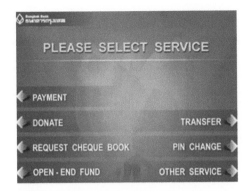

For each goal below, what on the screen would attract your attention?

- Pay a bill
- Transfer money to your savings account
- Pay your dentist by funds transfer
- Change your PIN
- Open a new account
- Purchase travelers' cheque

FIGURE 8.4

ATM screen—our attention is drawn initially toward items that match our goal literally.

et al., 2001; Nielsen, 2003). Consider the ATM machine display shown in Figure 8.4. What is the first thing on the screen that gets your attention when you are given each of the goals listed?

You probably noticed that some of the listed goals direct your attention initially to the wrong option. Is "Pay your dentist by funds transfer" under "Payment" or "Transfer"? "Open a new account" probably sent your eyes briefly to "Open-End Fund," even though it is actually under "Other Service." Did the goal "Purchase traveler's cheques" make you glance at "Request Cheque Book" because of the word they share?

The goal-seeking strategy of following the information scent, observed across a wide variety of situations and systems, suggests that interactive systems should be designed so that the scent is strong and really leads users to their goals. To do that, designers need to understand the goals that users are likely to have at each decision point in a task, and ensure that each choice point in the software provides options for every important user goal and clearly indicates which option leads to which goal.

For example, imagine that you want to cancel a reservation you made or a payment you scheduled. You tell the system to cancel it, and a confirmation dialog box appears asking if you really want to do that. How should the options be labeled? Given that people interpret words literally in following the information scent toward their goal, the standard confirmation button labels "OK" (for yes) and "Cancel" (for no) would give a misleading scent. If we compare a cancellation confirmation dialog box from Marriott.com to one from WellsFargo.com, we see that Marriott.com's labeling provides a clearer scent than Quicken.com's (see Fig. 8.5).

As a second example, imagine that you forgot that a certain document was already open, and you tried to open it again. The designers of Microsoft Excel did a better job than the designers of Microsoft Word in anticipating this situation, understanding the goals you might have at this point, and presenting you with instructions and options that make it clear what to do (see Fig. 8.6).

FIGURE 8.5

Marriott's cancellation confirmation (A) provides a clearer scent than Wells Fargo's (B).

FIGURE 8.6

Microsoft Excel's (A) warning when users try to open an already-open file is clearer than Microsoft Word's (B).

WE PREFER FAMILIAR PATHS

People know that their attention is limited, and they act accordingly. While pursuing a goal, they take *familiar* paths whenever possible rather than exploring *new* ones, especially when working under deadlines. As explained more fully in Chapter 10, exploring new paths is problem solving, which severely taxes our attention and short-term memory. In contrast, taking familiar, well-learned routes can be done fairly automatically and does not consume much attention and short-term memory.

Years ago, in a usability test session, a test participant in the middle of a task said to me:

I'm in a hurry, so I'll do it the long way.

He knew there probably was a more efficient way to do what he was doing, but he also knew that learning the shorter way would require time and thought, which he was unwilling to spend.

Once we learn one way to perform a certain task using a software application, we may continue to do it that way and *never* discover a more efficient way. Even if we discover or are told that there is a "better" way, we may stick with the old way because it is familiar, comfortable, and, most important, requires little thought. Avoiding thought when using computers is important. People are willing to type *more* to think *less*.

Why is that? Are we mentally lazy? Usually, yes. Conscious thought is slow, strains working memory, and consumes much energy. We essentially run on batteries—that is, the food we eat—so energy conservation is an important feature that is part of our makeup. Operating via automatic processes is fast, doesn't strain working memory, and conserves energy. So the brain tries to run on automatic as much as possible (Kahneman, 2011; Eagleman, 2012).

The human preference for familiar, mindless paths and "no-brainer" decisions has several design implications for interactive systems:

- *Sometimes mindlessness trumps keystrokes.* With software intended for casual or infrequent use, such as bank ATM machines or household accounting applications, allowing users to become productive quickly and reducing their need to problem-solve while working is more important than saving keystrokes. Such software simply isn't used enough for the number of keystrokes per task to matter much. On the other hand, in software that is used all day by highly trained users in intensive work environments, such as airline telephone reservation operators, unnecessary extra keystrokes needed to perform a task are very costly.

- *Guide users to the best paths.* From its first screen or homepage, software should show users the way to their goals. This is basically the guideline that software should provide a clear information scent.

- *Help experienced users speed up.* Make it easy for users to switch to faster paths after they have gained experience. The slower paths for newcomers should show users faster paths if there are any. This is why most applications show the keyboard accelerators for frequently used functions in the menu-bar menus.

OUR THOUGHT CYCLE: GOAL, EXECUTE, EVALUATE

Over many decades, scientists studying human behavior have found a cyclical pattern that seems to hold across a wide variety of activities:

- Form a *goal* (e.g., open a bank account, eat a peach, or delete a word from a document).

- Choose and *execute* actions to try to make progress toward the goal.

- *Evaluate* whether the actions worked—that is, whether the goal has been reached or is nearer than before.

- Repeat until the goal is reached (or appears unreachable).

People cycle through this pattern constantly (Card et al., 1983). In fact, we run through it at many different levels simultaneously. For example, we might be trying to insert a picture into a document, which is part of a higher-level task of writing a term paper, which is part of a higher-level task of passing a history course, which is part of a higher-level task of completing college, which is part of a higher-level goal of getting a good job, which we want to achieve our top-level goal of having a comfortable life.

As an example, let's run through the cycle for a typical computer task: buying an airline ticket online. The person first forms the primary goal of the task and then begins to break that down into actions that appear to lead toward the goal. Promising actions are selected for execution, executed, and then evaluated to determine if they have moved the person closer to the goal.

- *Goal:* Buy airline ticket to Berlin, using your favorite travel Web site.

- *Step 1:* Go to travel Web site. You are still far from the goal.

- *Step 2:* Search for suitable flights. This is a very normal, predictable step at travel Web sites.

- *Step 3:* Look at search results. Choose a flight from those listed. If no flights on the results list are suitable, return to Step 2 with new search criteria. You are not at the goal yet, but you feel confident of getting there.

- *Step 4:* Go to checkout. Now you are getting so close to your goal that you can almost smell it.

- ***Step 5:*** Confirm flight details. Check it—all correct? If no, back up; otherwise proceed. Almost done.

- ***Step 6:*** Purchase ticket with credit card. Check credit card information. Everything look okay?

- ***Step 7:*** Print e-ticket. Goal achieved.

In the airline ticket example, to keep the example short, we didn't get down into the details of each step. If we had, we would have seen substeps that followed the same *goal-execute-evaluate* cycle.

Let's try another example, this time examining the details of some of the higher-level steps. This time the task is sending flowers to a friend. If we simply look at the top level, we see the task like this:

Send flowers to friend.

If we want to examine the goal-execute-evaluate cycle for this task, we must break down this task a bit. We must ask: *How* do we send flowers to a friend? To do that, we break the top-level task down into subtasks:

Send flowers to friend.
  Find flower delivery Web site.
  Order flowers to be delivered to friend.

For many purposes, the two steps we have identified are enough detail. After we execute each step, we evaluate whether we are closer to our goal. But *how* is each step executed? To see that, we have to treat each major step as a subgoal, and break it down into substeps:

Send flowers to friend.
  Find flower delivery Web site.
    Open web browser.
    Go to Google web search page.
    Type "flower delivery" into Google.
    Scan the first page of search results.
    Visit some of the listed links.
    Choose a flower delivery service.
  Order flowers to be delivered to friend.
    Review service's flower selection.
    Choose flowers.
    Specify delivery address and date.
    Pay for flowers and delivery.

After each substep is executed, we evaluate to see if it is getting us closer to the subgoal of which it is part. If we want to examine how a substep is executed and evaluated, we have to treat it as a sub-subgoal and break it into its component steps:

Send flowers to friend.
  Find flower delivery Web site.
    Open web browser.
      • Click browser icon on taskbar, startup menu, or desktop.
    Go to Google web search page.
      • If Google isn't browser's starting page, choose "Google" from favorites list.
      • If Google is not on favorites list, type "Google.com" into browser's address box.
    Type "flower delivery" into Google.
      • Set text-insertion point in search box.
      • Type the text.
      • Correct typo: "floowers" to "flowers."
    Visit some of the resulting links.
      • Move screen pointer to link.
      • Click on link.
      • Look at resulting web page.
    Choose a flower delivery service.
      • Enter chosen service's URL into browser.
   ...

You get the idea. We could keep expanding, down to the level of individual keystrokes and individual mouse movements, but we rarely need that level of detail to be able to understand the task well enough to design software to fit its steps and the goal-execute-evaluate cycle that is applied to each step.

How can software support users in carrying out the goal-execute-evaluate cycle? Any of these ways:

- *Goal.* Provide clear paths—including initial steps—for the user goals that the software is intended to support.

- *Execute.* Software concepts (objects and actions) should be based on the task rather than the implementation (see Chapter 11). Don't force users to figure out how the software's objects and actions map to those of the task. Provide a clear information scent at choice points to guide users to their goals. Don't make them choose actions that seem to take them away from their goal to achieve it.

- *Evaluate.* Provide feedback and status information to show users their progress toward the goal. Allow users to back out of tasks that didn't take them toward their goal.

An example of the evaluate guideline—clear feedback about the user's progress through a series of steps—is provided by ITN.com's flight reservation system (see Fig. 8.7). By the way, does the figure seem familiar? If so, it is because you saw it in Chapter 4 (see Fig. 4.16B), and your brain recognized it.

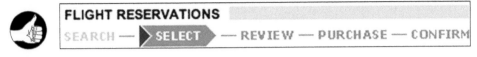

FIGURE 8.7

ITN.com's flight reservation system clearly shows users' progress toward making a reservation.

AFTER WE ACHIEVE A TASK'S PRIMARY GOAL, WE OFTEN FORGET CLEANUP STEPS

The goal–execute–evaluate cycle interacts strongly with short-term memory. This interaction makes perfect sense: short-term memory is really just what the focus of attention is at any given moment. Part of the focus of attention is our current goal. The rest of our attentional resources are directed toward obtaining the information needed to achieve our current goal. The focus shifts as tasks are executed and the current goal shifts from high-level goals to lower-level ones, then back to the next high-level goal.

Attention is a very scarce resource. Our brain does not waste it by keeping it focused on anything that is no longer important. Therefore, when we complete a task, the attentional resources focused on that task's main goal are freed to be refocused on other things that are now more important. The impression we get is that once we achieve a goal, everything related to it often immediately "falls out" of our short-term memory—that is, we forget about it.

One result is that people often forget loose ends of tasks. For example, people often forget to do these things:

- Turn car headlights off after arrival.
- Remove the last pages of documents from copiers and scanners.
- Turn stove burners and ovens off after use.
- Add closing parentheses and quotation marks after typing text passages.
- Turn off turn signals after completing turns.
- Take books they were reading on a flight with them when they exit the plane.
- Log out of public computers when finished using them.
- Set devices and software back into normal mode after putting them into a special mode.

These end-of-task short-term memory lapses are completely predictable and avoidable. When they happen to us, we call ourselves "absent-minded," but they are the result of how the brain works (or doesn't), combined with a lack of support from our devices.

To avoid such lapses, interactive systems can and should be designed to remind people that loose-end steps remain. In some cases, it may even be possible for the system to complete the task itself. For example:

- Cars already turn off turn signals after a turn.

- Cars should (and now do) turn off headlights automatically when the car is no longer in use, or at least remind drivers that the lights are still on.

- Copiers and scanners should automatically eject all documents when tasks are finished, or at least signal that a page has been left behind.

- Stoves should signal when a burner is left on with no pot present for longer than some suitable interval, and ovens should do likewise when left on with nothing in them.

- Computers should issue warnings if users try to power them down or put them to sleep before the computer has finished a background task (e.g., saving files or sending a document to a printer).

- Special software modes should revert to "normal" automatically, either by timing out—as some appliances do—or through the use of spring-loaded mode controls, which must be physically held in the non-normal state and revert to normal when released (Johnson, 1990).

Software designers should consider whether the tasks supported by a system they are designing have cleanup steps that users are likely to forget, and if so, they should design the system either to help users remember, or eliminate the need for users to remember.

Recognition is Easy; Recall is Hard

9

Chapter 7 described the strengths and limitations of long-term memory and their implications for the design of interactive systems. This chapter extends that discussion by describing important differences between two functions of long-term memory: recognition and recall.

RECOGNITION IS EASY

The human brain was "designed," through millions of years of natural selection and evolution, to recognize things quickly. By contrast, recalling memories—that is, retrieving them without perceptual support—must not have been as crucial for survival, because our brains are much worse at that.

Remember how our long-term memory works (see Chapter 7): Perceptions enter through our sensory systems, and their signals, when they reach the brain, cause complex patterns of neural activity. The neural pattern resulting from a perception is determined not only by the features of the perception, but also by the context in which it occurs. Similar perceptions in similar contexts cause similar patterns of neural activity. Repeated activation of a particular neural pattern makes that pattern easier to reactivate in the future. Over time, connections between neural patterns develop in such a way that activating one pattern activates the other. Roughly speaking, each pattern of neural activity constitutes a different memory.

Patterns of neural activity, which is what memories are, can be activated in two different ways:

1. By more perceptions coming in from the senses.

2. By other brain activity.

If a perception comes in that is similar to an earlier one and the context is close enough, it easily stimulates a similar pattern of neural activity, resulting in a sense of *recognition*. Recognition is essentially perception and long-term memory working in concert.

As a result, we assess situations very quickly. Our distant ancestors on the East African savannah had only a second or two to decide whether an animal emerging from the tall grasses was something they would regard as food or something that would regard *them* as food (see Fig. 9.1). Their survival depended on it.

Similarly, people recognize human faces very quickly—usually in a fraction a second (see Fig. 9.2). Until recently, the workings of this process were considered a mystery. However, that was when scientists assumed that recognition was a process

FIGURE 9.1

Early hominids had to recognize quickly whether animals they spotted were prey or predators.

FIGURE 9.2

How long did it take you to recognize these faces?[1]

---

[1] U.S. Presidents Barack Obama and Bill Clinton.

in which perceived faces were stored in a separate short-term memory and compared with those in long-term memory. Because of the speed with which the brain recognizes faces, cognitive scientists assumed that the brain must search many parts of long-term memory simultaneously, via what computer scientists call *parallel processing*. However, even a massively parallel search process could not account for the astounding rapidity of facial recognition.

Nowadays, perception and long-term memory are considered closely linked, which demystifies the speed of facial recognition somewhat. A perceived face stimulates activity in millions of neurons in distinct patterns. Individual neurons and groups of neurons that make up the pattern respond to specific features of the face and the context in which the face is perceived. Different faces stimulate different patterns of neural response. If a face was perceived previously, its corresponding neural pattern will already have been activated. The same face perceived again reactivates the same pattern of neural activity, only more easily than before. That *is* the recognition. There is no need to search long-term memory: the new perception reactivates the same pattern of neural activity, more or less, as the previous one. Reactivation of a pattern *is* the reactivation of the corresponding long-term memory.

In computer jargon, we could say that the information in human long-term memory is *addressed by its content*, but the word "addressed" wrongly suggests that each memory is located at a specific spot in the brain. In fact, each memory corresponds to a pattern of neural activity extending over a wide area of the brain.

That explains why, when presented with faces we have not seen before and asked if they are familiar, we don't spend a long time searching through our memories to try to see if that face is stored in there somewhere (see Fig. 9.3). There is no search.

FIGURE 9.3

How long did it take you to realize that you do not recognize these faces?[2]

---

[2] George Washington Carver (American scientist, educator, and inventor) and average male face (FaceResearch.org).

FIGURE 9.4

We can recognize complex patterns quickly.

A new face stimulates a pattern of neural activity that has not been activated before, so no sense of recognition results. Of course, a new face may be so similar to a face we have seen that it triggers a *misrecognition*, or it may be just similar enough that the neural pattern it activates triggers a familiar pattern, causing a feeling that the new face reminds us of someone we know.

An interesting aside is that face recognition is a special type of recognition: it has its own dedicated mechanisms in our brains, hardwired in by evolution; we do not have to learn to recognize human faces (Eagleman, 2012).

Similar mechanisms make our visual system fast at recognizing complex patterns, although unlike face recognition, they develop largely through experience rather than being wired in from birth. Anyone with at least a high school education quickly and easily recognizes a map of Europe and a chessboard (see Fig. 9.4). Chess masters who have studied chess history may even recognize the chess position as Kasparov versus Karpov 1986.

RECALL IS HARD

In contrast, *recall* is long-term memory reactivating old neural patterns without immediate similar perceptual input. That is much harder than reactivating a neural pattern with the same or similar perceptions. People *can* recall memories, so it obviously *is* possible for activity in other neural patterns or input from other areas of the brain to reactivate a pattern of neural activity corresponding to a memory. However, the coordination and timing required to recall a memory increase the likelihood that the wrong pattern or only a subset of the right pattern will be activated, resulting in a failure to recall.

Whatever the evolutionary reasons, our brain did not evolve to recall facts. Many schoolchildren dislike history class because it demands that they remember facts, such as the year the English Magna Carta was signed, the capital city of Argentina, and the names of all 50 U.S. states. Their dislike is not surprising; the human brain is not well suited for that sort of task.

Because people are bad at recall, they develop methods and technologies to help them remember facts and procedures (see Chapter 7). Orators in ancient Greece used the *method of loci* to memorize the main points of long speeches. They imagined a large building or plaza and mentally placed their talking points in spots around it. When presenting the speech, they mentally "walked" through the site, picking up their talking points as they passed.

Today we rely more on external recall aids than on internal methods. Modern-day speakers remember their talking points by writing them down on paper or displaying them in overhead slides or presentation software. Businesses keep track of how much money they have, owe, or are owed by keeping account books. To remember contact information of friends and relatives, we use address books. To remember appointments, birthdays, anniversaries, and other events, we use calendars and alarm clocks. Electronic calendars are best for remembering appointments, because they actively remind us; we don't have to remember to look at them.

RECOGNITION VERSUS RECALL: IMPLICATIONS FOR USER-INTERFACE DESIGN

The relative ease with which we recognize things rather than recall them is the basis of the graphical user interface (GUI) (Johnson et al., 1989). The GUI is based on two well-known user interface design rules:

- ***See and choose is easier than recall and type***. Show users their options and let them choose among them, rather than force users to recall their options and tell the computer what they want. This rule is the reason GUIs have almost replaced command-line user interfaces (CLIs) in personal computers (see Fig. 9.5).

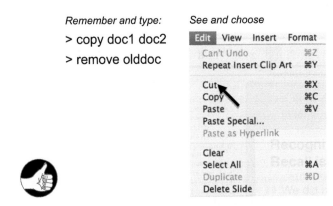

FIGURE 9.5

The main design rule behind today's GUI: "See and choose is easier than remember and type."

FIGURE 9.6

Desktop icons convey function via recognition—by analogy with physical objects or by experience.

FIGURE 9.7

Wordpress.com uses symbols plus text to label functional pages on the Dashboard.

"Recognition rather than recall" is one of Nielsen and Molich's (1990) widely used heuristics for evaluating user interfaces. By contrast, using language to control a software application sometimes allows more expressiveness and efficiency than a GUI would. Thus, *recall and type* remains a useful approach, especially in cases where users can easily recall what to type, such as when entering target keywords into a search box.

- *Use pictures where possible to convey function.* People recognize pictures very quickly, which also stimulates the recall of associated information. For this reason, today's user interfaces often use pictures to convey function (see Figs. 9.6 and 9.7), such as desktop or toolbar icons, error symbols, and graphically depicted choices. Pictures that people recognize from the physical world are useful because they can be recognized without needing to be taught. This recognition is good as long as the familiar meaning matches the intended meaning in the computer system (Johnson, 1987). However, using familiar pictures from the physical world is not absolutely crucial. Computer users can learn to associate new icons and symbols with their intended meaning if these graphics are well designed. Memorable icons and symbols hint at their meaning, are distinguishable from others, and consistently mean the same thing, even across applications.

The GUI originated in the mid-1970s and became widespread in the 1980s and 1990s. Since then, additional design rules have arisen that are based on human

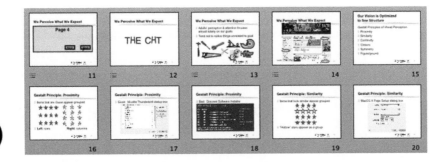

FIGURE 9.8

Microsoft PowerPoint can show slides as thumbnails, providing an overview based on recognition.

perception in general and on recognition and recall in particular. The following sections outline a few of these newer rules.

Use thumbnail images to depict full-sized images compactly

Recognition is fairly insensitive to the size in which objects and events are displayed. After all, we have to be able to recognize things independently of their distance from us. What is important are features: as long as most of the same features are present in the new picture that were in the original one, the new perception stimulates the same neural pattern, resulting in recognition.

Therefore, a great way to display pictures people have already seen is to present them as small thumbnail images. The more familiar a picture, the smaller the thumbnails of it can be and still be recognizable. Displaying small thumbnails instead of full-sized images allows people to see more of their options, their data, their history, etc., at once.

Photo management and presentation applications use thumbnail images to give users an overview of their images or slides (see Fig. 9.8). Web browsers use thumbnails to show pages a user has recently visited (see Fig. 9.9).

The larger the number of people who will use a function, the more visible the function should be

For the reasons described before, recall often fails. If a software application hides its functionality and requires its users to recall what to do, some percentage of users will fail. If the software has a lot of users, that percentage who fail to recall—even if it is small—adds up to a significant number. Software designers obviously don't want a significant number of users to fail in using their product.

The solution is to make functions that many people need highly visible, so users see and *recognize* their options rather than having to *recall* them. By contrast, functionality that few people will use—especially when those few people are highly trained—can be hidden, for example, behind "Details" panels, in right-click menus, or via special key combinations.

FIGURE 9.9

Apple Safari can show recently visited pages as thumbnail images, for quick recognition and choice.

Use visual cues to let users recognize where they are

Visual recognition is fast and reliable, so designers can use visual cues to show users instantly where they are. For example, it is a well-known Web design rule that all pages in a Web site should have a common distinctive visual style so people can easily tell whether they are still on the site or have gone to a different one. Slight but systematic variations on a site's visual style can show users which section of the site they are in.

Some desktop operating systems allow users to set up multiple desktops ("rooms" or "workspaces") as locations for different categories of work. Each has its own background graphic to allow easy recognition.

Some corporate Web sites use pictures to assure users that they are on a secure site. Users choose a picture as a personal account logo, and the site displays the logo whenever it recognizes the user from cookies or after the user has entered a valid login name but not yet a password (see Fig. 9.10). This lets users know they are at the real company site and not a fake site hosted by someone running a phishing scam.

Make authentication information easy to recall

People know that it is hard to recall arbitrary facts, words, and sequences of letters or digits. That is why they often write passwords and challenge-question answers down and keep the information in places that are easy to reach and thus insecure. Or they base passwords on their children's initials, their birthdates, their street

FIGURE 9.10

BankOfAmerica.com shows recognized customers their self-selected account logo (SiteKey) to assure them that it is the real bank's site.

address, and other information they know they can recall. Unfortunately, such passwords are too often easy for other people to guess (Schrage, 2005). How can designers help users avoid such unsafe behavior?

For starters, we can at least not make it hard for people to recall their login information, like the systems cited in Chapter 7 that impose burdensome password restrictions or offer a limited choice of challenge questions.

Instead, we can give users the freedom to create passwords they can remember and challenge questions for which they can remember the correct response. We can also let users supply password *hints* that the system can present to them, under the assumption that users can devise hints that will serve as a recall probe for them but not identify the password to third parties.

Authentication methods that do not rely on users to recall the authentication data would seem to be a solution. Biometric authentication methods, such as iris scans, digital fingerprint scans, and voice identification, fall into this category. However, many people regard these methods as privacy threats because they require the collection and storage of individuals' biometric data, creating the potential for information leaks and abuse. Therefore, while biometric authentication does not burden users' memory, it would have to be implemented in a way that meets stringent privacy requirements to be widely accepted.

Learning from Experience and Performing Learned Actions are Easy; Novel Actions, Problem Solving, and Calculation are Hard

10

As we saw in Chapter 9's comparison of recognition and recall, the human brain is good at some tasks and not so good at others. In this chapter, we compare several additional functions of the brain to show which ones it is good and bad at, and to see how to design computer systems to support human activity. But first, a bit more about the brain and mind.

WE HAVE THREE BRAINS

We really have three brains, or if you prefer, a brain with three main parts, each of which affects different aspects of our thought and behavior (Weinschenk, 2009):

- *The old brain.* This is mainly the brain stem, where the spinal cord enters the base of the brain. It has been around since the first fish evolved over 500 million years ago. (Insects and mollusks, which appeared before fish, don't have brains in the usual sense of the word; just collections of neural cells called ganglia.) The old brain classifies everything into three categories: edible, dangerous, or sexy. It also regulates the body's automatic functions, such as digestion, breathing, and reflexive movement. Reptiles, amphibians, and most fish have only the old brain.

- *The midbrain.* This part of the brain is "middle" in two ways: (1) physically, because it is located above the old brain and beneath the cortex, and (2) evolutionarily, because it evolved after the old brain and before the new brain. The midbrain controls emotions; it reacts to things with joy, sadness, fear, aggressiveness, apprehensiveness, anger, etc. Birds[1] and lower mammals have only an old brain and a midbrain.

- *The new brain.* This part of the brain mainly consists of the cerebral cortex. It controls intentional, purposeful, conscious activity, including planning. Most mammals have a cortex in addition to their old brain and midbrain, but only a few highly evolved mammals—elephants; porpoises, dolphins, and whales; and monkeys, apes, and humans—have a sizable one.

WE HAVE TWO MINDS

Cognitive psychologists these days usually lump the functions of the midbrain and old brain together, separate from the functions of the new brain. They view the human mind as consisting of two distinct "minds": an unconscious, automatic mind operating largely in the old brain and midbrain, and a conscious, monitored mind operating mainly in the new brain. Psychologists often call the unconscious, automatic mind *system one* because it evolved first and is the main controller of our perception and behavior. They refer to the conscious, monitored mind as *system two* because it came later in evolution and it usually takes a back seat in controlling human perception and behavior (Kahneman, 2011). Some scientists prefer the terms *emotional mind* and *rational mind*, respectively (Eagleman, 2012).

One noteworthy fact about our conscious, rational, monitored mind (system two) is that it is *us*—it is where our consciousness and self-awareness are. Of course, it thinks it is in charge of our behavior. It believes it runs the show because it is the only one of the two minds that *has* consciousness. But in fact system two is *rarely* in charge (Kahneman, 2011; Eagleman, 2012).

System one (the unconscious, automatic, emotional mind) operates quickly compared to system two—10 to 100 times as fast—but it does so by operating based on intuition, guesses, and shortcuts, which makes everything it does an approximation. For example, consider this math problem (adapted from Kahneman, 2011):

> A baseball and a bat together cost $110. The bat costs $100 more than the ball. How much does the ball cost?

Most likely, your system one instantly gave you (i.e., your system two) the answer: $10. Perhaps your system two accepted that answer. Or maybe after a moment of thought, it rejected it. If the ball costs $10 and the bat costs $100 more (i.e., $110),

---

[1] Corvids (ravens, crows, and magpies) and some types of parrots (e.g., New Zealand kia) have large brains compared to other birds, even though, like all birds, they have no cortex. They often exhibit intelligence rivaling elephants, porpoises, and monkeys. In these birds, other parts of their brains apparently serve functions that the cortex serves in mammals.

then their combined cost would be $120. But the two add up to $110, so the ball cannot cost $10. The correct answer for the cost of the ball is $5. System two can work that out; system one cannot.

System one is also easily biased. The perceptual biases described and illustrated in Chapter 1 are biases of system one. Look at Figure 10.1. System one sees the dogs getting larger as you go upward and to the right (i.e., toward the back in system one's view), but in fact they are the same size. Even after your system two *knows* this, it is hard to override system one.

System one has several other characteristics:

- When it encounters a problem it can't solve, it substitutes an easier problem and solves that. For example, accurately answering the question "Is asparagus a popular vegetable?" requires engaging system two and either conducting a survey or looking up and reading survey results, which takes time and effort. System one just tosses that question out and quickly answers the question "Do I like asparagus?"

- It bases judgments only on what it perceives; it doesn't care that important (potentially conflicting) information might exist. If such data is not present, it doesn't exist.

- It filters perceptions based on goals and beliefs given to it by system two: information that doesn't match is filtered out before reaching system two.

We all have both system one and system two, but system two is often lazy: it accepts the quick estimates and judgments of system one even though they are often

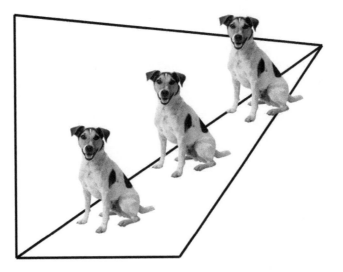

FIGURE 10.1

The three dogs are the same size, but the converging lines bias system one to see them as arranged in three dimensions and successively larger.

inaccurate. Why? Because the perceptions and judgments of system one come quickly, and are usually good enough to allow us to get by in most situations. Also, operating system two takes conscious will and mental effort, while system one is always running in the background and takes no conscious effort.

So why do we have a system two? Human behavior, like that of other animals, is run mainly by unconscious processes[2]: system one. But a fully automatic brain would be inflexible: it couldn't switch goals in midaction or quickly adjust its response to rapidly changing situations. To counter this, people—and perhaps a few other animals—also have a small conscious "CEO" process that can oversee and guide the operation of system one. Usually it isn't needed, so it "sleeps." But when needed, it wakes up and tries to assume control, sometimes successfully.

When is system two needed? When our goals require getting something not just *sort of* right but *exactly* right, when we are in situations system one does not recognize and therefore has no automatic response, or when system one has multiple conflicting responses and no quick-and-dirty way to resolve them.

Because system one is the primary controller of human perception and behavior, with system two intervening only as necessary, the human mind is not fully rational and conscious—it isn't even mostly rational and conscious. When we perceive something—an object or an event—both minds react and contribute to our thought and behavior. Since system one reacts faster than system two, we sometimes act based on what it tells us before we (i.e., our system two) reach a conscious decision or are even aware that action is required.

LEARNING FROM EXPERIENCE IS (USUALLY) EASY

People are pretty good at generalizing from specific experiences and observations to extract conclusions. We generalize constantly throughout our lives.

The neural basis of learning is not as well understood as that of recognition and recall (Liang et al., 2007). However, people learn from their experiences constantly and often automatically. Most people, if given the necessary experience, easily learn such lessons as:

- Stay away from leopards.

- Don't eat bad-smelling food.

- Ice cream tastes good, but it melts quickly in hot weather.

- Wait a day before replying to an email that makes you mad.

- Don't open attachments from unfamiliar senders.

- LinkedIn is useful, but Facebook is a waste of time (or vice versa, depending on your preference).

---

[2] Brain researcher David Eagleman calls them "zombie" or "robotic" processes (Eagleman, 2012).

In fact, learning from experience and adjusting our behavior accordingly does not require our being aware that we are learning and adjusting. System one can do it alone, without system two's involvement.

For example, imagine that you are in a casino, playing two slot machines that are next to each other. Unbeknownst to you, the machines are rigged so one pays out slightly more often than the other. After you've played hundreds of times, you may be able to identify the "good" machine. That is system two talking. But if we measure your galvanic skin response (GSR, a measure of anxiety), we would see that after only a few dozen trials, your system one has already identified the "bad" machine: whenever you reach for it, your GSR jumps. System one might even make you start to avoid that slot machine, unless overridden by your still-clueless system two.

Our ability to learn from experience is limited in several ways. First, complex situations that involve many variables or that are subject to a wide variety of forces are difficult for people to predict, learn from, and generalize about. For example:

- Experienced stock market investors still aren't sure what stocks to sell or buy now.

- People who have lived in Denver, CO, for years still have trouble predicting the weather there.

- Even after interacting with your sister's boyfriend on several occasions, you may still not be sure he is a good guy.

Second, experiences from our own lives or those of relatives and friends influence our conclusions more than experiences we read or hear about. For example, we may have read and seen reports, consumer reviews, and statistics indicating that the Toyota Prius is a great car, but if our Uncle Charlie had a bad experience with one, we will probably have a negative assessment of it. We do this because our system one considers family members to be like us and, therefore, more trustworthy than data about thousands of anonymous car buyers, even though from a rational standpoint the statistics are more reliable (Weinschenk, 2009; Kahneman, 2011; Eagleman, 2012).

Third, when people make a mistake, they don't always learn the right lesson from it. By the time they realize they are in a bad situation, they may not remember their recent actions well enough to be able to connect their situation with the true cause or causes.

A fourth problem people have in learning from experience is that they often overgeneralize—that is, make generalizations based on incomplete data. As explained earlier, this is a characteristic of system one. For example, many people assume all crows are black because all the crows they have seen are black. In fact, there are crows that are not black (see Fig. 10.2).

However, it can be argued that overgeneralizing isn't a problem—it's a feature. It is rare that one can see all possible examples of something. For example, a person can never see all crows, but it may still be useful in daily life (although not in scientific research) to assume that the many crows one has seen are enough evidence to conclude that all crows are black. Overgeneralization, therefore, seems like a

FIGURE 10.2

The common belief that all crows are black is false: (A) African pied crow (*photograph by Thomas Schoch*), and (B) white (nonalbino) crow, Ohio.

necessary adaptation for life in the real world. It is primarily when we overgeneralize in extreme ways—for example, making generalizations on the basis of few examples or atypical examples—that we get ourselves into trouble.

The ability to learn from experience has a long evolutionary history. A creature does not need a cerebral cortex (new brain) to be able to do it. Both the old brain and midbrain can learn from experience. Even insects, mollusks, and worms, without even an old brain—just a few neuron clusters—can learn from experience. However, only creatures with a cortex or brain structures serving similar functions[3] can learn from the experiences of others. A cortex is certainly necessary to be aware that one has learned from experience, and only creatures with the largest new brains (relative to body size)—possibly only humans—can articulate what they have learned from experience.

Bottom line: Even though there are limits on how well we learn from direct experience and from the experience of others, learning and generalizing from experience are relatively easy for the human mind.

PERFORMING LEARNED ACTIONS IS EASY

When we go somewhere we have been many times before, or do something we have done many times before, we do it almost automatically, without much conscious thought. The route, the routine, the recipe, the procedure, the action, has become semiautomatic or fully automatic. We are mainly using system one. Here are some examples:

- Riding a bicycle after many years of practice.

- Backing out of your driveway and driving to work for the 300th time.

- Brushing your teeth as an adult.

---

[3] The reason for the caveat is that some birds can learn from watching other birds.

- Playing a tune that you have played hundreds of times on a musical instrument.

- Using a mouse or a touchpad to move a cursor on a computer display after a few days of practice.

- Entering a banking transaction into your old familiar bank account software.

- Reading and then deleting a text message from your longtime mobile phone.

In fact, "automatic" is how cognitive psychologists refer to routine, well-learned behavior (Schneider and Shiffrin, 1977). Researchers have determined that performing this type of action consumes few or no conscious cognitive resources—that is, it is not subject to the limits of attention and short-term memory described in Chapter 7.

Automatic activities can even be done in parallel with other activities. Thus, you can tap your foot while humming a familiar song while beating an egg, while still leaving your mind "free" to keep an eye on your children or plan your upcoming vacation.

How does an activity become automatic? The same way you get to Carnegie Hall (as the old joke goes): practice, practice, practice.

PERFORMING NOVEL ACTIONS IS HARD

When a person first tries to drive a car—especially a car with a stick shift—every part of the activity requires conscious attention (i.e., the engagement of system two). Am I in the right gear? Which foot do I use to press the accelerator pedal, the brake pedal, and the clutch pedal? How hard should I press on each of these pedals? How hard am I pressing on the clutch pedal now? Which way am I headed? How fast am I going? What is ahead of me, behind me, beside me? Where are the mirrors I should be checking? Is that my street coming up ahead? "Objects in mirror are closer than they appear"—what does that mean? And what is that light blinking on the dashboard?

When everything involved in driving a car is still conscious, keeping track of it all far exceeds our attention capacity—remember that it is four items, plus or minus one (see Chapter 7). People who are still learning to drive often feel overwhelmed. That is why they often practice driving in parking lots, parks, rural areas, and quiet neighborhoods, where traffic is light: to reduce the number of things they have to attend to.

After a lot of practice, all the actions involved in driving a car become automatic; they are taken over by system one. They no longer compete for attention and they recede from consciousness. We may not even be fully aware of doing them. For example, which foot do you use to push the accelerator pedal? To remember, you probably had to pump your feet briefly.

Similarly, when music teachers teach students to play a musical instrument, they don't make students monitor and control every aspect of their playing at once. That would overwhelm the students' attention capacity. Instead, teachers focus students' attention narrowly on one or two aspects of their playing: the correct notes, the rhythm, the tone, the articulation, or the tempo. Only after students learn to control some aspects of their playing without thinking about them do music teachers require their students to control more aspects simultaneously.

To demonstrate to yourself the difference in conscious attention required by well-learned (automatic) versus novel (controlled) tasks, try these:

- Recite the letters of the alphabet from A to M. Then recite the letters of the alphabet from M to A.

- Count down from 10 to 0—think of a rocket launch. Then count down from 21 to 1 by odd numbers.

- Drive to work, using your normal route. The next day, use a very different, unfamiliar route.

- Hum the first measure of the song "Twinkle, Twinkle, Little Star." Then hum it backwards.

- Enter your phone number using a standard 12-key telephone pad. Then enter your phone number using the number keys at the top of your computer keyboard.

- Type your full name on a computer keyboard. Then cross your hands on the keyboard and type your full name again. (I was going to suggest riding a bicycle with your hands crossed, but that is actually dangerous, so I do *not* recommend trying it.)

Most real-world tasks have a mixture of automatic and controlled components. Driving to work along your usual route is mostly automatic, allowing you to focus on the radio news or think about your evening dinner plans. But if another vehicle near you does something unexpected or a child appears on the road ahead of you, your system two engages and your attention will be yanked back to the task of driving.

Similarly, if you check your email using your usual email program, the way you retrieve and view your email is well practiced and mostly automatic, and reading text is well practiced and automatic (see Chapter 6), but the *content* of any newly arrived email messages is new and therefore requires your conscious attention. If while on vacation you go into an Internet cafe and try to check your email using an unfamiliar computer, operating system, or email program, less of the task will be automatic, so it will require more conscious thought, take more time, and be more prone to error.

When people want to get something done—as opposed to challenging themselves mentally—they prefer to use methods that are automatic or at least semi-automatic to save time and mental effort, and to reduce the chance of error. If you are in a hurry to pick up your child from school, you take your tried-and-true route, even if your neighbor just told you yesterday about a faster route. Remember what the usability test subject said (previously mentioned in Chapter 8):

I'm in a hurry, so I'll do it the long way.

How can designers of interactive systems make the tasks that they support faster, easier, and less error-prone? By designing them so they can be handled by the automatic functions of system one, or quickly become so. How does one do that? Chapter 11 describes some of the ways.

PROBLEM SOLVING AND CALCULATION ARE HARD

Reptiles, amphibians, and most birds get along in their world quite well with just an old brain and a midbrain.[4] Insects, spiders, and mollusks survive in their environments with even less. Animals without a cortex (or its equivalent, as in a few birds) can learn from experience, but it usually takes a lot of experience and they can only learn minor adjustments to their behavior. Most of their behavior is stereotyped, repetitive, and predictable once we understand the demands of their environment (Simon, 1969). That may be just fine when their environment requires only the behaviors they already have automated.

But what if the environment throws a curve ball: it requires new behavior, and requires it *right now*? What if a creature faces a situation it has never encountered before, and may never encounter again? In short, what if it is faced with a *problem*? In such cases, creatures with no cortex or its equivalent cannot cope.

Having a cerebral cortex (new brain) frees creatures from relying solely on instinctive, reactive, automatic, well-practiced behaviors. The cortex is where conscious reasoning happens (Monti et al., 2007). In current cognitive theory, it is largely where system two resides. Generally speaking, the larger a creature's cerebral cortex relative to the rest of its brain, the greater its ability to interpret and analyze situations on-the-fly, plan or find strategies and procedures to cope with those situations, execute those strategies and procedures, and monitor their progress.

Expressed in computer jargon, having a large cortex gives us the ability to devise programs for ourselves on-the-fly and run them (in system two) in an emulated, highly monitored mode rather than a compiled or native mode. That is essentially what we are doing when we are following a cooking recipe, playing bridge, calculating income taxes, following instructions in a software manual, or figuring out why no sound is coming out of the computer when we play a video.

Although having a large new brain gives us the flexibility to deal with problems on short notice, that flexibility has a price. Learning from experience and performing well-learned actions are easy largely because they don't require constant awareness or focused attention and because they can occur in parallel. In contrast, controlled processing—including problem solving and calculation—requires focused attention and constant conscious monitoring, and executes relatively slowly and serially (Schneider and Shiffrin, 1977). It strains the limits of our short-term memory because all the chunks of information needed to execute a given procedure compete with each other for scarce attention resources. It requires conscious mental effort, as you saw when you tried to recite the alphabet backward from M to A.

---

[4]For example, salamanders choose a jar containing four fruit flies over one with two or three fruit flies (Sohn, 2003).

THE NEW BRAIN ALSO ACTS AS A BRAKE ON IMPULSIVE BEHAVIOR

The new brain—specifically the frontal cortex—also acts to inhibit reflexive and impulsive behavior coming from the midbrain and old brain that could interfere with the execution of the new-brain's carefully worked-out plans (Sapolsky, 2002). It keeps us from jumping up and getting off of a subway car when a smelly person boards, because, after all, we do have to get to work on time. It keeps us sitting quietly in our seats in classical music concerts, but lets us stand up and hoot and holler in rock concerts. It helps keep us out of fights (usually). It tries to stop us from buying that red sports car because preserving our marriage is a higher goal than having the car. And whereas the old brains and midbrains are tempted by the email that proposes a "BUSINESS OPPORTUNITY WORTH $12.5 MILLION DOLLARS," the new brain stops us from clicking, saying, "It's a spammer and a scammer; you know that, don't you?"

In computer jargon, the human mind has only one serial processor for emulation mode, or controlled execution of processes: system two. System two is severely limited in its temporary storage capacity and its clock is between one and two orders of magnitude slower than that of the brain's highly parallelized and compiled automatic processing (i.e., system one).

Modern humans evolved from earlier hominids between 200,000 and 50,000 years ago, but numbers and numerical calculation did not exist until about 3400 BCE, when people in Mesopotamia (modern-day Iraq) invented and started using a number system in commerce. By then, the human brain was more or less as it is today. Since the modern human brain evolved before numerical calculation existed, it is not optimized for calculation.

Calculation is done mainly in system two: the brain's controlled, monitored mode. It consumes scarce resources of attention and short-term memory, so when we try to perform calculations entirely in our heads, we have trouble. The exception is that some steps in a calculation may be memorized and therefore are automatic. For example, the overall process of multiplying 479×832 is controlled, but certain sub-steps of the process may be automatic if we have memorized the multiplication tables for single-digit numbers.

Problems and calculations that involve only one or two steps, in which some steps are memorized (automatic), don't involve much information, or all the relevant information is immediately available—and therefore need not be kept in short-term memory—are easy for most people to work out in their heads. For example:

- $9 \times 10 = ?$

- I need to move the washing machine out of the garage, but the car is in the way, and my car keys are in my pocket. What to do?

- My girlfriend has two brothers, Bob and Fred. I have met Fred, and the one here now isn't Fred, so it must be Bob.

However, problems that system one cannot resolve and require the engagement of system two, exceed our short-term memory limits, require certain information be retrieved from long-term memory, or in which we encounter distractions, strain our brains. For example:

- I need to move the washing machine out of the garage, but the car is in the way, and my car keys are … hmmm … they're not in my pocket. Where are they? … [Search car.] They're not in the car. Maybe I left them in my jacket. … Now where did I leave my jacket? [Search house; eventually find jacket in bedroom.] Okay, found the keys. … Boy is this bedroom messy—must clean it before wife gets home. … Hmmm. Why did I need the car keys? [Return to garage, see washer.] Oh, yeah: to move the car so I can move the washing machine out of the garage. *(Interim subgoals grabbed attention away from higher-level goals in short-term memory.)*

- Chapter 8 gave examples of tasks in which people have to remember to complete cleanup steps after achieving their primary goal—for example, remembering to turn your car headlights off after arrival at your destination, or to remove the last page of a document from a copier after you have the copy.

- John's cat is not black and likes milk. Sue's cat is not brown and doesn't like milk. Sam's cat is not white and doesn't like milk. Mary's cat is not yellow and likes milk. Someone found a cat that is yellow and likes milk. Whose cat is it?[5] *(The negations create more chunks of information than most people's short-term memory can hold at once.)*

- A man built a four-sided house. All four walls faced south. A bear walked by. What color was the bear? *(Requires deduction and knowing and retrieving specific facts about the world and its wildlife.)*

- If 5 factory workers can assemble 5 cars in 5 hours, how long does it take 100 factory workers to assemble 100 cars? *(System one offers a quick guess that system two is tempted to accept, but finding the correct answer requires rejecting that guess and engaging system two.)*

- Fred likes classic cars. He doesn't care much about the environment, but wants to reduce his gasoline costs. He replaces his '56 Cadillac (12 mpg), with a

---

[5] Answers provided at the end of this chapter.

'57 Chevy (14 mpg). Susan is an environmental activist. She decides to replace her Honda Fit (30 mpg) with a Toyota Prius (40 mpg). If they each drive 10,000 miles over the next year, who saves the most gas? *(Same as previous problem.)*

- You have to measure exactly four liters of water, but you only have a three-liter bottle and a five-liter bottle. How do you do it? *(Requires engaging system two to mentally simulate a series of pours until the right series is found, straining short-term memory and perhaps exceeding mental simulation abilities.)*

When solving such problems, people often use external memory aids, such as writing down interim results, sketching diagrams, and manipulating models of the problem. Such tools augment our limited short-term memory and our limited ability to imagine manipulating problem elements.

Problem solving and calculation are also difficult if they require a cognitive strategy, solution method, or procedure that we don't know and cannot devise or find. For example:

- $93.3 \times 102.1 = ?$ *(Requires arithmetic that exceeds short-term memory capacity, so must be done with a calculator or on paper. The latter requires knowing how to multiply multidigit decimal numbers on paper.)*

- A farmer has cows and chickens—30 animals total. The animals have a total of 74 legs. How many of each animal does the farmer have? *(Requires translation to two equations and then solving using algebra.)*

- A Zen master blindfolded three of his students. He told them that he would paint either a red dot or a blue dot on each one's forehead. In fact, he painted red dots on all three foreheads. Then he said, "In a minute I will remove your blindfolds. When I do, look at each other and if you see at least one red dot, raise your hand. Then guess which color your own dot is." Then he removed the blindfolds. The three students looked at each other, then all three raised a hand. After a minute, one of the students said, "My dot is red." How did she know? *(Requires reasoning by contradiction, a specialized method taught in logic and mathematics.)*

- You play a YouTube video on your computer, but there is no sound even though you can see people speaking. Is the problem in the video, the video player, the computer, the speaker cables, or the speakers? *(Requires devising and executing a series of diagnostic tests that successively narrow the possible causes of the problem, which requires computer and electronics domain knowledge.)*

These made-up examples demonstrate that certain problems and calculations require training that many people do not have. The sidebar on the next page gives real examples of people being unable to resolve technical problems, because they lack training in effective diagnosis in the technical problem domain and are not interested in learning how to do it.

SOLVING TECHNICAL PROBLEMS REQUIRES TECHNICAL INTEREST AND TRAINING

Software engineers are trained to do systematic diagnosis of problems. It is part of their job to know how to devise and execute a series of tests to eliminate possible causes of a fault until they find the cause. Engineers often design technology-based products as if the intended users of the technology were just as skilled as engineers are in technical problem diagnosis. However, most people who are not software engineers have not been trained in that sort of problem diagnosis, and therefore cannot do it effectively. Here are true examples of nontechnical people facing problems they could not solve without help:

- A friend wanted to book a flight, but couldn't because the airline Web site wouldn't let her. It demanded a password but she didn't have one. She called a computer engineer friend, who asked several questions to learn her situation. It turned out that the Web site assumed she was her husband, because he had previously bought tickets from that airline on that computer. The site wanted his login and password. She didn't know his password and he was out of town. The engineer told her to log out of the Web site, then return as a *new* customer and create her own account.

- San Francisco's Freecycle Network uses a Yahoo Group. Some people try to join, but fail because they cannot figure out how to complete the registration process. Therefore, they cannot participate in the group.

- At a church, one of two stage-monitor speakers in the audio system stopped working. The assistant music director assumed that one of the speakers had failed and said he would replace it. A musician who also is an engineer wasn't sure the speaker was bad, so he swapped the two monitor speaker cables at the speaker end. Now the "bad" speaker worked and the "good" one didn't, showing that the problem was *not* a bad speaker. The assistant music director concluded that one speaker cable was bad and said he would buy a new one. Before he did, the engineer–musician swapped the monitor cables where they connect to the monitor amplifier, to see if the problem was a faulty monitor amplifier output rather than the cable. The problem turned out to be a loose connection in the monitor amplifier output jack.

Even when people know they *could* solve a problem or perform a calculation if they put effort into it, sometimes they don't do it because they don't consider the potential reward worth the effort. This response is especially common when solving a problem is not required by one's job or otherwise. Some real examples:

- A posting on San Francisco Freecycle Network: "Free: Epson Stylus C86. Was working fine, then suddenly it couldn't recognize the new full ink cartridge. Not sure if it's the cartridge or the printer. So I bought a new printer and am giving the old one away."

- Fred and Alice, a schoolteacher and a nurse who are married, never install or update software on their home computer. They don't know how, and they don't want to know. They use only the software that came with the computer. If their computer says updates are available, they ignore it. If an application (e.g., a web browser) stops working because it is outdated, they stop using it. When necessary, they buy a new computer.

- Another couple, Ted and Samantha, have a television, a videotape player, and a DVD player. Remote controls for the devices lie in a pile near the TV, unused. Ted and Samantha control the devices by getting up and walking across the room. When asked why, they say it's too much trouble to learn to work the remotes and remember which one is for which device. Yet they use computers daily, for email and Web.

The nontechnical people in these examples are not stupid. Many have college degrees, putting them in the top 30% of educational attainment in the United States. Some are even trained to diagnose problems in different domains (e.g., medicine). They just have no training and/or interest in solving technical problems.

People invented calculators and computers mainly as tools for performing calculations and solving problems that humans cannot easily solve on their own. Computers and calculators do calculation and problem solving much more easily and reliably than we do, at least when the problems are well defined.

IMPLICATIONS FOR USER-INTERFACE DESIGN

People often intentionally challenge and entertain themselves by creating or solving puzzles that strain—or "exercise"—their minds (see Fig. 10.3). However, that fact does not imply that people will happily accept mind-straining problems foisted upon them by someone or something else. People have their own goals. They are using a computer to help them achieve a goal. They want—and need—to focus their attention on that goal. Interactive systems—and designers of them—should respect that and not distract users by imposing technical problems and goals that users don't want.

Here are some examples of technical problems that computers and web services impose upon their users:

- "It wants my 'member ID.' Is that the same as my 'username'? It must be." *(Requires reasoning by process of elimination.)*

- "Huh? It charged me the full price! It didn't give me my discount. What now?" *(Requires backtracking through the purchase process to try to figure out what happened.)*

- "I want page numbers in the chapter to start at 23 instead of 1, but I don't see a command to do that. I've tried Page Setup, Document Layout, and View Header and Footer, but it isn't there. All that's left is this Insert Page Numbers command. But I don't want to *insert* page numbers—the chapter already has page numbers. I just want to change the starting number." *(Requires searching methodically through the application's menus and dialog boxes for a way to change the starting page number, and if it isn't found, deciding by process of elimination that the Insert Page Numbers command must be the way.)*

- "Hmmm. This checkbox is labeled 'Align icons horizontally.' I wonder what happens if I uncheck it. Will my icons be aligned vertically, or will they simply not be aligned?" *(Requires setting the property to on to see what will happen.)*

FIGURE 10.3

We challenge ourselves by creating and solving puzzles that tax our mental abilities.

Interactive systems should minimize the amount of attention users must devote to operating them (Krug, 2005), because that pulls precious cognitive resources away from the task a user came to the computer to do. Here are some design rules:

- *Prominently indicate system status and users' progress toward their goal.* If users can always check their status easily by direct perception, using the system will not strain their attention and short-term memory.

- *Guide users toward their goals.* Designers can do this implicitly, by making sure every choice-point provides a clear information "scent" that leads users toward their goal, or explicitly, by using a wizard (multistep dialog box). Don't just display a bunch of options that appear equally likely and expect users to know how to start and get to their goal, especially if they won't perform the task very often.

- *Tell users explicitly and exactly what they need to know.* Don't expect them to deduce information. Don't require them to figure things out by a process of elimination.

- *Don't make users diagnose system problems.* For example, a faulty network connection. Such diagnosis requires technical training, which most users don't have.

- *Minimize the number and complexity of settings.* Don't expect people to optimize combinations of many interacting settings or parameters. People are really bad at that.

- *Let people use perception rather than calculation.* Some problems that might seem to require calculation can be represented graphically, allowing people to achieve their goals with quick perceptual estimates instead of calculation. A simple example: Suppose you want to go to the middle of a document. Document editing software of the 1970s and early 1980s forced you to look at the document's length, divide that in half, and issue a command to go to the middle page number. With modern-day document editing software, you just drag the scrollbar "elevator" to the middle of the bar, and you are there. Similarly, snap-to grids and alignment guides in drawing tools eliminate the need for users to determine, match, and compute coordinates of existing graphic elements when adding new ones.

- *Make the system familiar.* Use concepts, terminology, and graphics that users already know to make the system as familiar to them as possible, requiring them to think about it less. Designers can use this approach to a certain extent even if the system provides functionality that users have not seen before. One way to do it is to follow industry conventions and standards (e.g., Apple Computer, 2009; Microsoft Corporation, 2009). A second way is to make new software applications work like older ones that users have used before. A third approach is to base the design on metaphors, such as the desktop metaphor (Johnson et al., 1989). Finally, designers can study users to learn what is and is not familiar to them.

FIGURE 10.4

California's online unemployment form asks for data it could calculate itself in both of these questions.

- ***Let the computer do the math.*** Don't make people calculate things the computer can calculate itself (see Fig. 10.4).

ANSWERS TO PUZZLES

- The cat is John's.

- The bear was white, because to have four south-facing walls, the house must be on the North Pole.

- Five workers can assemble 5 cars in 5 hours, so 1 worker can assemble 1 car in 5 hours and 100 workers can assemble 100 cars in the same 5 hours. (*Adapted from Kahneman, 2011.*)

- Fred cuts his gas consumption from 833 gallons to 714 gallons, saving 119 gallons. Susan cuts her gas usage from 333 gallons to 250 gallons, saving 83 gallons. (*Adapted from Kahneman, 2011.*)

- To end with four liters of water, fill the three-liter bottle and pour it into the five-liter bottle, then fill the three-liter bottle again and fill up the five-liter bottle. That leaves one liter in the three-liter bottle. Empty the five-liter bottle, and pour the one liter from the three-liter bottle into the five-liter bottle. Then fill the three-liter bottle again and pour it into the five-liter bottle.

- Let A be the number of cows and B the number of chickens. "A farmer has cows and chickens—30 animals total" translates to $A + B = 30$. "The animals have a total of 74 legs" translates to $4A + 2B = 74$. Solving for A and B gives $A = 7$ and $B = 23$, so the farmer has 7 cows and 23 chickens.

- The Zen student saw three hands up and red dots on both other students. From this information, she didn't know whether her dot was red or blue. She started out assuming it was blue, and waited. She reasoned that the other students would see her (assumed) blue dot and one other red dot, realize that two red dots were required for all three hands to be up, and quickly figure out that their own dots had to be red. But after a minute neither of the other students had said anything, which told the Zen student that the other students couldn't figure out what color their dots were, which meant that her own dot was *not* blue; it had to be red.

Many Factors Affect Learning

11

Chapter 10 contrasted system one, the automatic processes our brain uses to carry out well-learned activities and make quick judgments, with system two, the conscious, highly monitored, controlled processes that we use to solve novel problems, make rational choices, and perform calculations. Automatic processes (system one) consume little or no short-term memory (attention) resources and can operate in parallel with each other, while controlled processes (system two) place high demands on short-term memory and operate one at a time (Schneider and Shiffrin, 1977; Kahneman, 2011; Eagleman, 2012).

OUR BRAIN REWIRES ITSELF CONSTANTLY

How does the brain learn? Recent brain research has found that the brain adapts to new situations and environmental requirements constantly, mainly by rewiring itself: neurons that formerly fired independently become connected and fire in concert or in opposition, and neurons that formerly participated in one perception or behavior are reused for others. This is known as *brain plasticity* (Doidge, 2007).

It has been known for over 40 years that infants' brains are highly plastic: within months of birth, somewhat random collections of neurons develop into highly organized neural networks. However, the degree to which brains remain plastic (i.e., reorganizable) into adulthood was unknown until nuclear magnetic resonance imagery (NMRI) and similar brain observation methods became available.

149

One dramatic example of brain plasticity is the fact that blind people can be taught to "see" by connecting a video camera to an array of tactile stimulators resting on the person's back. The stimulators touch the person's back in patterns corresponding to images captured by the camera, vibrating for dark areas of the image but not for light areas. With training, participants in these studies can read, perceive scenes in three dimensions, and recognize objects. Initially, they perceive the stimulation as tactile patterns on their back, but after a while they report it as actually "seeing."

Brain plasticity is also exemplified by a new approach to stroke rehabilitation. People who have strokes sometimes lose the use of an arm or leg on one side of their body. Recovering use of the limb has traditionally been difficult—often impossible—and stroke victims often learn to compensate by ignoring their bad limbs and relying on their good ones. However, some stroke doctors have recently started placing patients' good limbs in casts to immobilize them, literally forcing patients to use their bad limbs. Results have been positive. Apparently, the brain reassigns different neurons to the bad arm, for example, allowing it to function again (Doidge, 2007).

The first time or even the first several times we perform an activity, we do it in a highly controlled and conscious manner, but with practice it becomes more automatic. Examples include peeling an apple, driving a car, juggling balls, riding a bicycle, reading, playing a musical instrument, and using an app on your mobile phone. Even an activity that might seem to require our attention, such as sorting good cherries from bad ones, can become automated to the point that we can do it as a background task, with plenty of cognitive resources left over for having a conversation, watching the news on television, etc.

This progression from controlled to automatic raises an obvious question for designers of interactive applications, online services, and electronic appliances: How can we design them so that using them becomes automatic within a reasonable amount of time?

This chapter explains and demonstrates factors that affect how quickly people can learn to use interactive systems. To preview the factors, we learn faster when:

- Practice is frequent, regular, and precise.

- Operation is task focused, simple, and consistent.

- Vocabulary is task focused, familiar, and consistent.

- Risk is low.

WE LEARN FASTER WHEN PRACTICE IS FREQUENT, REGULAR, AND PRECISE

Obviously, practice facilitates learning. Here are some details about practice.

Frequency of practice

If people use an interactive system only rarely (e.g. once every few weeks or less) it is hard for them to remember from one time to the next the details of how to use it. However, if they use an interactive system frequently, familiarity develops quickly. Most user-interface designers are well aware of this, and therefore design applications, appliances, and online service differently depending on whether people will use them casually and rarely or intensively and often.

For example, automated teller machines (ATMs) for banks are designed under the assumption that people will not remember much from one usage to the next. They are designed to be simple and to remind people what they do and how they work. ATMs present a short list of anticipated user goals (e.g., withdraw cash, deposit funds, transfer funds), then guide users through the steps of the selected task. Airline and hotel booking websites are similarly task oriented: "Tell me your goal and I'll guide you to it." In contrast, document editing applications, electronic calendars, smartphone texting apps, air-traffic control systems, and online accounting services are designed with the understanding that people will be using them daily—perhaps even minute-by-minute—and will quickly learn and remember details about how to use them.

Regularity of practice

How long does it take for an activity to become an automatic habit? Lally and her colleagues conducted a study to measure this (Lally et al., 2010). They asked about 100 volunteer participants to choose a new eating, drinking, or physical activity to do every day for at least two months. They monitored the participants and measured how long it took for the new behavior to become automatic—that is, to be executed without conscious thought or effort.

They found that forming automatic habits takes from 18 to 254 days, with more complex activities taking more time. They also found that habits formed faster if practiced regularly (e.g., daily). Skipping a practice session now and then didn't make much difference, but skipping a lot of practice sessions significantly slowed participants' progress toward habit formation.

Bottom line: If you want the use of your software to become habitual and automatic for users, design it so as to encourage people to use it regularly.

Precision of practice

Unorganized collections of neurons are noisy: they fire randomly; not in an organized way. When people practice an activity repeatedly, the brain organizes itself to support and control that activity: networks of neurons get "trained up" to fire in concert. Their firing becomes more systematic and less "noisy." This is true regardless of whether the activity is perceptual like identifying a word, motor like skiing, cognitive like counting numbers, or a combination like singing a song.

The more carefully and precisely a person practices an activity, the more systematic and predictable the activation of the corresponding neural network. If a person practices an activity carelessly and sloppily, the supporting neural networks remain somewhat disorganized (i.e., noisy), and the execution of the activity will remain sloppy and imprecise (Doidge, 2007).

Stated simply: Practicing the same activity imprecisely just strengthens the imprecision, because the neural networks controlling it remain noisy. To train the neural networks to make the activity precise, one must practice precisely and carefully, even if that requires practicing slowly at first or breaking down the activity into parts.

If efficiency and precision are important for a task, design the supporting software and its documentation to (1) help people be precise (e.g., by providing guides and grids), and (2) encourage people to use it purposefully and carefully rather than absentmindedly and sloppily. The following section explains how providing users with a clear conceptual model can support (2). Consistency of keystrokes and gestures, discussed later in this chapter, is also important.

WE LEARN FASTER WHEN OPERATION IS TASK FOCUSED, SIMPLE, AND CONSISTENT

When we use a tool—whether it is computer based or not—to do a task, we have to translate what we want to do into the operations provided by the tool. Some examples:

- You are an astronomer. You want to point your telescope at the star Alpha Centauri. Most telescopes don't let you specify a star to observe. Instead, you have to translate that goal into how the telescope's positioning controls operate: in terms of a vertical angle (azimuth) and a horizontal angle, or perhaps even the *difference* between where the telescope is pointing now and where you want it to point.

- You want to call someone who isn't in your phone's contact list. To call this person, you have to translate the person into a telephone number and give that to the phone.

- You want to create an organization chart for your company using a generic drawing program. To indicate organizations, suborganizations, and their managers, you have to draw boxes, label them with organization and manager names, and connect them with lines.

- You want to make a two-sided copy of a two-sided document, but the copier only makes single-sided copies. To make your copy, you must first copy one side of each document sheet, take those copies and put them back into the copier's paper tray upside down, and then copy the other side of each document sheet.

Cognitive psychologists call the gap between what a tool user wants and the operations the tool provides "the gulf of execution" (Norman and Draper, 1986). A person using a tool must expend cognitive effort to translate what he or she wants into a plan based on the tool's available operations and vice versa. That cognitive effort pulls the person's attention away from the task and refocuses it on the requirements of the tool. The smaller the gulf between the operations that a tool provides and what its users want to do, the less the users need to think about the tool and the more they can concentrate on their task. As a result, the tool becomes automatic more quickly.

The way to reduce the gulf is to design the tool to provide operations that match what users are trying to do. To build on the preceding examples:

- A telescope's control system could have a database of celestial objects, so users could simply indicate which object they want to observe, perhaps by pointing to it on a display.

- Telephones with contact lists allow users to simply specify the person or organization they want to call, rather than having to translate that to a number first.

- A special-purpose organization chart editing application would let users simply enter the names of organizations and managers, freeing users from having to create boxes and connect them.

- A copier that can make double-sided copies allows users who want such copies to simply choose that option on the copier's control panel.

To design software, services, and appliances to provide operations matching users' goals and tasks, designers must thoroughly understand the user goals and tasks the tool is intended to support. Gaining that understanding requires three steps:

1. Perform a task analysis.

2. Design a task-focused conceptual model, consisting mainly of an objects/actions analysis.

3. Design a user interface based strictly on the task analysis and conceptual model.

Task analysis

Describing in detail how to analyze users' goals and tasks is beyond the scope of this book. Entire chapters—even whole books—have been written about it (Beyer and Holtzblatt, 1997; Hackos and Redish, 1998; Johnson, 2007). For now, it is enough to say that a good task analysis answers these questions:

- What goals do users want to achieve by using the application?
- What set of human tasks is the application intended to support?
- Which tasks are common, and which ones are rare?
- Which tasks are most important, and which ones are least important?
- What are the steps of each task?

- What are the result and output of each task?
- Where does the information for each task come from?
- How is the information that results from each task used?
- Which people do which tasks?
- What tools are used to do each task?
- What problems do people have performing each task? What sorts of mistakes are common? What causes them? How damaging are mistakes?
- What terminology do people who do these tasks use?
- What communication with other people is required to do the tasks?
- How are different tasks related?

Conceptual model

Once these questions are answered (by observing and/or interviewing people who do the tasks that the tool supportss), the next step is *not* to start sketching possible user interfaces. The next step is to design a conceptual model for the tool that focuses on the users' tasks and goals (Johnson and Henderson, 2002, 2011, 2013).

A conceptual model of an application is the one that the designers want users to understand. By using the application, talking with other users, and reading the documentation, users build a model in their minds of how to use it. Hopefully, the model that users build in their minds is close to the one the designers intended. That is more likely when designers explicitly design a clear conceptual model as a key part of their development process.

A conceptual model describes abstractly what tasks a user can perform with the system and what concepts they must be aware of to complete them. The concepts should be those that came out of the task analysis, so the conceptual model is focused on the task domain. It should include few, if any, concepts for users to master that are not in the target task domain. The more direct the mapping between the application's concepts and those of the tasks it is intended to support, the less translating users will have to do, and the easier the tool will be to learn.

In addition to being focused on users' tasks, a conceptual model should be as simple as possible. Simpler means fewer concepts. The fewer concepts a model has for users to master, the better, as long as it provides the required functionality. Less is more, as long as what is there fits well with users' goals and tasks.

For example:

- In a to-do list application, do users need to be able to assign priorities of 1 to 10 to items, or are two priority levels, low and high, enough?

- Does a Search function need to allow users to enter full Boolean expressions? If it allowed that, would a significant number of people use it? If not, leave it out.

- Does a ticket machine in a train station need to be able to offer tickets for train routes other than the routes that this station is on?

In most development efforts, there is pressure to add extra functionality in case a user might want it. Resist such pressure unless there is considerable evidence that a significant number of potential customers and users really need the extra functionality. Why? Because every extra concept increases the complexity of the software. It is one more thing users have to learn. But actually it is not just *one* more thing. Each concept in an application interacts with most of the other concepts, and those interactions result in more complexity. Therefore, as concepts are added to an application, the application's complexity grows not just linearly, but multiplicatively.

For a more comprehensive discussion of conceptual models, including some of the difficulties that arise in trying to keep them simple and task focused while providing the required functionality and flexibility, see Johnson and Henderson (2002, 2011, 2013).

After you have designed a conceptual model that is task focused, as simple as possible, and as consistent as possible, you can design a user interface for it that minimizes the time and experience required for using the application to become automatic.

EXCESS COMPLEXITY DUE TO SEPARATE CONCEPTS BEING TOO SIMILAR

Some software applications are too complex because they have concepts that overlap in meaning or functionality. For example, one company's customer-support Web site presented four concepts that the developers considered quite different:

- *Membership.* Whether a company had paid for the customer-support service.
- *Subscription.* Whether a company had subscribed to a customer-support newsletter.
- *Access.* Which areas of the customer-support web site users in a company could access.
- *Entitlements.* Services provided for each membership level.

Users confused these four concepts. The four concepts should have been collapsed into *one*, or at least fewer than four.

Another company developed a Web site for people seeking to buy a home. There were two ways to start looking for a home: (1) name the state, county, or town; and (2) point to a location on a map. The site called these two methods "by location" or "by map," respectively, and required users to choose one. A usability test found that many users did not think of those as different ways of finding a home. To them, both methods were *by location*; they just differed in how the location was specified.

Consistency

The *consistency* of an interactive system strongly affects how quickly its users progress from controlled, consciously monitored, slow operation to automatic, unmonitored, faster operation (Schneider and Shiffrin, 1977). The more predictable the operation of a system's different functions, the more consistent it is. In a highly consistent system, the operation of a particular function is predictable from its *type*, so people quickly learn how everything in the system works and its use quickly becomes habitual. In an inconsistent system, users cannot predict how its different functions work, so they must learn each one anew, which slows their learning of the overall system and keeps their use of it a controlled, attention-consuming process.

The designer's goal is to devise a conceptual model that is task focused, as simple as possible, and as consistent as possible. From such a model, one can design a user interface for it that minimizes the time and experience required for using the application to become automatic.

Interactive systems can be consistent or inconsistent on at least two different levels: the conceptual level and keystroke level. Consistency at the conceptual level is determined by the mapping between the objects, actions, and attributes of the conceptual model (see earlier). Do most objects in the system have the same actions and attributes, or not? Consistency at the keystroke level is determined by the mapping between the conceptual actions and the physical movements required to execute them. Are all conceptual actions of a certain type initiated and controlled by the same physical movements, or not?

Keystroke consistency

When a designer moves from conceptual design to actual user-interface design, keystroke-level consistency becomes important.

Keystroke-level consistency is *at least* as important as conceptual consistency in determining how quickly the operation of an interactive system becomes automatic. The goal is to foster the growth of what is often called "muscle memory," meaning motor habits. A system that is inconsistent at the keystroke level does not let people quickly fall into muscle memory motor habits. Rather, it forces them to remain consciously aware of, and guess about, which keystrokes to use in each context, even when the gestures in different contexts differ only slightly. In addition, it makes it likely that people will make errors—that is, accidentally do something they did not intend.

Achieving keystroke-level consistency requires standardizing the physical actions for all activities of the same type. An example of a type of activity is editing text. Keystroke-level consistency for text editing requires the keystrokes, pointer movements, and gestures to be the same regardless of the context in which text is being edited (e.g., documents, form fields, filenames, etc.). Keystroke-level consistency is also desirable for other types of activity, such as opening documents, following links, choosing from a menu, choosing from a displayed set of options, and clicking buttons.

Consider three alternative designs for the keyboard shortcuts for Cut and Paste in a hypothetical multimedia document editor. The document editor supports the creation of documents containing text, sketches, tables, images, and videos. In design

A, Cut and Paste have the same two keyboard shortcuts regardless of what type of content is being edited. In design B, the keyboard shortcuts for Cut and Paste are different for every type of content. In design C, all types of content *except* videos have the same Cut and Paste keyboard shortcuts (see Table 11.1).

The first question is: Which of these designs is easiest to learn? It is fairly clear that design A is the easiest.

The second question is: Which design is hardest to learn? That is a tougher question. It is tempting to say design B because that one seems to be the least consistent of the three. However, the answer really depends on what we mean by "hardest to learn." If we mean "the design for which users will require the most time to become productive," that is certainly design B. It will take most users a long time to learn all the different Cut and Paste keyboard shortcuts for the different types of content. But people are remarkably adaptable if sufficiently motivated—they can learn amazingly arbitrary things if, say, using the software is required for their job. Eventually—maybe in a month—users would be comfortable and even quick with design B. In contrast, users of design C would begin to be productive in about the same short time as users of design A—probably a matter of minutes.

However, if we interpret "hardest to learn" as meaning "the design for which users will take the longest to be error-free," that is design C. All the types of document content use the same shortcut keys for Cut and Paste except videos. Although users of design C will be productive quickly, they would continue to make the error of trying to use CTRL-X and CTRL-V with videos for at least several months—perhaps forever.

Consistency is extremely important for learning hand–eye coordination activities such as scrolling, panning, and zooming a display, especially on touch-controlled screens. If those actions require users to make different gestures in different contexts (e.g., different apps), the corresponding neural networks in users' brains will remain noisy, preventing the users from ever being able to pan and scroll automatically (i.e., without conscious thought).

For example, on Apple Macintosh computers running Mac OS X,[1] panning and scrolling is usually accomplished by dragging two fingers across the trackpad in the desired direction, and zooming is controlled by spreading or pinching two fingers. But

Table 11.1 Which UI Design Will be Easiest/Hardest to Learn and Remember?

| Object | Document Editor Keyboard Shortcuts: Alternative Designs | | | | | |
| | Design A | | Design B | | Design C | |
	Cut	Paste	Cut	Paste	Cut	Paste
Text	CTRL-X	CTRL-V	CTRL-X	CTRL-V	CTRL-X	CTRL-V
Sketch	CTRL-X	CTRL-V	CTRL-C	CTRL-P	CTRL-X	CTRL-V
Table	CTRL-X	CTRL-V	CTRL-Z	CTRL-Y	CTRL-X	CTRL-V
Image	CTRL-X	CTRL-V	CTRL-M	CTRL-N	CTRL-X	CTRL-V
Video	CTRL-X	CTRL-V	CTRL-Q	CTRL-R	CTRL-E	CTRL-R

[1] As this was being written, the current version of Mac OS X was Lion 10.8.5.

what if a Mac user is using Google Maps? In the column on the left listing search results (see Fig. 11.1), scrolling/panning the list uses the standard Mac OS X gesture: sliding two fingers up or down, and the text is zoomed by spreading or pinching two fingers. But over the map, oops, sorry: dragging two fingers there doesn't *pan* it, it *zooms* it. Panning the map requires clicking the trackpad down with one finger and dragging it. And spreading or pinching two fingers over the map doesn't zoom it, it zooms the entire contents of the browser window. Needless to say, such inconsistencies effectively block scrolling, panning, and zooming from becoming automatic for users.

A common way that developers promote keystroke-level consistency is to follow look-and-feel standards. Such standards can be presented in style guides or they can be built into common user-interface construction tools and component sets. Style guides exist for the entire industry and they exist separately for desktop software (Apple Computer, 2009; Microsoft Corporation, 2009) and web design (Koyani et al., 2006). Ideally, companies also have internal style guides that augment the industry style guides to define a look and feel for their own products.

However conventions are encapsulated, the goal is to stick to conventions at the keystroke level while perhaps innovating at the conceptual and task levels. We as designers really don't want our software's users to have to keep thinking about their keystroke-level actions as they work, and users don't want to think about them either.

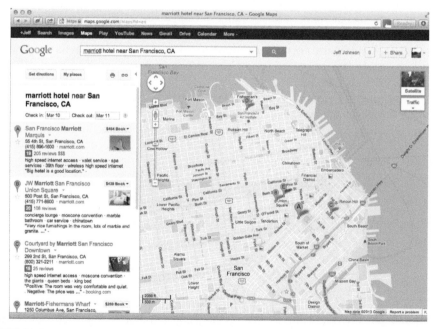

FIGURE 11.1

Inconsistent gestures block scrolling, panning, and zooming from becoming automatic.

WE LEARN FASTER WHEN VOCABULARY IS TASK FOCUSED, FAMILIAR, AND CONSISTENT

Ensuring that an application, web service, or appliance exposes a small, consistent, and task-appropriate set of concepts to its users is a big first step, but it is not enough to minimize the time it takes for people to learn an interactive system. You also have to make sure that the *vocabulary*—what concepts are called—fits the task, is familiar, and is consistent.

Terminology should be task focused

Just as the user-visible concepts in an interactive system should be task focused, so should the *names* for the concepts. Usually, task-focused terms for concepts emerge from the interviews and observations of users that designers conduct as part of the task analysis. Occasionally, software needs to expose a concept that is new to users; the challenge for a designer is keeping such concepts and their names focused on the task, not on the technology.

Some examples of interactive software systems using terminology that is not task focused are as follows:

- A company developed a desktop software application for performing investment transactions. The application let users create and save templates for common transactions. It gave users the option of saving templates either on their own PC or on a network server. Templates stored on the PC were private; templates stored on the server were accessible to other people. The developers used "database" for templates on the server because they were kept in a database. They used "local" for templates on the users' own PC because that is what "local" meant to them. Terms that would be more task focused are "shared" or "public" instead of "database," and "private" instead of "local."

- iCasualties.org provides up-to-date tallies of the number of coalition military personnel killed or injured in the Iraq and Afghanistan wars. It starts by asking site visitors to select a "database." However, visitors to this site don't care or need to know that the Web site's data is stored in multiple databases. Task-focused instructions would ask them to select a "country" in which there is an ongoing conflict, not a "database" (see Fig. 11.2).

Terminology should be familiar

To reduce the time it takes for people to master your application, Web site, or appliance, so that using it becomes automatic or nearly so, don't force them to learn a whole new vocabulary. Chapter 4 explained that familiar words are easier to read and understand because they can be recognized automatically. Unfamiliar words cause people to use more conscious decoding methods, which consumes scarce short-term memory resources and thereby lowers comprehension.

FIGURE 11.2

iCasualties.org uses language that is not task focused ("database") in its instructions.

FIGURE 11.3

Unfamiliar computer jargon (a.k.a. "geek speak") slows learning and frustrates users.

Unfortunately, many computer-based products and services present users with unfamiliar terms from computer engineering—often called "geek speak"—and require them to master those terms (see Fig. 11.3). Why? Operating a stove doesn't require us to master terminology about the pressure and chemical composition of natural gas, or terminology about the production and delivery of electricity. Why should shopping on the Web, sharing photographs, or checking email require us to learn "geek speak" such as "USB," "TIFF," or "broadband"? But in many cases, it does.

Some examples of interactive software systems using unfamiliar terminology are as follows:

- A development team was designing a video-on-demand system for schoolteachers to use in classrooms. The purpose of the system was to allow teachers to find videos offered by their school district, download them, and show them in their classrooms. The developers' initial plan was to organize the videos into a hierarchy of "categories" and "subcategories." Interviews with teachers showed, however, that they use the terms "subject" and "unit" to organize instructional content, including videos. If the system had used the developers' terminology,

FIGURE 11.4

An update message from SPRINT mobile-phone service uses the computer jargon term "UI themes."

teachers who used it would have to *learn* that "category" meant "subject" and "subcategory" meant "unit," making the system harder to master.

- SPRINT, a mobile-phone service provider, sends announcements of software updates to customers' phones. These announcements often indicate new features that the update includes. One SPRINT update announcement offered "the option to select between Light and Dark UI themes from the Settings menu" (see Fig. 11.4). Most consumers won't know what a user-interface theme is, as that is a technical term used mainly by software designers and developers.

- Windows Media Player sometimes displays error messages that use familiar terms in unfamiliar, "geeky" ways (see Fig. 11.5). The error message in the figure

FIGURE 11.5

An error message in Windows Media Player uses a familiar term ("current state") in an unfamiliar way.

is referring to the state of the *software*, but the average Media Player user is likely to interpret it as referring to the *state* in which he or she lives.

In contrast to these examples, Southwest Airlines' Web site tries to prevent errors from occurring, but when they do occur, it explains the problem using task-focused, familiar language (see Fig. 11.6).

FIGURE 11.6

Error messages at Southwest Airlines' Web site are task focused and clear, fostering learning.

Terminology should be consistent

People want to focus their cognitive resources on their own goals and tasks, not on the software they are using. They just want to accomplish their goal, whatever it is. They are not interested in the software. They interpret what the system presents only superficially and very literally. Their limited attentional resources are so focused on their goal that if they are looking for a Search function but it is labeled "Query" on the current screen or page, they may miss it. Therefore, the terminology in an interactive system should be designed for maximum consistency.

The terminology used in an interactive system is consistent when each concept has *one and only one* name. Caroline Jarrett, an authority on user-interface and forms design, provides this rule:

Same name, same thing; different name, different thing (FormsThatWork.com).

This means that terms and concepts should map strictly 1:1. Never use *different* terms for the *same* concept, or the *same* term for *different* concepts. Even terms that are ambiguous in the real world should mean only one thing in the system. Otherwise, the system will be harder to learn and remember.

An example of different terms for the same concepts is provided by Earthlink's frequently asked questions (FAQs) page in the web-hosting section of its site (see Fig. 11.7). In the *question*, the two available web-hosting platforms are called "Windows-

What are the differences between Windows-based and UNIX-based platforms?
For detailed information on choosing between these two operating systems, please visit our Windows or UNIX page.

For a quick look at which features and programs each platform supports, please consult the chart below:

Feature	Standard	ASP
Microsoft FrontPage Extensions	YES	YES
RealVideo and RealAudio	YES	NO
ASP (Active Server Pages)	NO	YES
ADO (ActiveX Data Objects)	NO	YES
ODBC Data Sources	NO	YES
Windows Media Server	NO	YES
PHP	YES	NO
MySQL Databases	YES	NO
Free ready-to run scripts, such as a hit counter, forum, e-mail form, blog, and guestbook	YES	NO

FIGURE 11.7

Earthlink's web-hosting FAQs use different terms for the same options in the question and in the table.

based" and "UNIX-based," but in the *table* they are referred to as "Standard" and "ASP." Customers have to stop and try to figure out which one is which. Do you know?

An example from Adobe Photoshop shows that inconsistent terminology can impede learning. Photoshop has two functions for replacing a target color in an image: Replace Color, which replaces the target color throughout an image with a new color, and Paint Bucket, which replaces the target color in an enclosed area with a new color. Both functions have a parameter that specifies how similar a color in the image must be to the target color before it will be replaced. The inconsistency is that the Replace Color function calls this parameter "Fuzziness," but the Paint Bucket function calls it "Tolerance" (see Fig. 11.8). Photoshop's online Help documentation

FIGURE 11.8

Photoshop uses different names for the tolerance parameter in two color-replacement functions: (A) "Fuzziness" in Replace Color, and (B) "Tolerance" in Paint Bucket.

for Replace Color even says "Adjust the *tolerance* of the mask by dragging the *Fuzziness* slider or entering a value" [emphasis added]. If the parameter were simply called "Tolerance" in *both* color replacement functions, people who learned one function could quickly transfer that learning to the other. But it isn't, so people have to learn the two functions separately.

Finally, WordPress.com provides an example of the *same* term for *different* concepts—also called *overloading* a term. For administering a blog, WordPress.com provides each blogger with a Dashboard consisting of monitoring and administrative functions organized into several pages. The problem is that one of the administrative function pages in the Dashboard is also called the "Dashboard," so the same name refers to both the whole Dashboard and one page of it (see Fig. 11.9). Therefore, when new bloggers are learning to use WordPress.com, they have to discover and remember that sometimes "Dashboard" means the entire administrative area and sometimes it means the Dashboard *page* of the administrative area.

FIGURE 11.9

At WordPress.com, "Dashboard" means both a blog's entire administrative area and a certain page in it.

Developing task-focused, familiar, consistent terminology is easier with a good conceptual model

The good news is that when you perform a task analysis and develop a task-focused conceptual model, you also get the vocabulary your target user population uses to talk about the tasks. You don't have to make up new terms for the user-visible concepts in your application—you can use the terms that people who do the task *already* use. In fact, you *shouldn't* assign new names for those concepts, because any names you assign will likely be computer technology concepts, foreign to the task domain.[2]

---

[2] Unless you are designing software development tools.

From the conceptual model, a software development team should create a product *lexicon*. The lexicon gives a name and definition for each object, action, and attribute that the product—including its documentation—exposes to users. The lexicon should map terms onto concepts 1:1. It should not assign multiple terms to a single concept, or a single term to multiple concepts.

Terms in the lexicon should come from the software's supported *tasks*, not its implementation. Terms should fit well into the users' normal task vocabulary, even if they are new. Typically, technical writers, user-interface designers, developers, managers, and users all help create the lexicon.

Certain concepts in GUIs have industry-standard names. These are the GUI equivalents of "reserved words" in programming languages. If you rename such concepts or assign new meanings to the standard names, you will confuse users. One such reserved term is "select." It means clicking on an object to highlight it, marking it as the object for future actions. The word "select" should not be used for any other purpose in a GUI (e.g., adding an item to a list or a collection). Other reserved GUI terms are "click," "press," "drag," "button," and "link".

Follow the product lexicon consistently throughout the software, user manuals, and marketing literature. Treat it as a living document: as the product evolves, the lexicon changes based on the basis of new design insights, changes in functionality, usability test results, and market feedback.

WHEN RISK IS LOW, WE EXPLORE MORE AND LEARN MORE

Imagine you are visiting a foreign city on business for a week or two. You have spare time after your work duties are finished in the evenings and on weekends. Compare two possible cities:

- You have been told that this city is easy to get around in: it is laid out in a consistent grid of streets and avenues with clear street and subway signs written in a language you understand, and the residents and police speak your language and are friendly and eager to help tourists.

- You have been warned that this city has a convoluted, confusing layout, with winding, poorly marked streets; the few street and subway signs are in a language you cannot read, and residents don't speak your language and are generally contemptuous of tourists.

In which city are you more likely to go out exploring?

Most interactive systems—desktop software, web services, electronic appliances—have far more functionality than most of their users ever try. Often people don't even know about most of the functionality provided by software or gadgets they use every day. One reason for this is fear of being "burned."

People make mistakes. Many interactive systems make it too easy for users to make mistakes, do not allow users to correct mistakes, or make it costly or time consuming to correct mistakes. People won't be very productive in using such systems: they will waste too much time correcting or recovering from mistakes.

Even more important than the impact on *time* is the impact on *practice and exploration*. A high-risk system, in which mistakes are easy to make and costly, discourages both: people who are anxious and afraid of making mistakes will avoid using the system, and when they do use it, they will tend to stick to familiar, safe paths and functions.

Imagine a violin or trumpet that gave mild electric shocks to its players when they made a mistake. Musicians would avoiding practicing with it and would never use it to play new, unfamiliar tunes.

When practice and exploration are discouraged, learning suffers.[3] In contrast, a low-risk system—in which mistakes are hard to make, low in cost, and easy to correct—reduces stress and encourages practice and exploration, and therefore supports learning. With such systems, users are more willing to try new paths: "Hmmm, I wonder what *that* does." Creating a low-risk environment means doing the following:

- Prevent errors where possible.

- Deactivate invalid commands.

- Make errors easy to detect by showing users clearly what they have done (e.g., deleting a paragraph by mistake).

- Allow users to undo, reverse, or correct errors easily.

---

[3] The benefits of practice were described earlier in this chapter.

Human Decision Making is Rarely Rational

12

Theories of decision making and economics have long been based on the assumption that decision making is rational, selfish, and stable over time. However, research in cognitive science has shown that at least two of those attributes—rationality and stability—are not attributes of *human* decision making (Kahneman, 2011; Eagleman, 2012). These findings have had a strong impact on economic and decision theory.

Chapter 10 explained that we have three brains—old, mid, and new—giving rise to two separate minds, which psychologists call *system one* (automatic, unconscious, unmonitored, highly parallel, irrational, approximate, fast) and *system two* (controlled, conscious, monitored, single-process, rational, precise, slow). Although system two believes that it governs our thoughts and actions, it only rarely does. Its main role is to override the quick-and-dirty and often faulty judgments of system one. However, system two is lazy[1] and does that only when necessary.

PEOPLE ARE OFTEN IRRATIONAL

Classic decision and economic theory is based on studies of people's choices between simple gambles. Economists and decision scientists do this to simplify their research, just as some biologists study fruit flies, flatworms, and white rats to help them understand more general biological processes. A basic axiom of rational decision making is this: If you prefer an X to a Y, then you will prefer a 40% chance of winning an X over a 40% chance of winning a Y. From this and similar basic axioms, plus the assumptions that humans are rational, selfish, and stable in their preferences, economists and decision theorists derived complex economic and decision theories. Those theories are

---

[1] System two is also a source of individual differences. Some people have a less lazy, more proactive system two than others (Kahneman, 2011; Eagleman, 2012).

useful for calculating how people and organizations *should* make decisions, but when it comes to predicting how humans *actually* make decisions, they are just plain wrong.

LOSSES MEAN MORE TO US THAN GAINS

If you ask people if they would prefer (1) a 50% chance of winning $100 or nothing, or (2) a gift of $45, most choose the gift. A rational agent would choose the bet because its expected value is $50.[2] But for system one—the one that actually makes most of our decisions before we are aware of it—the 50% chance of ending up with nothing is just too scary. The gift's value has to be *much* less than the expected value of the bet for people to prefer the bet. An exception is professional gamblers, who would probably choose the bet because they know that over *many* such choices, they would come out ahead. Their system one has learned to accept risky but favorable bets.

Not convinced? Consider this example: A friend offers you a bet based on a coin toss: heads, he pays you $150; tails, you pay him $100. Would you take that bet? Although the odds are in your favor, studies show that most people would *not* take the bet (Kahneman, 2011). They fear losing more than they rejoice at winning. Most people want two-to-one odds (heads you win $200; tails you lose $100) before they will take the bet. Again, professional traders are less risk-averse; they know they will be taking a lot of bets, so if the odds are even slightly in their favor, they will probably come out ahead overall even if they lose many individual bets.

Also, according to Kahneman (2011), the pain people feel from a loss is not linear with the size of the loss. For example, for a cattle rancher, the pain of losing 900 cows is more than 90% of the pain of losing 1,000 cows.

Based on years of research on how people actually make decisions on gambles and other risky conditions (e.g., whether to settle a lawsuit out of court), Daniel Kahneman and his colleague Amos Tversky developed a 2 × 2 matrix, which they named *fourfold pattern*, to summarize their theory's predictions (see Table 12.1). It says that when we face a big chance of a large gain (top left) or a small chance of a large loss (bottom right), we prefer to play it safe (i.e., are risk-averse), but when we face a big chance of a large loss (top right) or a small chance of a large gain (bottom left), we prefer to gamble (i.e., are risk-seeking).

The fourfold pattern predicts human behavior in risky situations—for example, our willingness to:

- Accept settlements in lawsuits.

- Buy insurance (when not required).

- Play lotteries.

- Gamble in casinos.

---

[2] The *expected value* of a bet is the amount you can win multiplied by the probability of winning—in this case, $100 × 0.5 = $50. It is what you can expect to win each time, on average, if you bet many times.

Table 12.1 Fourfold Pattern: Predictions of Human Choice under Risk

	Gain	Loss
High probability	Gamble: 95% chance to win $10,000 (5% chance to win $0) Alternative: definite gain of $8,000 (less than expected value of gamble) • Fear to lose gain • People are risk-averse • Most accept "safe" definite gain	Gamble: 95% chance to lose $10,000 (5% chance to lose $0) Alternative: definite loss of $8,000 (less than expected loss of gamble) • Hope to avoid loss • People are risk-seeking • Most prefer to gamble
Low probability	Gamble: 5% chance to win $10,000 (95% chance to win $0) Alternative: definite gain of $2,000 (more than expected value of gamble) • Hope for large gain • People are risk-seeking • Most prefer to gamble	Gamble: 5% chance to lose $10,000 (95% chance to lose $0) Alternative: definite loss of $2,000 (more than expected loss of gamble) • Fear of large loss • People are risk-averse • Most accept "safe" definite loss

Adapted from: Kahneman, 2011.

WE ARE BIASED BY HOW CHOICES ARE WORDED

Imagine that your doctor informs you that you have a terminal disease. She tells you that there is a treatment that has a 90% survival rate. Sounds good, doesn't it? Rewind now to the doctor informing you of your terminal illness. In this version, she tells you the treatment has a 10% mortality rate. Sounds bad, doesn't it?

The two statements about the treatment's effectiveness are equivalent. A rational agent's decision would not be affected by how the doctor phrases it. But people's decisions are. That is system one at work, with system two rarely bothering to intervene.

Here is another nice example of biasing by choice of words, adapted from Kahneman (2011): An outbreak of a dangerous flu is about to hit your country. Health officials predict that if the population is not vaccinated against it, about 600 people will die. Two vaccines are available:

- Vaccine A has been used before; an estimated 200 (of the 600) people would be saved.

- Vaccine B is experimental, with a one-third chance of saving all 600 people and a two-thirds chance of saving no one.

Most people presented with this choice choose vaccine A. They like the certainty. Now look at these slightly differently worded options for the same choice:

- Vaccine A has been used before; an estimated 400 (of the 600) people would die.

- Vaccine B is experimental, with a one-third chance of nobody dying and a two-thirds chance of all 600 people dying.

With this alternative wording, most people choose vaccine B. In this case, the certainty is unappealing because it is about deaths. According to Kahneman, system one not only treats losses as more important than gains, it also is risk-averse for gains and risk-seeking for losses. Therefore, people usually prefer a sure thing over a gamble when options are worded as gains, and gambles over sure things when the identical options are worded as losses.

Psychologists call this the *framing* effect: how choices are framed affects people's decisions.

Framing can also bias our decisions by presetting our mental "accounting" to a certain level, after which we perceive gains and losses from that *new* level. For example, imagine you are on a TV game show and have just won $1,000. Before you leave, the game-show host offers you a choice: (1) 50% chance (coin toss) in which you could win either $1,000 more or $0 more, or (2) get $500 more for sure. Most people choose the sure thing; they'd rather end up with a sure $1,500 than gamble for $2,000 and risk ending up with only $1000. Although system one made the decision, system two rationalizes it by thinking "Why be greedy?"

But now let's start over. Assume you initially won $2,000, and now your choice is: (1) a 50% chance you could *lose* either $1,000 or $0 of the $2,000 just won, or (2) lose $500 for sure. In this case, most people don't like the sure loss; they prefer to gamble to keep all $2,000, even though there is a good chance they may end up with only $1,000. System two rationalizes by thinking, "I'm hoping to keep it all."

Framing effects are one reason people's judgments and preferences are unstable over time: phrase a choice one way, people decide one way; phrase it differently, people decide differently.

WE ARE BIASED BY OUR VIVID IMAGINATIONS AND MEMORIES

In addition to being biased by gain versus loss and by how choices are framed, people tend to overestimate the probability of improbable events, especially when we can picture or easily recall those events. Furthermore, we tend to give more weight to such events in our decisions.

As an example, if people are asked to estimate the number of murders in the U.S. state of Michigan last year, those who remember that Detroit is in Michigan give a larger number than those who don't—and many don't remember that. Many people would even estimate the number of murders per year as higher for Detroit than for Michigan. The explanation is system one gives quick answers based on heuristics, such as how easily relevant information comes to mind. Murders in Detroit are often mentioned in news reports, thereby associating Detroit with murder in people's memories, but news reports about "murders in Michigan" are rare, so "murder" and "Michigan" are not strongly associated in memory. If system one does not recall that Michigan includes Detroit, its estimate is low, and system two rarely intervenes (Kahneman, 2011).

Similarly, if asked whether politicians or pediatricians are more likely to have extramarital affairs, most people immediately say "politicians, of course." This answer comes from system one, which can easily recall lurid stories about politicians' affairs due to all the press coverage that such affairs receive. But unless the person happens to know a pediatrician who had an affair, system one can't recall any such affairs because they seldom are reported in the press.

System one is also easily biased by the vividness of imagery and the old-brain and mid-brain's visceral responses to events. This is why people use vague or euphemistic terms in polite company: it avoids causing strong reactions to terms associated with unpleasant topics. For example, at a dinner party we would say that our spouse was absent because he or she was ill; we wouldn't say that our spouse was vomiting or had diarrhea.

A related bias is that people give more weight to coherent, compelling stories than to statistical evidence. In Chapter 10, the "Uncle Charlie" effect was explained: a person may have seen mountains of statistics showing that a Nissan Leaf is a great car, but if that person's Uncle Charlie (or other relative or friend) had a bad experience with one, the person's system one[3] will consider the car a "lemon," which will bias their opinion of the car unless system two overrides it.

Similarly, system one does not care about sample sizes. If you read that a door-to-door survey of potential voters found 63% support for the U.S. President, your system one doesn't worry about whether 300 or 3,000 voters were polled. However, if you read that 30 voters were polled, that will get your system two's attention and it will intervene and override system one, saying "that's not a valid survey" (Kahneman, 2011).

Finally, system one bases decisions on what is immediately before it: current perceptions and strong, easy-to-recall memories. System one does not—cannot—take into account other, possibly contrary evidence and experiences. Since what is immediately available to system one changes over time, its responses and choices are subject to change.

EXPLOITING STRENGTHS AND WEAKNESSES OF HUMAN COGNITION

How can designers use knowledge of the previously described characteristics of human decision making to achieve their goals? Here are some ways.

Support rational decision making: Help system two override or co-opt system one

People invented computer technology for the same reason that we invented arithmetic, calculators, rolodexes, and checklists: to augment our weak and unreliable rational thought processes. Early computers performed numerical calculations too complex or lengthy for people to perform reliably and quickly, but they now perform for us—or help us perform—a wide variety of information processing tasks.

---

[3] As Kahneman (2011) points out, the distinction between system one and system two is itself a story, concocted by psychologists to help explain the dual character of human cognition. The truth is more complex.

Computers are good—reliable, fast, and accurate—at precisely what we are bad at: remembering, calculating, deducing, monitoring, searching, enumerating, comparing, and communicating, so people use computers to support those activities. Decision making is another such activity.

For example, many people these days won't sign a new home mortgage without first using a mortgage calculator to compare different loan options and compute their monthly payments and the total amount they will pay (see Fig. 12.1). The calculator supports our decision making.

An example of problems that arise when people *don't* use computer systems to augment their all-too-human capabilities is provided by a recent airliner crash at San Francisco International Airport (SFO). The crash was allegedly caused at least in

FIGURE 12.1

Sorted.org.nz's mortgage calculator helps people understand and choose a loan.

part[4] by the pilots trying to land the plane manually rather than with the autopilot (Weber, 2013).

It could be argued that a great many software applications and commercial websites exist to help people make decisions. Usually the decisions supported are mundane, as in websites that help people choose which product to buy (see Fig. 12.2). Such websites support rational choice (system two) by displaying products side by side, allowing people to compare their price, features, and reliability, as well as customer satisfaction as indicated by product ratings and reviews.

However, many software applications support decision making that is anything but mundane, such as where to drill for oil, how much water to store in a reservoir, what the suggested retail price of a new car should be, how many endangered rhinos and elephants a game reserve can hold, or what the most efficient route for a snow-plow is (see Fig. 12.3). In fact, software for supporting complex decision making is such an important and well-studied category that it has a title and acronym (decision support systems, DSS), a scientific journal (*Decision Support Systems*), textbooks, regular conferences, and even a Wikipedia page.

Whether the supported decisions are mundane or of monumental importance, the primary goal of decision support software (and websites) is to help people engage their system two, see all their options, evaluate them rationally and fairly, and make an unbiased decision. Achieving that goal isn't easy, because as is explained earlier and in Chapter 1, human perception and cognition are *usually* biased. But it is possible, if decision support software follows these guidelines:

FIGURE 12.2

PriceSpy.co.nz is a comparison shopping website.

---

[4] According to preliminary assessments by National Transportation Safety Board (NTSB) officials.

FIGURE 12.3

Decision support system for choosing efficient snowplow routes.

- ***Provide all options.*** If there are too many to simply list, organize or abstract them into categories and subcategories, and provide summary information for those, so people can evaluate and compare entire categories of options at once.

- ***Help people find alternatives.*** Some solutions may be so counterintuitive that people don't consider them. Decision support systems can expose options users might miss and can generate variants on user solutions that are minor or even major improvements.

- ***Provide unbiased data.*** That is, data created or collected in an objective, reproducible manner.

- ***Don't make people calculate.*** Perform calculations, inferences, and deductions for users where possible. Computers are good at that; people aren't.

- ***Check assertions and assumptions.*** Decisions are based not only on data, but also on assumptions and assertions. Decision support systems—especially those supporting critical or complex decisions—should let users declare any assumptions and assertions upon which a decision will be based, and then should "sanity check" them for the user.

Data visualization: Harnessing system one to support system two

One might assume that a secondary goal of decision support systems is to shut system one—with all its biases, satisficing, and approximating—out of the decision-making loop. In some decision support systems, that may indeed be a design goal. However, there is another way.

To understand the other way, one must realize that system one is *not* an inner "evil twin" trying to bias and mess up our decisions. It doesn't have any goal to thwart or undermine system two. Because it has no consciousness, system one has no goals. Strictly speaking, it isn't even a single thing. System one is a large collection of semi-independent automatic "robotic" or "zombie" processes, each of which handle a specific situation (Eagleman, 2012). Although, as described earlier, some of those automatic processes have characteristics that are detrimental to rational decision making, overall the brain's collection of automatic processes help us react, survive, and thrive. Many of those automatic processes are skills that can be harnessed—one could say "hijacked" or "co-opted"—by system two to *support* its analysis. That is the basis of the "other way."

An approach that utilizes this other way is called *data visualization*, or data viz for short. Think of it as business graphics on steroids. Data visualization exploits the strengths of the human visual system—which consists mainly of automatic processes—to allow people to perceive relationships in complex data. Some of those strengths were described earlier in this book: perception of structure (Chapter 2), analysis of complex scenes (Chapter 2), edge detection (Chapter 4), motion detection (Chapter 5), and face recognition (Chapter 9). Another strength is three-dimensional vision. Like decision support, data visualization is a large (and growing) field, with a name,[5] regular conferences, journals, textbooks, and a Wikipedia page.

A relatively simple but familiar example of data visualization is provided by schematic (i.e., nongeographic) maps of urban subway systems (see Fig. 12.4), which have largely replaced geographic subway maps over the past 100 years. Geographic location, landmarks, and even distances are of little importance in subway maps. All people usually want to see from these maps is which subway line(s) go to which stations, where lines connect, and whether a given destination is near or far. Geographic maps confuse the issue by providing unnecessary information. Schematic maps make it easy to see what people want to know.

A more complex and interactive example of data visualization is the GapMinder application described in Chapter 2 (see Fig. 2.21). It exploits human perception of motion and several Gestalt principles to show changes in the socioeconomic status of the world's nations and relationships between nations. It shows how nations and groups of nations have "moved" over the years along dimensions, such as average life expectancy, per capita income, gross national product, etc. Another example of interactive data visualization of time-varying data is a graph depicting the evolution of the Web from 2003 to 2012 (see Fig. 12.5). It uses horizontal scrolling along a timeline rather than animated motion of objects.

---

[5] Some researchers prefer the term *information visualization*, or info viz for short.

FIGURE 12.4

Maps of the London Underground: (A) geographic map, 1919, and (B) schematic map, 2013.

Some of the same graphical techniques, except motion, are used in a graph show-ing important data visualization publications, their relative number of citations, and how they are related to each other, such as in cross-citations (see Fig. 12.6).[6] Motion isn't needed in this visualization because the data depicts a moment in time rather than a time period.

---

[6]More data viz examples can be found at http://www.webdesignerdepot.com/2009/06/50-great-examples-of-data-visualization.

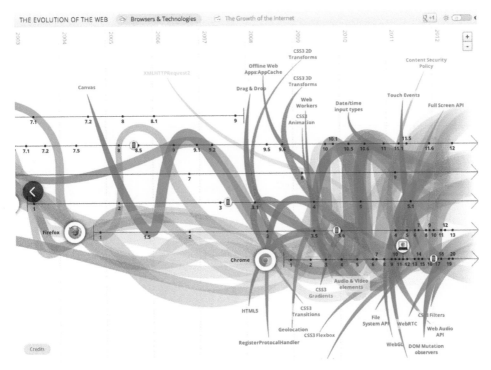

FIGURE 12.5

Evolution of the Web (2012). *Source: Hyperakt, Vizzuality, Google Chrome team* (http://www.evolutionoftheweb.com).

An imaginative example of data visualization goes by the name of *Chernoff faces*, named after Herman Chernoff, who invented the idea (Tufte, 2001). Scientists, engineers, and even administrators often must analyze and categorize data in which each data point has many dimensions. A simple example: a person in a police database can be represented by his name, address, phone number, date of birth, height, weight, eye color, hair color, number of traffic citations, number of convictions, and other variables. Bank accounts can be represented by their owner's name, a debit card number, a bank branch number, a balance, an interest rate, a minimum allowed balance, a required term of deposit, date of opening, etc. Displaying data in anything more than three dimensions is difficult, especially if scientists need to be able to see when data points form clusters or follow predictable patterns.

Chernoff realized that human faces are multidimensional: they vary in overall height, width, cheekbone height, nose length, nose width, chin width, eye distance, mouth width, ear height, ear width, ear vertical position, etc. He decided that 18 dimensions could characterize most human faces. He also knew that people are very

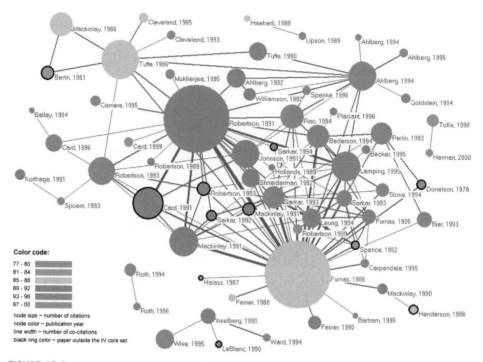

FIGURE 12.6

Visualization of data viz publications, their citations, and relationships.

good at recognizing human faces and differences, even slight differences, between faces. As is mentioned in Chapter 9, our ability to recognize faces is hardwired; we don't need to learn it.

Chernoff reasoned that because human faces are multidimensional, any multidimensional data can be represented as schematic faces, thereby exploiting our built-in face-recognition ability to allow people to recognize similarities, relationships, and patterns. Chernoff faces (see Fig. 12.7) have been used to represent a wide variety of data, from planets in the solar system to financial transactions.

Data visualization is a way to employ automatic visual perception processes built into system one to help system two understand complex data. For a visualization to succeed, it must present data in a way consistent with human visual capabilities and not trigger any of the visual system's flaws (Robertson et al., 1993; Ware, 2012).

Recent research on information visualization provides additional support for Chernoff's use of human faces. Researchers at MIT and Harvard found that data visualizations are much more memorable if they include "human-recognizable objects", such as pictures of people (Borkin et al, 2013).

FIGURE 12.7

Chernoff faces.

Convincing and persuading: Seducing system one and bypassing system two

Given how easily system one can be biased and even fooled, it goes almost without saying that *how* an interactive system presents information influences the decisions and behavior of users *at least* as strongly as *what* information it presents. If designers *want* to influence or persuade people to respond in a specific way—for example, buy a product, join an organization, subscribe to a service, donate to a charity, form a certain political opinion, vote a certain way—they can "exploit" the characteristics of system one to achieve that (Weinschenk, 2009; Kahneman, 2011).

Advertisers and political action committees are well aware of this, and so *often* design their messages to communicate with their audience's system one (and undermine system two). One can easily distinguish amateur advertisers and neophyte political copywriters from professionals. Amateurs present rational arguments and statistics supporting their point of view, hoping to convince our system two to agree. The pros skip the statistics; they design messages based on powerful stories evoking fear, hope, satisfaction, enjoyment, sex, money, prestige, food, and more fear, thereby bypassing our system two and aiming straight at our system one (see Fig 12.8).

Software and web designers can do the same if convincing and persuading people is their intent (Weinschenk, 2009). That has given rise to *persuasive* systems (Fogg, 2002), the opposite side of the coin from decision support systems. And, of course, persuasive software is a growing field of study, with a name, conferences, textbooks, and—you guessed it—a Wikipedia page.

FIGURE 12.8

Successful ads appeal to our emotions.

Contrasting decision support and persuasive systems

To better see the difference between decision support systems and persuasive systems, let's compare one of each, both of which concern charitable donations. One is CharityNavigator.org (see Fig. 12.9), which assesses and compares charitable

Top Ten Lists
10 Most Followed Charities
10 Celebrity-Related Charities
10 Super-Sized Charities
10 Charities Expanding in a Hurry
10 Most Frequently Viewed Charities
10 Charities Routinely in the Red
10 Highly Rated Charities Relying on Private Contributions
10 of the Best Charities Everyone's Heard Of
10 Charities in Deep Financial Trouble
10 Charities Worth Watching
10 Highly Paid CEOs at Low-Rated Charities

10 Highly Rated Charities Relying on Private Contributions

[f] Like 672   [y] Tweet 86   [P] Pin it   [+] Share 63   [🖶] Print

Most charities derive large chunks of revenue from earned income, membership fees, and government contracts and grants. **Ranked by overall score, these 10 excellent charities draw revenue solely from direct and indirect public support.** They report no government funding, no membership fees, and no revenue from earned income. As a result, **more than 95% of their total revenue comes from private contributions,** which makes the efficiency of their fundraising operations all the more impressive.

Rank	Charity	Overall Score
1	Books For Africa	69.94
2	Midwest Food Bank	69.89
3	Orphan Grain Train	69.80
4	Vitamin Angels	69.58
5	Palestine Children's Relief Fund	69.56
6	Helping Hand for Relief and Development	69.25
7	Feed My Starving Children	69.08
8	Just Detention International	69.05
9	Homes for Our Troops	68.97
10	Navy SEAL Foundation	68.76

FIGURE 12.9

CharityNavigator.org is a decision support website comparing charities.

organizations. The other is Feed My Starving Children, one of the charities listed at CharityNavigator.org (see Fig. 12.10).

CharityNavigator.org is a decision support site: it helps people decide, free of bias, which charities to support. To do this, it evaluates charities according to several criteria, such as the percentage of donations used for overhead costs, and assigns each organization an overall score, allowing people to compare the organizations.

In contrast, the clear goal of FMSC's website is to persuade visitors to donate to the organization so they can provide food-aid to families around the world. Everything on the site—photographs, logos, link labels, textual descriptions, even the organization's name—serves that goal (see Fig. 12.10). Their website is not about helping site visitors make a rational decision about whether to support FMSC versus other food-aid organizations. Decision support is neither their goal nor their responsibility. Their site exists to persuade.

I am not saying decision support is *good* and persuasion is *bad*, or that CharityNavigator.org is good and FMSC.org is bad. Both organizations have worthy missions and do good work. Persuasion can be good and often is necessary. Someone might decide to donate to FMSC because their friend recommended it and they trust

FIGURE 12.10

Feed My Starving Children (FMSC.org) is a charitable relief organization.

their friend. Furthermore, engaging system two to methodically enumerate all options and rationally compare them can be a waste of time if system one can produce an acceptable decision quickly. My only purpose in comparing the two sites is to illustrate the difference between decision support and persuasive systems.

Computer security: Worth the cost?

Setting up security (e.g., data backup and virus protection) on computers and smartphones costs time, effort, and money. In the terms used by decision theorists, the setup costs constitute a small to medium loss. People compare that small sure loss to a small chance of a large loss: losing all their data or having unauthorized people access their data. Some people buy the protection while others decide to take the risk.

This situation seems to fall into the bottom-right cell of Kahneman and Tversky's fourfold pattern: low probability of large loss. The pattern predicts that most people would take the risk-averse path and purchase backup and virus protection systems. In fact, however, many people practice denial and don't bother purchasing protection, and as a result occasionally suffer big losses. Recent surveys found that:

- Between 39% and 51% of American consumers have not backed up their files in over a year, if ever (Budman, 2011; Husted, 2012).

- 31% of personal computer users have at some point lost all of their files, and those files are on the average valued at over $10,000—that is, the files are much more valuable than the computers (McAfee, 2012).

- 17% of PCs worldwide have no virus protection; the United States is slightly worse at 19% (McAfee, 2012).

These findings prompt two sets of questions: one for researchers and one for designers. The question for researchers concerns the apparent deviation from Kahneman and Tversky's prediction that people are risk-averse and pay extra for protection when they face a small chance of a large loss. The relatively low percentage of PCs with no virus protection (17%) does not contradict the fourfold pattern: the majority of people (83%) do what the theory predicts. One could argue that even the 39-51% of PCs that are rarely or never backed up does not contradict the theory because it means that 49-61% of PCs *are* backed up. However, it *does* seem problematic for the theory that such a high percentage of computer systems—even a slight majority according to some surveys—are not.

Why do so many people not back up their data, when the fourfold pattern seems to predict that most people will? How reliable are the surveys that have been conducted? Is the variability in this case related to variability in people's willingness to gamble in casinos, buy lottery tickets (bottom left cell in Table 12.1), ride motorcycles without helmets, install smoke alarms, or fail to purchase insurance or extended product warranties? Knowing the answers to these questions would provide guidance for designers seeking to increase the use of computer security.

For designers, the question is: How can we design computer and smartphone security (data backup, virus protection, etc.) to get more people to use it. One way is obvious: reduce the costs of money, time, and effort. Make computer security inexpensive, simple and quick to set up, and easy to use, and more people will use it. For nearly everyone to use it, it would need to be as inexpensive and easy to set up and use as a toaster.

Many companies have tried to simplify backup, and most claim that their backup products and services are easy to set up and use. But the 40% non-backup and 19% no-virus-protection rates cited here are from surveys conducted in 2011 and 2012, so obviously the various costs of computer security are still not low enough for anything close to universal adoption. This should be seen as a challenge to user-interface designers.

Another answer for designers is less obvious: since people are influenced more by coherent stories than by statistics, companies offering backup and antivirus software should focus less on quoting statistics and instead share stories about how people lost their data or had their computers infected by viruses, or better: how they *recovered* their data and *avoided* viruses.

Our Hand–Eye Coordination Follows Laws

13

Have you ever had trouble hitting a tiny button or link on a computer screen or smartphone, or trouble keeping a screen pointer inside a narrow path required to reach a menu item or link?

Perhaps your hand was jittery because you had recently consumed too much coffee or taken a medication. Maybe it was shaking due to high anxiety, anger, or fear. Maybe you have Parkinson's disease, which makes your hands shake, or arthritis in your hands and arms, restricting your hand movement. Maybe your arm was restricted because it was temporarily in a cast or sling. Maybe you were using an unfamiliar pointing device. Or maybe the target was simply too small, or the allowed path too narrow.

It turns out that pointing at objects on a display and moving pointers along constrained paths follow consistent, quantitative laws.

FITTS' LAW: POINTING AT DISPLAYED TARGETS

The law for pointing at targets is called Fitts' law, named after the man who discovered it, Paul Fitts[1] (Fitts, 1954; Card et al., 1983). It basically says what makes intuitive sense: the larger your target on a screen and the nearer it is to your starting point, the faster you can point to it. That is all most user-interface designers need to know about Fitts' law, but in case you ever need to know the precise relationship between target size, distance, and placement time, here is the formula:

$$T = a + b \log_2 (1 + D/W)$$

where T is the time to move to the target, D is the distance to target, and W is the width of the target along the direction of movement of the pointer. From the formula, you can

---

[1] The law is not "Fitt's law"; the "s" is in his name. Some researchers prefer "Fitts's," but I prefer "Fitts'."

see that as the distance (*D*) increases, the time (*T*) to reach the target increases, and as the target width (*W*) increases, the time to reach it decreases (see Fig. 13.1).

Fitts' law is quite general. It applies to *any* type of pointing: mouse, trackball, track pad, joystick, even fingers on touchscreens. It also applies to everyone, regardless of age, physical abilities, or mental state. But people vary in how fast they can move, and devices vary in how fast they can be moved, so the formula includes the parameters *a* and *b* to adjust it for those sorts of differences: *a* is the ease of starting and stopping the movement, and *b* is a measure of the average difficulty of moving the hand and pointing the device (if any).

The dependency of pointing time on target size and distance codified in Fitts' law can be understood by considering how screen-pointers move. A person sees a target on a screen and decides to hit it. Hands and pointing devices have inertia, so movement toward the target starts slowly, but rapidly accelerates until reaching some maximum speed. This initial movement is fairly gross: it is essentially a shot in the general direction of the target, without much control. We call the initial shot *ballistic*, like a shell fired from a cannon. As the pointer nears the target, the movement speed slows as the person's hand–eye feedback loops take control. The movement ends slowly, with finer and finer corrections, until the pointer is on the target (see Fig. 13.2).

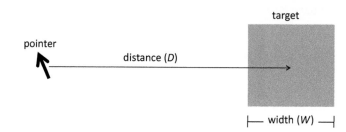

FIGURE 13.1

Fitts' law: pointing time depends on distance (*D*) and the width (*W*) of the target.

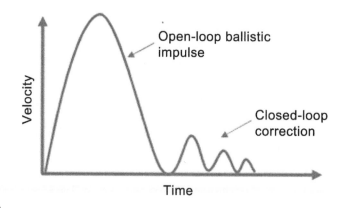

FIGURE 13.2

Graph of velocity over time as pointer moves to target. *Courtesy of Andy Cockburn.*

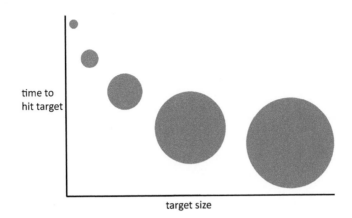

time to hit target

target size

FIGURE 13.3

Diminishing marginal benefit of increasing click-target size (if *D* is constant).

Although the basic prediction of Fitts' law—people hit on-screen targets faster the closer they are and the larger they are—seems pretty intuitive, the law also predicts something less intuitive: the *more* the distance decreases or the target grows, the *less* the decrease in pointing time. If a target is tiny and you double its size, the time people take to hit it decreases, but if you double the size *again*, the pointing time doesn't improve quite as much. So beyond a certain size, making a target even larger provides little added benefit (see Fig. 13.3), and below a certain distance, moving a target even closer doesn't help much.

A final noteworthy prediction of Fitts' law is that, if the pointer or finger is blocked from moving past the edge of the screen, targets at the edge will be very easy to hit: people can just yank the pointer toward the target until the edge stops it, with no need for slow, fine adjustments at the end of the movement. Thus, from the point of view of Fitts' law, targets at the screen's edge behave as if they were much larger than they actually are. However, this edge-pointing detail of the law applies mainly to desktop and laptop computers, because modern smartphones and tablet computers don't have raised edges that physically stop fingers.

Design implications of Fitts' law

Fitts' law is the basis of several common user-interface design guidelines:

- Make click-targets—graphical buttons, menu items, links—big enough that they are easy for people to hit. Don't make people click on tiny targets, as Bank of the West does on their online banking website (see Fig. 13.4).

- Make the *actual* click-target at *least* as large as the *visible* click-target. Above all, don't frustrate users by presenting big buttons that only accept clicks on a small area (e.g., the text label,) as the Aging in America (AIA) 2011 conference did in the navigation buttons on its website (see Fig. 13.5). Accept clicks over at least

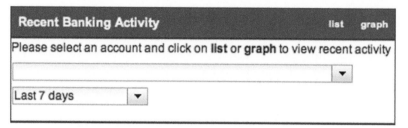

FIGURE 13.4

Bank Of The West.com's "list" and "graph" links are too small to hit easily.

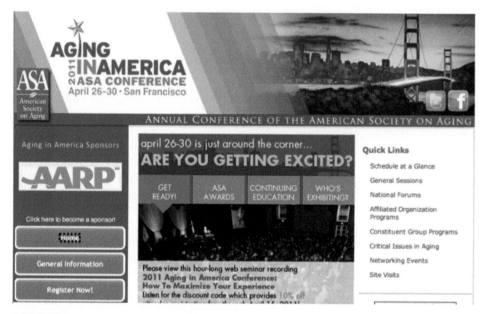

FIGURE 13.5

AIA 2011 conference website's navigation buttons (left) accept clicks only on the label.

the entire area of the visible click-target, as ElderLawAnswers.com does (see Fig. 13.6). If the visible target must be small (e.g., a small word embedded in text), design the user interface to treat clicks *near* the link as if they were *on* it.

- Checkboxes, radio buttons, and toggle switches should accept clicks on their labels as well as on the buttons, thereby increasing the clickable area.

- Leave plenty of space between buttons and links so people don't have trouble hitting the intended one.

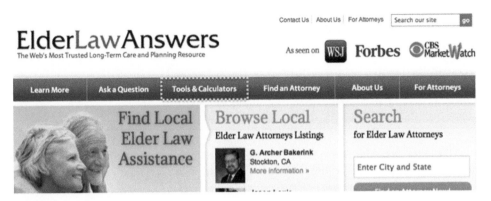

FIGURE 13.6

ElderLawAnswers.com's navigation buttons accept clicks over the entire area.

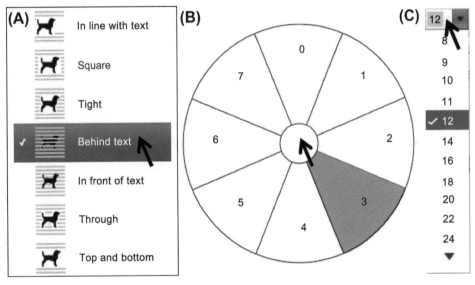

FIGURE 13.7

Types of menus: (A) pop-up menu, (B) pie menu, and (C) pull-down menu.

- Place important targets near the edge of the screen to make them very easy to hit.

- Display choices in pop-up and pie menus if possible (see Fig. 13.7). They are faster to use than pull-down menus on average, because they open "around" the screen pointer rather than below it, so users need to move the pointer less to reach most of the items. However, even pull-down menus are faster than pull-right ("walking") menus.

STEERING LAW: MOVING POINTERS ALONG CONSTRAINED PATHS

A law derived from Fitts' law governs the time it takes to steer a screen-pointer along a constrained path to a target. Appropriately, it is named the *Steering law* (Accot and Zhai, 1997). It says that if you must keep a pointer within a certain confined path while moving it to a target, then the wider the path, the faster you can move the pointer to the target (see Fig. 13.8). Its formula is simpler than that of Fitts' law:

$$T = a + b\,(D/W)$$

Like Fitts' law, the Steering law seems like common sense: a wider path means you need not move the pointer carefully; you can move it ballistically—that is, fast.

Design implications of the Steering law

Anyone who has used devices that have point-and-click or touchscreen user interfaces can probably think of situations where they had to steer the screen pointer or their finger along a constrained path. Those are situations in which the Steering law applies. The following are two examples:

- Pull-right menus (also called "walking" menus) where you must keep the pointer within a menu item as you move it sideways to a submenu; otherwise, the menu switches to the item above or below. The narrower each menu item is, the slower the menu will be to use.

- Page rulers (e.g., for setting tabs) where you must keep the pointer within the ruler as you drag a tab to a new location; otherwise, the tab doesn't move (as in recent versions of Microsoft Word). The narrower the ruler, the slower your movement.

Pull-right menus are fairly common in software applications. For example, Apple's Safari browser uses them (see Fig. 13.9). Some software applications, such as DataTaker's DataLogger product (see Fig. 13.10), have pull-right menus going out to several levels.

To see how widening pointer-movement paths can speed the use of pull-right menus, compare the former and current websites of RoadScholar.org, a travel

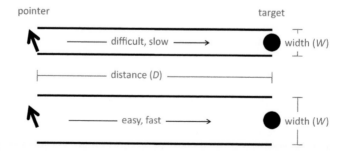

FIGURE 13.8

Steering law: pointing time depends on distance (*D*) and width (*W*) of path.

website aimed at older adult travelers. In mid-2012, a usability test of the website showed that people in the site's target age group had trouble choosing travel destinations using the site's pull-right menus (Finn and Johnson, 2013). By early 2013, the site's designers widened the menu items significantly, making it easier and faster for users to choose travel destinations that interested them (see Fig. 13.11). That's the Steering law at work.

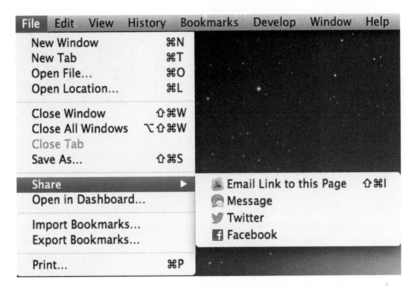

FIGURE 13.9

Pull-right menus in Apple's Safari browser.

FIGURE 13.10

Pull-right menus in DataTaker's DataLogger application.

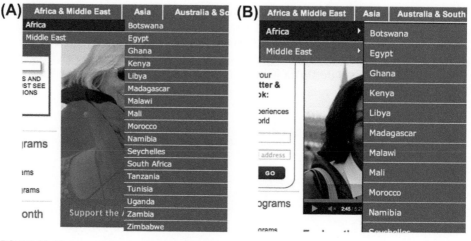

FIGURE 13.11

RoadScholar.org travel website: (A) in 2012, narrow menu items, and (B) in 2013, wider items.

Once upon a time, scroll bars in graphical user interfaces (GUIs) were constrained paths: you had to keep the pointer within the narrow vertical or horizontal scrollbar as you dragged the "elevator" along; otherwise, you lost control of the scrollbar. GUI designers soon realized that this made scrollbars slow, tedious, and error-prone to use, so they eliminated the constraint. Modern scrollbars allow you to move the pointer outside of the bar while you drag the "elevator." They track motion in the direction of the scrollbar only, and ignore any perpendicular motion. This change effectively made the constrained path as wide as the entire screen, greatly speeding scrollbar operation and eliminating a source of errors. Another case of the Steering law at work.

We Have Time Requirements

14

Events in the world take time to play out. *Perceiving* objects and events also takes time. So does remembering perceived events, thinking about past and future events, learning from events, acting on plans, and reacting to perceived and remembered events. How much time? And how does knowing the duration of perceptual and cognitive processes help us design interactive systems?

This chapter answers those questions. It presents the *durations* of perceptual and cognitive processes, and based on those, provides real-time *deadlines* that interactive systems must meet to synchronize well with human users. Interactive systems that don't synchronize well with users' time requirements are (1) less effective, and (2) users perceive them as unresponsive.

Issue (2), perceived responsiveness, may seem less important than effectiveness, but in fact it is *more* important. Over the past five decades, researchers have found consistently that an interactive system's responsiveness—its ability to keep up with users, keep them informed about its status, and not make them wait unexpectedly—is the *most* important factor in determining user satisfaction. It is not just *one* of the most important factors; it is *the* most important factor.[1] It is more important than ease of learning. It is more important than ease of use. Study after study has confirmed this finding (Barber and Lucas, 1983; Carroll and Rosson, 1984; Lambert, 1984; Miller, 1968; Rushinek and Rushinek, 1986; Shneiderman, 1984; Thadhani, 1981). Thus, with interactive systems, as in show business, timing is everything.

This chapter first defines responsiveness. It then enumerates important time constants of human perception and cognition. It ends with real-time guidelines for interactive system design, including examples.

---

[1] Some researchers have suggested that for users' perception of the loading speed of Web sites, the causality may go the other way: the more success people have at a site, the faster they think it is, even when their ratings don't correlate with the sites' actual speed (Perfetti and Landesman, 2001).

RESPONSIVENESS DEFINED

Responsiveness is related to performance, but is different. Performance is measured in terms of computations per unit of time. Responsiveness is measured in terms of compliance with human time requirements and user satisfaction.

Interactive systems can be responsive despite low performance. If you call a friend to ask a question, she can be responsive even if she can't answer your question immediately: she can acknowledge the question and promise to call back. She can be even more responsive by saying *when* she will call back.

Responsive systems keep a user informed even if they cannot fulfill the user's requests immediately. They provide feedback about what the user has done and what is happening, and they prioritize the feedback based on *human* perceptual, motor, and cognitive deadlines (Duis and Johnson, 1990). Specifically, they:

- Let you know immediately that your input was received.
- Provide some indication of how long operations will take (see Fig. 14.1).
- Free you to do other things while waiting.
- Manage queued events intelligently.
- Perform housekeeping and low-priority tasks in the background.
- Anticipate your most common requests.

Software can have poor responsiveness even if it is fast. Even if a camera repairman is very fast at fixing cameras, he is unresponsive if you walk into his shop and he ignores you until he finishes working on another camera. He is unresponsive if you hand him your camera and he silently walks away without saying whether he is going to fix it now or go to lunch. Even if he starts working on your camera immediately, he is unresponsive if he doesn't tell you whether fixing it will take five minutes, five hours, five days, or five weeks.

Systems that display poor responsiveness do not meet human time deadlines. They don't keep up with users. They don't provide timely feedback for user actions, so users are unsure of what they have done or what the system is doing. They make users wait at unpredictable times and for unpredictable periods. They limit users'

FIGURE 14.1

Mac OS X file transfer: good progress indicator, useful time estimate, and cancel button (circled X).

FIGURE 14.2

No progress bar (just a busy bar) and no cancel for (A) Mac OS X and (B) iMovie.

work pace—sometimes severely. Here are some specific examples of poor responsiveness:

- Delayed feedback for button presses, scrollbar movement, or object manipulations.
- Time-consuming operations that block other activity and cannot be aborted (see Fig. 14.2).
- Providing no clue how long lengthy operations will take (see Fig. 14.2).
- Jerky, hard-to-follow animations.
- Ignoring user input while performing "housekeeping" tasks users did not request.

These problems impede users' productivity and frustrate and annoy them. Unfortunately, despite all of the research showing that responsiveness is critical to user satisfaction and productivity, a lot of today's interactive systems have poor responsiveness (Johnson, 2007).

THE MANY TIME CONSTANTS OF THE HUMAN BRAIN

To understand the time requirements of human users of interactive systems, let's start with neurophysiology.

The human brain and nervous system are not really a single organ; rather, they are made up of a collection of neuron-based organs that appeared at vastly different points in the evolutionary chain from worms to people. This collection provides a large variety of sensory, regulatory, motor, and cognitive functions. Not surprisingly, these functions operate at different speeds. Some work very fast, executing functions in small fractions of a second, while others are many, many times slower, executing over many seconds, minutes, hours, or even longer timespans.

For example, Chapter 10 explained that automatic processing, such as playing a memorized musical piece, operates on a "clock" that is at least 10 times faster than the one governing highly monitored, controlled processing, such as composing a

HOW LONG DOES THE BRAIN TAKE TO …?

Table 14.1 shows durations of perceptual and cognitive functions that affect our perceptions of system responsiveness, from shortest to longest (Card et al., 1991; Johnson, 2007; Sousa, 2005; Stafford and Webb, 2005). Those that are not self-explanatory are explained more fully later.

Table 14.1 Durations of Perceptual and Cognitive Functions

Perceptual and Cognitive Functions	Duration
Shortest gap of silence that we can detect in a sound	1 millisecond (0.001 second)
Minimum time between spikes in auditory neurons, the fastest neurons in the brain	2 milliseconds (0.002 second)
Shortest time a visual stimulus can be shown and still affect us (perhaps unconsciously)	5 milliseconds (0.005 second)
Minimum noticeable lag in ink as someone draws with a stylus	10 milliseconds (0.01 second)
Maximum interval for auditory fusion of successive sound pulses into a pitched tone	20 milliseconds (0.02 second)
Maximum interval for visual fusion of successive images	50 milliseconds (0.05 second)
Speed of flinch reflex (involuntary motor response to possible danger)	80 milliseconds (0.08 second)
Time lag between a visual event and our full perception of it (or perceptual cycle time)	100 milliseconds (0.1 second)
Threshold for perceptual "locking" of events and sounds	100 milliseconds (0.1 second)
Duration of saccade (involuntary eye movement), during which vision is suppressed	100 milliseconds (0.1 second)
Maximum interval between events for perception that one event caused another event	140 milliseconds (0.14 second)
Time for a skilled reader's brain to comprehend a printed word	150 milliseconds (0.15 second)
Time to subitize (determine the number of) up to four to five items in our visual field	200 milliseconds (0.2 second; 50 milliseconds/item)
Editorial "window" within which the brain edits the presence and order of events	200 milliseconds (0.2 second)

Table 14.1 Durations of Perceptual and Cognitive Functions—cont'd

Perceptual and Cognitive Functions	Duration
Time to identify (i.e., name) a visually presented object	250 milliseconds (0.25 second)
Time to mentally count each item in a scene when there are more than four items	300 milliseconds (0.3 second)
Attentional "blink" (inattentiveness to other input) following recognition of an object	500 milliseconds (0.5 second)
Visual-motor reaction time (intentional response to unexpected event)	700 milliseconds (0.7 second)
Maximum duration of silent gap between turns in person-to-person conversation	About 1 second
Duration of unbroken attention to a single task (unit task)	6–30 seconds
Time to make critical decisions in emergency situations (e.g., medical triage)	1–5 minutes
Duration of important purchase decision (e.g., buying a car)	1–10 days
Time to choose a lifetime career	20 years

musical piece. Another example is the flinch reflex: a region of the brain called the superior colliculus—part of the evolutionarily ancient old brain—can "see" a rapidly approaching object and make you flinch or raise your arms long before your cortex has perceived and identified the object.

The sidebar "How long does the brain take to …?" gives the durations of some important perceptual and cognitive brain functions. Most are self-explanatory, but a few require additional explanation.

Shortest gap of silence that we can detect in a sound: 1 millisecond (0.001 second)

Our hearing is much more sensitive to short events and small differences than our vision is. Our ears operate using mechanical sound transducers, not electrochemical neural circuitry. The eardrum transmits vibration to the ossicles (middle-ear bones), which in turn transmit vibration to the cochlea's hair cells, which, when vibrated, trigger electrical pulses that go to the brain. Because the connection is mechanical, our ears respond to sound much faster than the rods and cones in our retina respond to light. This speed allows our auditory system to detect very small differences in the time when a sound arrives at our two different ears, from which the brain calculates the direction of the sound's source.

Shortest time a visual stimulus can be shown and still affect us (perhaps unconsciously): 5 milliseconds (0.005 second)

This is the basis of so-called subliminal perception. If you are shown an image for 5–10 milliseconds, you won't be aware of seeing it, but low-level parts of your visual system will register it. One effect of such exposure to an image is that your familiarity with it will increase: if you see it again later, it will seem familiar. Brief exposure to an image or a looming object can also trigger responses from your old brain and midbrain— avoidance, fear, anger, sadness, joy—even if the image disappears before the conscious mind identifies it. However, contrary to popular myth, subliminal perception is not a strong determinant of behavior. It cannot make you do things you wouldn't otherwise do or want things you wouldn't otherwise want (Stafford and Web, 2005).

Speed of flinch reflex (involuntary motor response to possible danger): 80 milliseconds (0.08 second)

When an object—even a shadow—approaches you rapidly, if you hear a loud sound nearby, or if something suddenly pushes, jabs, or grabs you, your reflex is to flinch: pull away, close your eyes, throw up your hands in defense, etc. This is the flinch reflex. It is very fast compared to intentional reaction to a perceived event: about 10 times faster. Evidence of the speed of the flinch reflex has been seen not only experimentally but also in examining the injuries that occur when people are attacked or involved in vehicle accidents: often their arms and hands are injured in ways that indicate that they managed to get their hands up in a split second (Blauer, 2007).

Time lag between a visual event and our full perception of it (or perceptual cycle time): 100 milliseconds (0.1 second)

From the time that light from an external event hits your retina to the time that neural impulses from that event reach your cerebral cortex, about 0.1 second elapses. Suppose our conscious awareness of the world lagged behind the real world by a tenth of a second. That lag would not be conducive to our survival: a tenth of a second is a long time when a rabbit you are hunting darts across a meadow. The brain compensates by extrapolating the position of moving objects by 0.1 second. Therefore, as a rabbit runs across your visual field, you see it where your brain estimates it is *now*, not where it was 0.1 second ago (Stafford and Web, 2005). However, your brain also edits the order of events before you are aware of them (see explanation of editorial window, page 202), so if the running rabbit suddenly turns left, your extrapolating brain doesn't falsely make you see it continuing straight ahead and then have to backtrack.

Threshold for perceptual "locking" of events and sounds: 100 milliseconds (0.1 second)

The brain "locks" a visual event to a corresponding sound if the delay between them is less than 0.1 second. If you watch a man beat a drum but are several hundred meters from him, you first see him hit the drum and then hear the sound.

The closer you are to the drummer, the less the delay. However, if the delay goes under 100 milliseconds (which it does at about 33.5 meters, or 100 feet, distance), the brain "locks" the visual perception to the auditory one, and you no longer notice the delay. This fact means that editors of television, movie, videogame, and other visual media can allow up to 100 milliseconds of "slop" in synchronizing visuals with audio before people notice (Bilger, 2011).

Duration of saccade (involuntary eye movement), during which vision is suppressed: 100 milliseconds (0.1 second)

As described in Chapter 6, our eyes move frequently and to a great extent involuntarily, about three times per second. These are called saccadic eye movements, or *saccades*. Each saccade takes about one-tenth of a second, during which vision is suppressed (i.e., turned off). This brief shutdown of vision is called *saccadic masking*. However, we don't notice these blank intervals. The brain edits out the blank intervals and stitches together the visual clips before they reach our awareness, making it seem to us as if they didn't exist. You can demonstrate this to yourself by facing a mirror and looking at your left eye, then your right eye, etc. You don't see blank intervals while your eyes move, and you also never see your eyes move. It's as if the movement took no time. However, someone else watching you will see your eyes moving back and forth, taking a noticeable amount of time to move from left to right (Bilger, 2011; Eagleman, 2012).

Maximum interval between events for perception that one event caused another event: 140 milliseconds (0.14 second)

This interval is the deadline for perception of cause and effect. If an interactive system takes longer than 0.14 second to respond to your action, you won't perceive your action as having caused the response. For example, if the echoing of characters you type lags more than 140 milliseconds behind your typing, then you will lose the perception that you are typing those characters. Your attention will be diverted away from the meaning of the text and toward the act of typing, which slows you down, pulls typing out of automatic processing and into conscious processing, and increases your chances of making an error.

Time to subitize (determine the number of) up to four to five items in our visual field: 200 milliseconds (0.2 second; 50 milliseconds/item)

If someone tosses two coins onto the table and asks how many coins there are, it takes only a glance for you to see that there are two. You don't have to explicitly count them. You can do the same with three coins, or four. Some people can do it with five. This function is called *subitizing*. Beyond four or five, it gets harder: now you are starting to have to count, or, if the coins happen to fall into separate groups on the table, you can subitize each subgroup and add the results. This phenomenon is why when we count objects using tick-marks, we write the tick-marks in groups of four, then draw the fifth tick-mark across the group, like this: ┼┼┼┼ ┼┼┼┼ ││. Subitizing feels instantaneous, but it isn't. It takes about 50 milliseconds per item (Card et al., 1983; Stafford and Webb, 2005). However, that is much less time per item than explicit counting, which takes about 300 milliseconds per item.

Editorial "window" within which the brain edits the presence and order of events: 200 milliseconds (0.2 second)

The order in which we perceive events is not necessarily the order in which they occur. The brain has a moving "editorial window" of about 200 milliseconds, during which perceived and recalled items vie for promotion to consciousness. Within that time window, events and objects that might otherwise have made it to consciousness may be superseded by others—even ones that occurred later in time (within the window). Within the window, events can also be resequenced on the way to consciousness. An example: We see a dot that disappears and immediately reappears in a new position as moving. Why? Our brain certainly does not do it by "guessing" the second dot's position and showing us "phantom" motion in that direction, because we see motion in the correct direction *regardless* of where the new object appears. The answer is that we don't actually perceive motion until the dot appears in the new position, but the brain resequences things so that we seem to see the motion *before* the dot reappears. The second dot must appear less than 0.2 second after the first dot disappears for the brain to be able to resequence the events (Stafford and Webb, 2005; Eagleman, 2012).

Attentional "blink" (inattentiveness to other objects) following recognition of an object: 500 milliseconds (0.5 second)

As described in Chapter 1, this is one way in which our perception is biased. Briefly: if you spot or hear something or someone that captures your attention, you are essentially deaf and blind to other events for about a half-second. Your brain is in "busy" mode.

With a colleague's help, you can demonstrate the "blink." Choose two words. Tell the colleague the two words. Then explain that you will read a list of words and at the end you want to know if either of the two words was in the list. Quickly read a long list of words at a rate of three words per second. Somewhere in the list, include one target word. If the second target word is presented right after the first—within one or two items—your colleague probably won't hear it.

Visual-motor reaction time (intentional response to unexpected event): 700 milliseconds (0.7 second)

This interval is the combined time for your visual system to notice something in the environment and initiate a conscious motor action, and for the motor system to execute the action. If you are driving your car toward an intersection and the light turns red, this is the time required for you to notice the red light, decide to stop, and put your foot on the brake pedal. How long it takes your car to actually *stop* is not included in the 700 milliseconds. The vehicle stopping time depends on how fast the car is going, the condition of the pavement under the wheels, etc.

This reaction time is different from the flinch reflex—the old brain responding to rapidly approaching objects, making you automatically close your eyes, dodge, or throw up your hands to protect yourself. That reflex operates about 10 times faster (see earlier).

The visual-motor intentional reaction time is approximate. It varies a bit among people. It also increases with distractions, drowsiness, blood-alcohol level, and possibly age.

Maximum duration of silent gap between turns in person-to-person conversation: About 1 second

This is the approximate normal length of gaps in a conversation. When gaps exceed this limit, participants—either speakers or listeners—often say something to keep the conversation going: they interject "uh" or "uh-huh," or take over as speaker. Listeners respond to such pauses by turning their attention to the speaker to see what caused it. The precise length of such gaps varies by culture, but it is always in the range of 0.5-2 seconds.

Duration of unbroken attention to a single task ("unit task"): 6–30 seconds

When people perform a task, they break it down into little pieces: subtasks. For example, buying airline tickets online consists of: (1) going to a travel or airline Web site, (2) entering the trip details, (3) scanning the results, (4) selecting a set of flights, (5) providing credit card information, (6) reviewing the purchase, and (7) finalizing the purchase. Some subtasks are broken down further, for example, entering the trip details consists of entering the trip origin, destination, dates, time, etc., piece by piece. This breaking down of tasks into subtasks ends with small subtasks that can be completed without a break in concentration, with the subgoal and all necessary information either held in working memory or directly perceivable in the environment. These bottom-level subtasks are called *unit tasks* (Card et al., 1983). Between unit tasks, people typically look up from their work, check to see if anything else requires attention, perhaps look out the window or take a sip of coffee, etc. Unit tasks have been observed in activities as diverse as editing documents, entering checkbook transactions, designing electronic circuits, and maneuvering fighter jet planes in dogfights, and they always last somewhere in the range of 6-30 seconds.

ENGINEERING APPROXIMATIONS OF TIME CONSTANTS: ORDERS OF MAGNITUDE

Interactive systems should be designed to meet the temporal requirements of their human users. However, trying to design interactive systems for the wide variety of perceptual and cognitive time constants would be nearly impossible.

But people who design interactive systems are engineers, not scientists. We don't have to account for the full variety of brain-related time constants and clock-cycle times. We just have to design interactive systems that work for human beings. This more approximate requirement gives us the freedom to consolidate the many perceptual and cognitive time constants into a smaller set that is easier to teach, remember, and use in design.

Examining the list of critical durations presented in Table 14.1 yields some useful groupings. Times related to sound perception are all on the order of a millisecond, so we can consolidate them all into that value. Whether they are really 1 millisecond, or 2, or 3—we don't care. We only care about factors of 10.

Similarly, there are groups of durations around 10 milliseconds, 100 milliseconds, 1 second, 10 seconds, and 100 seconds. Above 100 seconds, we are beyond durations that most interaction designers care about. Thus, for designing interactive systems, these consolidated deadlines provide the required accuracy.

Notice that these deadlines form a convenient series: each successive deadline is 10 times—one order of magnitude—greater than the previous one. That makes the series fairly easy for designers to remember, although remembering what each deadline is for may be challenging.

DESIGNING TO MEET REAL-TIME HUMAN INTERACTION DEADLINES

To be perceived by users as responsive, interactive software must follow these guidelines:

- Acknowledge user actions instantly, even if returning that the answer will take time; preserve users' perception of cause and effect.
- Let users know when the software is busy and when it isn't.
- Free users to do other things while waiting for a function to finish.
- Animate movement smoothly and clearly.
- Allow users to abort (cancel) lengthy operations they don't want.
- Allow users to judge how much time lengthy operations will take.
- Do its best to let users set their own work pace.

In these guidelines, *instantly* means within about 0.1 second. Much longer than that, and the user interface will have moved out of the realm of cause and effect, reflexes, perceptual-motor feedback, and automatic behavior, into the realm of conversational gaps and intentional behavior (see sidebar: "How long does the brain take to ...?"). After 2 seconds, a system has exceeded the expected time for turn taking in dialog and has moved into the time range of unit tasks, decision making, and planning.

Now that we have listed time constants of human perception and cognition, and consolidated them into a simplified set, we can quantify terms such as *instantly*, *take time*, *smoothly*, and *lengthy* in the preceding guidelines (see also Table 14.2).

0.001 second (1 millisecond)

As described earlier, the human auditory system is sensitive to very brief intervals between sounds. If an interactive system provides audible feedback or content, its audio-generation software should be engineered to avoid network bottlenecks, getting swapped out, deadlocks, and other interruptions. Otherwise, it may produce noticeable gaps, clicks, or lack of synchrony between audio tracks. Audio feedback and content should be provided by well-timed processes running with high priority and sufficient resources.

0.01 second (10 milliseconds)

Subliminal perception is rarely, if ever, used in interactive systems, so we needn't concern ourselves with that issue. Suffice it to say that if designers wanted to boost the familiarity of certain visual symbols or images without the users' awareness, the designers could do so by presenting the images or symbols repeatedly for 10 milliseconds at a time. It is also worth mentioning that while extremely brief exposure to an image can increase its familiarity, the effect is weak—certainly not strong enough to make people like or dislike specific products.

One way for software to generate tones is by sounding clicks at various rates. If the clicks are less than 10 milliseconds apart, they will be heard as a single sustained buzz, in which the pitch is determined in part by the click frequency. Users will hear clicks as distinct if the clicks are separated by intervals of more than 10 milliseconds.

Systems that use stylus-based input should ensure that electronic "ink" does not lag behind the stylus by more than 10 milliseconds; otherwise, users will notice the lag and be annoyed.

0.1 second (100 milliseconds)

If software waits longer than 0.1 second to show a response to a user's action, the perception of cause and effect is broken: the software's reaction will not seem to be a result of the user's action. Therefore, onscreen buttons have 0.1 second to show they've been clicked; otherwise, users will assume they missed and click again.

Table 14.2 Time Deadlines for Human–Computer Interaction

Deadline	Perceptual and Cognitive Functions	Deadlines for Interactive System Design
0.001 sec	• Minimum detectable silent audio gap	• Maximum tolerable delay or dropout time for audio feedback (e.g., tones, "earcons," music)
0.01 sec	• Preconscious perception • Shortest noticeable pen-ink lag	• Inducing unconscious familiarity of images or symbols • Generating tones of various pitches • Electronic ink maximum lag time
0.1 sec	• Subitizing (perceiving the number of) one to four items • Involuntary eye movement (saccade) • Audiovisual "lock" threshold • Flinch reflex • Perception of cause and effect • Perceptual-motor feedback • Visual fusion • Object identification • Editorial window of consciousness • The perceptual "moment"	• Assume users can "count" one to four screen items in ~100 msec, but more than four takes 300 msec/item • Feedback for successful hand–eye coordination (e.g., pointer movement, object movement, or resizing, scrolling, drawing with mouse) • Tolerable "slop" in synching sound with visual events • Feedback for click on button or link • Displaying "busy" indicators • Allowable overlap between speech utterances • Max interval between animation frames
1 sec	• Max conversational gaps • Visual-motor reaction time for unexpected events • Attentional "blink"	• Displaying progress indicators for long operations • Finishing user-requested operations (e.g., open window) • Finishing unrequested operations (e.g., auto-save) • Time after information presentation that can be used for other computations (e.g., to make inactive objects active) • Required wait time after presenting important information before presenting more
10 sec	• Unbroken concentration on a task • Unit task: one part of a larger task	• Completing one step of a multistep task (e.g., one edit in a text editor) • Completing user input to an operation • Completing one step in a wizard (multistep dialog box)
100 sec	• Critical decision in emergency situation	• Assure that all information required for a decision is provided or can be found within this time

This does not mean that buttons have to complete their *function* in 0.1 second—only that buttons must show that they have been *pressed* by that deadline.

The main design point about the flinch reflex is that interactive systems should not startle users and cause flinching. Other than that, the flinch reflex and its duration don't seem very relevant to interactive system design. It is difficult to imagine beneficial uses of the flinch reflex in human-computer interaction, but one can imagine games with loud noises, joysticks with sudden tactile jolts, or three-dimensional virtual environments that cause their users to flinch under some circumstances, perhaps purposefully. For example, if a vehicle detects a pending collision, it could do something to make riders flinch to help protect them upon impact.

If an object the user is dragging or resizing lags more than 0.1 second behind the user's pointer movements, users will have trouble placing or resizing the object as desired. Therefore, interactive systems should prioritize feedback for hand–eye coordination tasks so that the feedback never lags past this deadline. If meeting that deadline is unachievable, then the system should be designed so that the task does not require close hand–eye coordination.

If an operation will take more than a perceptual "moment" (0.1 second) to complete, it should display a busy indicator. If a busy indicator can be displayed within 0.1 second, it can double as the action acknowledgment. If not, the software's response should come in two parts: a quick acknowledgment within 0.1 second, followed by a busy (or progress) indicator within 1 second. More guidance for displaying busy indicators is given later.

The brain can reorder events within this approximate time window before the events reach consciousness. Human speech is highly prone to such reordering if it occurs out of order. If you listen to several people talking and some people start talking just before the person before them has finished talking (within the time window), your brain automatically "untangles" the utterances so that you seem to hear them sequentially, without perceived overlap. Television and movies sometimes take advantage of this phenomenon to speed up conversations that normally would take too long.

We also regard 10 frames per second as an approximate minimum frame rate for perception of smooth animation, even though smooth animation really requires a rate more like 20 frames per second.

1 second

Because 1 second is the maximum gap expected in conversation, and because operating an interactive system is a form of conversation, interactive systems should avoid lengthy gaps in their side of the conversation. Otherwise, the human user will wonder what is happening. Systems have about 1 second to either do what the user asked or indicate how long it will take. Otherwise, users get impatient.

If an operation will take more than a few seconds, a progress indicator is needed. Progress indicators are an interactive system's way of keeping its side of the expected conversational protocol: "I'm working on the problem. Here's how much progress

I've made and an indication of how much more time it will take." More guidelines for progress indicators are provided later.

One second is also the approximate minimum time a user needs to respond intentionally to an unanticipated event. Therefore, when information suddenly appears on the screen, designers can assume that users will take at least 1 second to react to it (unless it causes a flinch response; see earlier discussion). That lag time can be useful in cases when the system needs to display an interactive object but cannot both render the object and make it interactive within 0.1 second. Instead, the system can display a "fake," inactive version of the object, and then take its time (1 second) to fill in details and make the object fully interactive. Today's computers can do a lot in 1 second.

10 seconds

Ten seconds is the approximate unit of time into which people usually break down their planning and execution of larger tasks. Examples of unit tasks are: completing a single edit in a text-editing application, entering a transaction into a bank account program, and executing a maneuver in an airplane dogfight. Software should support segmentation of tasks into these 10-second pieces.

Ten seconds is also roughly the amount of time users are willing to spend setting up "heavyweight" operations like file transfers or searches—if it takes any longer, users start to lose patience. Computing the result can then take longer if the system provides progress feedback.

Similarly, each step in a multipage "wizard" dialog box should have at most about 10 seconds of work for a user to do. If a step of a wizard takes significantly longer than 10 seconds to complete, it probably should be broken up into multiple smaller steps.

100 seconds (~1.5 minutes)

Interactive systems that support rapid critical decision making should be designed so that all the necessary information is either already in front of the decision maker or can be easily obtained with minimal browsing or searching. The best user interface for this type of situation is one in which users can obtain all crucial information simply by moving their eyes to where it is displayed[2] (Isaacs and Walendowski, 2001).

ADDITIONAL GUIDELINES FOR ACHIEVING RESPONSIVE INTERACTIVE SYSTEMS

In addition to design guidelines specific to each of the consolidated human–computer interaction deadlines, there are general guidelines for achieving responsiveness in interactive systems.

---

[2] Sometimes called "no-click" user interfaces.

Use busy indicators

Busy indicators vary in sophistication. At the low end, we have simple, static wait-cursors (e.g., an hourglass). They provide very little information: only that the software is temporarily occupied and unavailable to the user for other operations.

Next, we have wait-animations. Some of these are animated wait-cursors, such as the Mac OS rotating color wheel. Some wait-animations are not cursors but, rather, larger graphics elsewhere on the screen, such as the "downloading data" animations displayed by some web browsers. Wait animations are more "friendly" to users than static wait-cursors because they show that the system is working, not crashed or hung up waiting for a network connection to open or data to unlock. Of course, busy animations should cycle in response to the actual computations they represent. Busy animations that are simply started by a function but run independently of it are not really busy animations: they keep running even when the process they represent has hung or crashed and thereby potentially misleading users.

A common excuse for not displaying a busy indicator is that the function is supposed to execute quickly and so doesn't need to display one. But how quickly is "quickly"? What if the function doesn't always execute quickly? What if the user has a slower computer than the developer, or one that is not optimally configured? What if the function tries to access data that is temporarily locked? What if the function uses network services and the network is hung or overloaded?

Software should display a busy indicator for *any* function that blocks further user actions while it is executing, even if the function normally executes quickly (e.g., in less than 0.1 second). This indicator can be very helpful to a user if for some reason the function gets bogged down or hung up. Furthermore, it harms nothing: when the function executes at the normal speed, the busy indicator appears and disappears so quickly that users barely see it.

Use progress indicators

Progress indicators are better than busy indicators because they let users see how much time remains. Again, the deadline for displaying a progress indicator is 1 second.

Progress indicators can be graphical (e.g., a progress bar), textual (e.g., a count of files yet to be copied), or a combination of graphical and textual. They greatly increase the perceived responsiveness of an application, even though they don't shorten the time to complete operations.

Progress indicators should be displayed for any operation that will take longer than a few seconds. The longer the operation, the more important they are. Many noncomputer devices provide progress indicators, so we often take them for granted. Elevators that don't show the elevator's progress toward your floor are annoying. Most people wouldn't like a microwave oven that didn't show the remaining cooking time.

Here are some guidelines for designing effective progress indicators (McInerney and Li, 2002):

- Show work remaining, not work completed. Bad: "3 files copied." Good: "3 of 4 files copied."

- Show total progress, not progress on the current step. Bad: "5 seconds left on this step." Good: "15 seconds left."

- To show the percentage of an operation that is complete, start at 1%, not 0%. Users worry if the bar stays at 0% for more than 1–2 seconds.

- Similarly, display 100% only very briefly at the end of an operation. If the progress bar stays at 100% for more than 1–2 seconds, users assume it's wrong.

- Show smooth, linear progress, not erratic bursts of progress.

- Use human-scale precision, not computer precision. Bad: "240 seconds." Good: "About 4 minutes."

Delays between unit tasks are less bothersome than delays within unit tasks

Unit tasks are useful not only as a way of understanding how (and why) users break down large tasks. They also provide insight into when system response delays are most and least harmful or annoying.

During execution of a unit task, users keep their goal and necessary information in working memory or within their perceptual field. After they complete one unit task, before moving onto the next one, they relax a bit, and then pull the information needed for the next unit task into memory or view.

Because unit tasks are intervals during which the content of working memory and the perceptual field must remain fairly stable, unexpected system delays *during* a unit task are particularly harmful and annoying. They can cause users to lose track of some or all of what they were doing. By contrast, system delays *between* unit tasks are not as harmful or annoying, even though they may slow the user's overall work rate.

This difference between the impact of system response delays during and between unit tasks is sometimes expressed in user-interface design guidelines in terms of task closure, as in the classic user-interface design handbook *Human–Computer Interface Design Guidelines* (Brown, 1988):

A key factor determining acceptable response delays is level of closure. … A delay after completing a major unit of work may not bother a user or adversely affect performance. Delays between minor steps in a larger unit of work, however, may cause the user to forget the next planned steps. In general, actions with high levels of closure, such as saving a completed document to a file, are less sensitive to response time delays. Actions at the lowest levels of closure, such as typing a character and seeing it echoed on the display, are most sensitive to response time delays.

Bottom line: If a system has to impose delays, it should do so between unit tasks, not during tasks.

Display important information first

Interactive systems can appear to be operating fast by displaying important information first, then details and auxiliary information later. Don't wait until a display is fully rendered before letting users see it. Give users something to think about and act upon as soon as possible.

This approach has several benefits. It distracts users from the absence of the rest of the information and it fools them into believing that the computer did what they asked quickly. Research indicates that users prefer progressive results to progress indicators (Geelhoed et al., 1995). Displaying results progressively lets users start planning their next unit task. Finally, because of the aforementioned minimum reaction time for users to respond intentionally to what they see, this approach buys at least one more second for the system to catch up before the user tries to do anything. Here are some examples:

- *Document editing software.* When you open a document, the software shows the first page as soon as it has it, rather than waiting until it has loaded the entire document.

- *Web or database search function.* When you do a search, the application displays items as soon as it finds them, while continuing to search for more.

High-resolution images sometimes render slowly, especially in web browsers. To decrease the perceived time for an image to render, the system can display the image quickly at low resolution and then re-render it at a higher resolution. Because the visual system processes images holistically, this appears faster than revealing a full-resolution image slowly from top to bottom (see Fig. 14.3). Exception: For text, rendering a page at low resolution first and then substituting a higher-resolution version is *not* recommended: it annoys users (Geelhoed et al., 1995).

Fake heavyweight computations during hand–eye coordination tasks

In interactive systems, some user actions require rapid successive adjustments—with hand–eye coordination—until the goal is achieved. Examples include scrolling through a document, moving a game character through a landscape, resizing a window, or dragging an object to a new position. If feedback lags behind user actions by more than 0.1 second, users will have trouble hitting their goal. When your system cannot update its display fast enough to meet this hand–eye coordination deadline, provide lightweight simulated feedback until the goal is clear and then apply the real operation.

Graphics editors fake feedback when they provide rubberband outlines of objects that a user is trying to move or resize. Some document editing applications make quick-and-dirty changes to internal document data structures to represent the effect of user actions, and then straighten things out later.

FIGURE 14.3

If displaying images takes more than two seconds, display the whole image first at low resolution (A), not at full resolution from the top down (B).

Work ahead

Work ahead of users when possible. Software can use periods of low load to precompute responses to high-probability requests. There will be periods of low load because the users are human. Interactive software typically spends a lot of time waiting for input from the user. Don't waste that time! Use it to prepare something the user will probably want. If the user never wants it, so what? The software did it in "free" time; it didn't take time away from anything else. Here are some examples of using background processing to work ahead of users:

- A text search function looks for the *next* occurrence of the target word while you look at the current one. When you tell the function to find the next occurrence of the word, it already has it and so it seems very fast.

- A document viewer renders the next page while you view the current page. When you ask to see the next page, it is already ready.

Process user input according to priority, not the order in which it was received

The order in which tasks are done often matters. Blindly doing tasks in the order in which they were requested may waste time and resources or even create extra work. Interactive systems should look for opportunities to reorder tasks in their queue. Sometimes reordering tasks can make completing the entire set more efficient.

Airline personnel use nonsequential input processing when they walk up and down long check-in lines looking for people whose flights are leaving very soon so they can pull them out of line and get them checked in. In web browsers, clicking the "Back" or "Stop" buttons or on a link *immediately* aborts the process of loading and displaying the current page. Given how long it can take to load and display a web page, the ability to abort a page load is critical to user acceptance.

Monitor time compliance; decrease the quality of work to keep up

An interactive system can measure how well it is meeting the real-time deadlines. If it is missing deadlines or determines that it is at risk of missing a pending deadline, it can adopt simpler, faster methods, usually resulting in a temporary reduction in the quality of its output. This approach must be based on *real* time, not on processor cycles, so that it yields the same responsiveness on different computers.

Some interactive animation uses this technique. As described earlier, animation requires a frame rate of about 20 frames per second to be seen as smooth. In the late 1980s, researchers at Xerox Palo Alto Research Center (PARC) developed a software engine for presenting interactive animations that treats the frame rate as the most important aspect of the animation (Robertson et al., 1989, 1993). If the graphics engine has trouble maintaining the minimum frame rate because the images are complex or the user is interacting with them, it simplifies its rendering, sacrificing details such as text labels, three-dimensional effects, highlighting and shading, and

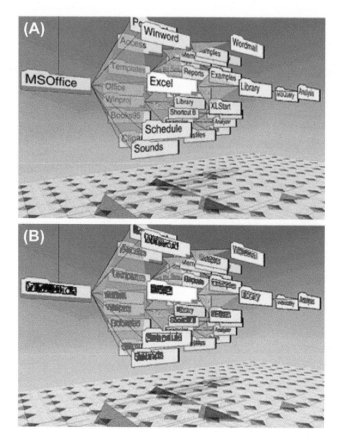

FIGURE 14.4

A cone tree (A) renders folder labels as blobs while a user rotates the tree (B).

color. The idea is that it is better to reduce an animated three-dimensional image temporarily to a line drawing than it is to let the frame rate drop below the limit.

The cone tree, developed at PARC, is based on this graphics engine. It is an interactive display of a hierarchical data structure, such as file directories and subdirectories (see Fig. 14.4). Users can grab any part of the tree and rotate it. While the tree rotates, the software might not have time to render all details of each frame while maintaining smooth animation. In that case, it might, for example, save time by rendering the filename labels on each folder as black blobs instead of as text. When the user stops rotating the tree, it is again rendered in full detail. Most users wouldn't even notice a degradation of the image during the movement, because they would attribute their inability to read the labels to motion blur.

Provide timely feedback even on the Web

Developers of web applications may have dismissed the time deadlines presented earlier in this chapter as pure fantasy.

It is true that meeting those deadlines on the Web is difficult—often impossible. However, it is also true that those deadlines are psychological time constants, wired into us by millions of years of evolution, governing our perception of responsiveness. They are not arbitrary targets that we can adjust at will to match the limitations of the Web or of any technology platform. If an interactive system does not meet those deadlines, even if it is a web application, users *will* consider its responsiveness to be poor. That means most web software has poor responsiveness. The question is: How can designers and developers maximize responsiveness on the Web? Here are some approaches:

- Minimize the size and number of images.

- Provide quick-to-display thumbnail images or overviews, with ways to show details only as needed.

- When the amount of data is too large or time consuming to display all at once, design the system to give an overview of *all* the data, and allow users to drill down into specific parts of the data to the level of detail they need.

- Style and lay out pages using Cascading Style Sheets (CSSs) instead of presentational HTML, frames, or tables, so browsers can display them faster.

- Use built-in browser components (e.g., error dialog boxes) instead of constructing them in HTML, for the same reason.

- Download applets and scripts to the browser so user interactions require less Internet traffic.

ACHIEVING RESPONSIVENESS IS IMPORTANT

By following the guidelines described in this chapter and additional responsiveness guidelines given in Johnson (2007), interaction designers and developers can create systems that meet human real-time deadlines, and that users therefore perceive as responsive.

However, the software industry must first recognize these facts about responsiveness:

- It is of great importance to users.

- It is different from performance; responsiveness problems are not solvable merely by tuning performance or making hardware faster.

- It is a *design* issue, not just an implementation issue.

History shows that faster processors will not solve the problem. Today's personal computers are as fast as supercomputers were 30 years ago, yet people still wait for their computers and grumble about a lack of responsiveness. Ten years from now, when personal computers and electronic appliances are as powerful as today's most powerful supercomputers, responsiveness will still be an issue because the software of that day will demand much more from the machines and the networks connecting them. For example, whereas today's text and document-editing applications do *spell* checking in the background, future versions may do Internet-based *fact* checking in the background. Additionally, applications 10 years from now will probably be based on these capabilities and technologies:

- Deductive reasoning.
- Image recognition.
- Real-time speech generation and recognition.
- Downloading terabyte-sized files.
- Wireless communication among dozens of household appliances.
- Collation of data from thousands of remote databases.
- Complex searches of the entire Web.

The result will be systems that place a much heavier load on the computer than today's systems do. As computers grow more powerful, history shows that much of that power is eaten up by applications that demand ever more processing power. Therefore, despite ever-increasing performance, responsiveness will never disappear as an issue.

For design flaws (bloopers) that hurt responsiveness, principles for designing responsive systems, and more techniques for achieving responsiveness, see Johnson (2007).

SUMMARY

The Introduction stated that applying interaction design guidelines in real designs is not simple and mindless. Constraints happen and force tradeoffs. Sometimes designers have to violate one guideline to follow another one, so they must be able to determine which guideline takes precedence in that situation.

That is why interaction design is a *skill*, not something that anyone can do by following a recipe. Learning that skill amounts to learning not only what the design guidelines are, but also how to recognize which rules to follow in each design situation.

The purpose of this book was to provide a brief background in the human perceptual and cognitive psychology that underlies interaction design guidelines. Now that you have that background knowledge, hopefully any user-interface guidelines you have been following will make more sense—they should no longer seem like arbitrary edicts by some user-interface guru. It should also now be clearer that the basis of all sets of user-interface design guidelines (see the Appendix) is the same. Finally, you are now better equipped to interpret, trade off, and apply user-interface design guidelines in real-world design situations.

CAVEAT

Technology—especially computer technology—advances quickly. The state of the art of computer-based interactive systems changes so quickly that it is difficult to get a book out before some of the technologies and designs mentioned in it are obsolete.

On the other hand, the fundamentals of how people perceive, learn, and think do not change quickly. The basic operations of human perception and cognition have remained fairly stable for tens—perhaps even hundreds—of thousands of years. In the long term, human perceptual and cognitive function will continue to evolve, but not in the timespan during which this book will be in circulation. However, people already use technology to improve their perception, memory, and reasoning; that trend will continue. Thus, human perception and thinking *will* change in a matter of decades, as our tools proliferate and improve and our reliance on them increases.

On the *third* hand, humanity's *knowledge* of human perception and cognition is, like computer technology, advancing rapidly. The past 20 years, especially, have seen a tremendous surge in our understanding of how the human brain works, aided by research tools such as functional MRI, eye-tracking systems, and neural network simulations. This has allowed cognitive psychology to move beyond "black box" models that merely *predicted* behavior to ones that *explain* how the brain processes and stores information and produces behavior. In this book, I have tried to digest and present some of these exciting new findings because of their value to designers. I do this knowing that, like the state of the art of computer technology, the state of knowledge of human cognitive/perceptual psychology will continue to advance, possibly rendering some of what the book says obsolete. It is better for designers to proceed using mostly correct knowledge of how people perceive and think than to design with *no* knowledge.

Well-known User-Interface Design Rules

Here is a sampling of user-interface design guidelines that have been published.

NORMAN (1983A)

Inferences from research

- Mode errors suggest the need for better feedback.
- Description errors suggest the need for better system configuration.
- Lack of consistency leads to errors.
- Capture errors imply the need to avoid overlapping command sequences.
- Activation issues suggest the importance of memory reminders.
- People will make errors, so make the system insensitive to them.

Lessons

- *Feedback.* The state of the system should be clearly available to the user, ideally in a form that is unambiguous and that makes the set of options readily available so as to avoid mode errors.

- *Similarity of response sequences.* Different classes of actions should have quite dissimilar command sequences (or menu patterns) so as to avoid capture and description errors.

- *Actions should be reversible.* As much as possible and where both irreversible and of relatively high consequence, they should be difficult to do, thereby preventing unintentional performance.

- *Consistency of the system.* The system should be consistent in its structure and design of command so as to minimize memory problems in retrieving the operations.

219

SHNEIDERMAN (1987); SHNEIDERMAN AND PLAISANT (2009)

- Strive for consistency.
- Cater to universal usability.
- Offer informative feedback.
- Design task flows to yield closure.
- Prevent errors.
- Permit easy reversal of actions.
- Make users feel they are in control.
- Minimize short-term memory load.

NIELSEN AND MOLICH (1990)

- Consistency and standards.
- Visibility of system status.
- Match between system and real world.
- User control and freedom.
- Error prevention.
- Recognition rather than recall.
- Flexibility and efficiency of use.
- Aesthetic and minimalist design.
- Help users recognize, diagnose, and recover from errors.
- Provide online documentation and help.

NIELSEN AND MACK (1994)

- Visibility of system status.
- Match between system and real world.
- User control and freedom.
- Consistency and standards.
- Error prevention.
- Recognition rather than recall.
- Flexibility and efficiency of use.
- Aesthetic and minimalist design.
- Help users recognize, diagnose, and recover from errors.
- Provide online documentation and help.

STONE *et al.* (2005)

- *Visibility.* First step to goal should be clear.
- *Affordance.* Control suggests how to use it.
- *Feedback.* Should be clear what happened or is happening.

- *Simplicity.* As simple as possible and task focused.
- *Structure.* Content organized sensibly.
- *Consistency.* Similarity for predictability.
- *Tolerance.* Prevent errors, help recovery.
- *Accessibility.* Usable by all intended users, despite handicap, access device, or environmental conditions.

JOHNSON (2007)

Principle 1: Focus on the users and their tasks, not on the technology

- Understand the users.
- Understand the tasks.
- Consider the context in which the software will function.

Principle 2: Consider function first, presentation later

- Develop a conceptual model.

Principle 3: Conform to the users' view of the task

- Strive for naturalness.
- Use users' vocabulary, not your own.
- Keep program internals inside the program.
- Find the correct point on the power/complexity tradeoff.

Principle 4: Design for the common case

- Make common results easy to achieve.
- Two types of "common": how many users versus how often.
- Design for core cases; don't sweat "edge" cases.

Principle 5: Don't complicate the users' task

- Don't give users extra problems.
- Don't make users reason by elimination.

Principle 6: Facilitate learning

- Think outside-in, not inside-out.
- Consistency, consistency, consistency.
- Provide a low-risk environment.

Principle 7: Deliver information, not just data

- Design displays carefully; get professional help.
- The screen belongs to the user.
- Preserve display inertia.

Principle 8: Design for responsiveness

- Acknowledge user actions instantly.
- Let users know when software is busy and when it isn't.
- Free users to do other things while waiting.
- Animate movement smoothly and clearly.
- Allow users to abort lengthy operations they don't want.
- Allow users to estimate how much time operations will take.
- Try to let users set their own work pace.

Principle 9: Try it out on users; then fix it

- Test results can surprise even experienced designers.
- Schedule time to correct problems found by tests.
- Testing has two goals: informational and social.
- There are tests for every time and purpose.

Bibliography

Accot, J., Zhai, S., 1997. Beyond Fitts' law: Models for trajectory-based HCI tasks. Proc. of ACM CHI 1997 Conf. Hum. Factors in Comput. Syst., 295–302.

Alvarez, G., Cavanagh, P., 2004. The capacity of visual short-term memory is set both by visual information load and by number of objects. Psychol. Sci. 15 (2), 106–111.

Angier, N., 2008. Blind to change, even as it stares us in the face. New York Times. April 1, 2008. Retrieved from www.nytimes.com/2008/04/01/science/01angi.html.

Arons, B., 1992. A review of the cocktail party effect. J. Am. Voice I/O Soc. 12, 35–50.

Apple Computer, 2009. Apple human interface guidelines. Retrieved from developer.apple.com/mac/library/documentation/UserExperience/Conceptual/AppleHIGuidelines.

Baddeley, A. (2012). Working Memory: Theories, Models, and Controversies. Annual Review of Psychology. 63, 1–29.

Barber, R., Lucas, H., 1983. System response time, operator productivity, and job satisfaction. Commun. ACM. 26 (11), 972–986.

Bays, P.M., Husain, M., 2008. Dynamic shifts of limited working memory resources in human vision. Science 321, 851–854.

Beyer, H., Holtzblatt, K., 1997. Contextual design: A customer-centered approach to systems design. Morgan Kaufmann, San Francisco.

Bilger, B., 2011. The Possibilian: David Eagleman and the Mysteries of the Brain. The New Yorker. April 25, 2011, retrieved from www.newyorker.com/reporting/2011/04/25/110425fa_fact_bilger.

Blauer, T., 2007. On the startle/flinch response. Blauer tactical intro to the spear system: Flinching and the first two seconds of an ambush. YouTube video, Retrieved from www.youtube.com/watch?v5jk_Ai8qT2s4.

Borkin, M.A., Vo, A.A., Bylinskii, Z., Isola, P., Sunkavalli, S., Oliva, A., Pfister, H., 2013. What makes a visualization memorable? IEEE Transactions on Visual Computer Graphics, Dec 19 (12), 2306–2315. Retrieved from, http://www.ncbi.nlm.nih.gov/pubmed/24051797, http://dx.doi.org/10.1109/TVCG.2013.234.

Boulton, D., 2009. Cognitive science: The conceptual components of reading and what reading does for the mind. Interview of Dr. Keith Stanovich, Children of the Code website. Retrieved from www.childrenofthecode.org/interviews/stanovich.htm.

Broadbent, D.E., 1975. The magical number seven after fifteen years. In: Kennedy, A., Wilkes, A. (Eds.), Studies in long-term memory. Wiley, London, pp. 3–18.

Brown, C.M., 1988. Human–computer interface design guidelines. Ablex Publishing Corporation, Norwood, NJ.

Budman, G., 2011. 94% of computer users still risk data loss. Backblaze blog July 12, 2011. Retrieved from blog.backblaze.com/2011/07/12/94-of-computer-users-still-risk-data-loss/.

Card, S., 1996. Pioneers and settlers: Methods used in successful user interface design. In: Rudisill, M., Lewis, C., Polson, P., McKay, T. (Eds.), Human-computer interface design: Success cases, emerging methods, real-world context. Morgan Kaufmann, San Francisco.

Card, S., Moran, T., Newell, A., 1983. The psychology of human–computer interaction. Lawrence Erlbaum Associates, Hillsdale, NJ.

Card, S., Robertson, G., Mackinlay, J., 1991. The information visualizer, an information workspace. Proc. of ACM CHI'91, 181–188.

Carroll, J., Rosson, M., 1984. Beyond MIPS: Performance is not quality. BYTE, 168–172.

Cheriton, D.R., 1976. Man–machine interface design for time-sharing systems. Proc. ACM Natl. Conf., 362–380.

Chi, E.H., Pirolli, P., Chen, K., Pitkow, J., 2001. Using information scent to model user information needs and actions on the web. Proc. ACM SIGCHI Conf. Comput.–Hum. Interact. (CHI 2001), 490–497.

Clark, A., 1998. Being there: Putting brain, body, and world together again. MIT Press, Cambridge, MA.

Cooper, A., 1999. The Inmates are running the asylum. SAMS, Indianapolis.

Cowan, N., Chen, Z., Rouder, J., 2004. Constant capacity in an immediate serial-recall task: A logical sequel to Miller (1956). Psychol. Sci. 15 (9), 634–640.

Doidge, N., 2007. The brain that changes itself. Penguin Group, New York.

Duis, D., Johnson, J., 1990. Improving user-interface responsiveness despite performance limitations. Proc. IEEE CompCon'90, 380–386.

Eagleman, D., 2012. Incognito: The secret lives of the brain. Vintage Books, New York.

Finn, K., Johnson, J., 2013. A usability study of websites for older travelers. Proceedings of HCI International 2013. Springer-Verlag, Las Vegas.

Fitts, P.M., 1954. The information capacity of the human motor system in controlling the amplitude of movement. J. Exp. Psychol. 47 (6), 381–391.

Fogg, B.J., 2002. Persuasive technology: Using computers to change what we think and do. Morgan Kaufmann.

Gazzaley, A., 2009. The aging brain: At the crossroads of attention and memory. User Experience 8 (1), 6–8.

Geelhoed, E., Toft, P., Roberts, S., Hyland, P., 1995. To influence time perception. Proc. ACM CHI'95 5, 272–273.

Grudin, J., 1989. The case against user interface consistency. Commun. ACM. 32 (10), 1164–1173.

Hackos, J., Redish, J., 1998. User and task analysis for interface design. Wiley, New York.

Herculano-Houzel, S., 2009. The human brain in numbers: A linearly scaled-up primate brain. Front. Hum. Neurosci. 3 (31). Retrieved from http://www.ncbi.nlm.nih.gov/pmc/articles/PMC2776484.

Herrmann, R., 2011. How do we read words and how should we set them? OpenType.info blog, June 14. Retrieved from http://opentype.info/blog/2011/06/14/how-do-we-read-words-and-how-should-we-set-them.

Husted, B., 2012. Backup your data, then backup your backup. Ventura County Star. September 8. Retrieved from Web http://www.vcstar.com/news/2012/sep/08/back-up-your-data-then-back-up-your-backup.

Isaacs, E., Walendowski, A., 2001. Designing from both sides of the screen: How designers and engineers can collaborate to build cooperative technology. SAMS, Indianapolis.

Johnson, J., 1987. How faithfully should the electronic office simulate the real one? SIGCHI Bulletin 19 (2), 21–25.

Johnson, J., 1990. Modes in non-computer devices. Int. J. Man–Machine Stud. 32, 423–438.

Johnson, J., 2007. GUI bloopers 2.0: Common user interface design don'ts and dos. Morgan Kaufmann, San Francisco.

Johnson, J., Henderson, D.A., 2002. Conceptual models: Begin by designing what to design. Interactions 9 (1), 25–32.

Johnson, J., Henderson, D.A., 2011. Conceptual models: Core to good design. San Rafael, CA: Morgan and Claypool.

Johnson, J., Henderson, D.A., 2013. Conceptual models in a nutshell. Boxes and Arrows (online magazine). January 22. Retrieved from http://boxesandarrows.com/conceptual-models-in-a-nutshell.

Johnson, J., Roberts, T., Verplank, W., Smith, D.C., Irby, C., Beard, M., Mackey, K., 1989. The Xerox star: A retrospective. IEEE Comput. 22 (9), 11–29.

Jonides, J., Lewis, R.L., Nee, D.E., Lustig, C.A., Berman, M.G., Moore, K.S., 2008. The mind and brain of short-term memory. Annu. Rev. Psychol. 59, 193–224.

Kahneman, D., 2011. Thinking fast and slow. Farrar Straus and Giroux, New York.

Koyani, S.J., Bailey, R.W., Nall, J.R., 2006. Research-based web design and usability guidelines. U.S. Department of Health and Hum. Serv. Retrieved from usability.gov/pdfs/guidelines.html.

Krug, S., 2005. Don't make me think: A common sense approach to web usability, 2nd ed. New Riders Press, Indianapolis.

Lally, P., van Jaarsveld, H., Potts, H., Wardie, J., 2010. How are habits formed: Modeling habit formation in the real world. Eur. J. Soc. Pyschology 40 (6), 998–1009.

Lambert, G., 1984. A comparative study of system response time on program developer productivity. IBM Syst. J. 23 (1), 407–423.

Landauer, T.K., 1986. How much do people remember? Some estimates of the quantity of learned information in long-term memory. Cogn. Sci. 10, 477–493.

Larson, K., 2004. The Science of word recognition, Microsoft.com. July 2004, http://www.microsoft.com/typography/ctfonts/WordRecognition.aspx.

Liang, P., Zhong, N., Lu, S., Liu, J., Yau, Y., Li, K., Yang, Y., 2007. The neural mechanism of human numerical inductive reasoning process: A combined ERP and fMRI study. Springer-Verlag, Berlin.

Lindsay, P., Norman, D.A., 1972. Human information processing. Academic Press, New York and London.

Marcus, A., 1992. Graphic design for electronic documents and user interfaces. Addison-Wesley, Reading, MA.

Mastin, L., 2010. Short-term (working) memory. The human memory: What it is, how it works, and how it can go wrong. Retrieved from http://www.human-memory.net/types_short.html.

McAfee, 2012. Consumer alert: McAfee releases results of global unprotected rates study. McAfee blog, May 29. Retrieved from https://blogs.mcafee.com/consumer/family-safety/mcafee-releases-results-of-global-unprotected-rates.

McInerney, P., Li, J., 2002. Progress indication: Concepts, design, and implementation, IBM. Developer Works. Retrieved from www-128.ibm.com/developerworks/web/library/us-progind.

Microsoft Corporation, 2009. Windows user experience interaction guidelines. Retrieved from, http://www.msdn.microsoft.com/en-us/library/aa511258.aspx.

Miller, G.A., 1956. The magical number seven, plus or minus two: Some limits on our capacity for processing information. Psychol. Rev. 63, 81–97.

Miller, R., 1968. Response time in man–computer conversational transactions. Proc. IBM Fall Joint Comput. Conf. vol. 33, 267–277.

Minnery, B., Fine, M., 2009. Neuroscience and the future of human–computer interaction. Interactions 16 (2), 70–75.

Monti, M.M., Osherson, D.N., Martinez, M.J., Parsons, L.M., 2007. Functional neuroanatomy of deductive inference: A language-independent distributed network. NeuroImage 37 (3), 1005–1016.

Mullet, K., Sano, D., 1994. Designing visual interfaces: Communications oriented techniques. Prentice-Hall, Englewood Cliffs, NJ.

Nielsen, J., 1999. Designing web usability: The practice of simplicity. New Riders Publishing, Indianapolis.

Nielsen, J., 2003. Information foraging: Why Google makes people leave your site faster. Nielsen-Norman Group, June 30. http://www.nngroup.com/articles/information-scent/.

Nielsen, J., Molich, R., 1990. Heuristic evaluation of user interfaces. Proc. ACM CHI'90 Conf., Seattle, 249–256.

Nielsen, J., Mack, R.L., (Eds.), 1994. *Usability Inspection Methods*. John Wiley & Sons, Inc, New York.

Nichols, S., 2013. Social network burnout affecting six in ten Facebook users. V3.co.uk. Feb. 6. Retrieved from http://www.v3.co.uk/v3-uk/news/2241746/social-network-burnout-affecting-six-in-ten-facebook-users.

Norman, D.A., 1983a. Design rules based on analysis of human error. Commun. ACM. 26 (4), 254–258.

Norman, D.A., 1983b. Design principles for human–computer interfaces. In: Janda, A. (Ed.), Proceedings of the CHI-83 conference on human factors in computing systems, Boston. ACM Press, New York. Reprinted in R. M. Baecker and William A. S. Buxton (Eds.), Readings in human–computer interaction. San Mateo, CA: Morgan Kaufmann, 1987.

Norman, D.A., Draper, S.W., 1986. User-centered system design: New perspectives on human-computer interaction. CRC Press, Hillsdale, NJ.

Larson, K., 2004. The Science of word recognition, Microsoft.com, July 2004, http://www.microsoft.com/typography/ctfonts/WordRecognition.aspx.

Oracle Corporation/Sun Microsystems, 2001. Java look and feel design guidelines, 2nd ed. Retrieved from http://www.java.sun.com/products/jlf/ed2/book/index.html.

Perfetti, C., Landesman, L., 2001. The truth about download time. User Interface Engineering, Jan. 31. Retrieved from http://uie.com/articles/download_time/.

Rainie, L., Smith, A., Duggan, M., 2013. Coming and going on Facebook. Report from Pew Internet and American Life Project, Feb 5. Retrieved from http://www.pewinternet.org/~/media//Files/Reports/2013/PIP_Coming_and_going_on_facebook.pdf.

Raymond, J.E., Shapiro, K.L., Arnell, K.M., 1992. Temporary suppression of visual processing in an RSVP task: An attentional blink? J. Exp. Psychol. Hum. Percept. Perform. 18 (3), 849–860.

Redish, G., 2007. Letting go of the words: Writing web content that works. Morgan Kaufmann, San Francisco.

Robertson, G., Card, S., Mackinlay, J., 1989. The cognitive co-processor architecture for interactive user interfaces. Proceedings of the ACM Conference on User Interface Software and Technology (UIST'89). ACM Press. 10–18.

Robertson, G., Card, S., Mackinlay, J., 1993. Information visualization using 3D interactive animation. Commun. ACM. 36 (4), 56–71.

Rushinek, A., Rushinek, S., 1986. What makes users happy? Commun. ACM. 29, 584–598.

Sapolsky, R.M., 2002. A primate's memoir: A neuroscientist's unconventional life among the Baboons. Scribner, New York.

Schneider, W., Shiffrin, R.M., 1977. Controlled and automatic human information processing: 1. Detection, search, and attention. Psychol. Rev. 84, 1–66.

Schrage, M., 2005. The password is fayleyure. Technol. Rev. Retrieved from http://www. technologyreview.com/read_article.aspx?ch5specialsectionsandsc5securityandid516350.

Shneiderman, B., 1984. Response time and display rate in human performance with computers. ACM Comput. Surveys 16 (4), 265-285.

Shneiderman, B., 1987. Designing the user interface: Strategies for effective human–computer interaction, 1st ed. Addison-Wesley, Reading, MA.

Shneiderman, B., Plaisant, C., 2009. Designing the user interface: Strategies for effective human-computer interaction, 5th ed. Addison-Wesley, Reading, MA.

Simon, H.A., 1969. The sciences of the artificial. MIT Press, Cambridge, MA.

Simons, D.J., 2007. Scholarpedia 2 (5), 3244, http://www.scholarpedia.org/article/Inattentional_blindness.

Simons, D.J., Levin, D.T., 1998. Failure to detect changes in people during a real-world interaction. Psychon. Bull. Rev. 5, 644-669.

Simons, D.J., Chabris, C.F., 1999. Gorillas in our midst: Sustained inattentional blindness for dynamic events. Perception 28, 1059-1074.

Smith, S.L., Mosier, J.N., 1986. Guidelines for designing user interface software. National Technical Information Service, Springfield, VA Technical Report ESD-TR-86-278.

Soegaard, M., 2007. Gestalt principles of form perception. Interaction-Design.org. Retrieved from http://www.interaction-design.org/encyclopedia/gestalt_principles_of_form_perception.html.

Sohn, E., 2003. It's a math world for animals. Sci. News for Kids. Oct. 8. Retrieved from http://www.sciencenewsforkids.org/articles/20031008/Feature1.asp.

Sousa, D.A., 2005. How the brain learns to read. Corwin Press, Thousand Oaks, CA.

Stafford,T., Webb, M., 2005. Mind hacks:Tips and tools for using your brain. O'Reilly, Sebastapol, CA.

Stone, D., Jarrett, C., Woodroffe, M., Minocha, S., 2005. User interface design and evaluation. Morgan Kaufmann, San Francisco.

Thadhani, A., 1981. Interactive user productivity. IBM Syst. J. 20 (4), 407-423.

Thagard, P., 2002. Coherence in thought and action. MIT Press, Cambridge, MA.

Tufte, E., 2001. The visual display of quantitative information, 2nd ed. Graphics Press, Cheshire, Connecticut.

van Duyne, D.K., Landay, J.A., Hong, J.I., 2002. The design of sites: Patterns, principles, and processes for crafting a customer-centered web experience. Addison-Wesley, Reading, MA.

Waloszek, G., 2005. Vision and visual disabilities: An introduction, SAP Design Guild. Retrieved from, http://www.sapdesignguild.org/editions/highlight_articles_01/vision_physiology.asp.

Ware, C., 2008. Visual thinking for design. Morgan Kaufmann, San Francisco.

Ware, C., 2012. Information visualization: Perception for design, 3rd ed. Morgan Kaufmann, San Francisco.

Weber, P., 2013. Why Asiana Flight 214 crashed at San Francisco International Airport, The Week. July 8. Retrieved from, http://theweek.com/article/index/246523/why-asiana-flight-214-crashed-at-san-francisco-international-airport.

Weinschenk, S.M., 2009. Neuro web design: What makes them click? New Riders, Berkeley, CA.

Wolfmaier, T., 1999. Designing for the color-challenged: A challenge. ITG Publication. Retrieved from http://www.internettg.org/newsletter/mar99/accessibility_color_challenged.html.

Index

Note: Page numbers with "*b*" denote boxes; "*f*" figures; "*t*" tables.

Related Titles from Morgan Kaufmann

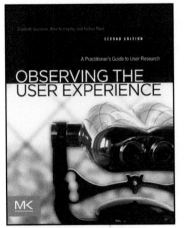

**Observing the User Experience,
2nd Edition**
A Practitioner's Guide to User Research
Elizabeth Goodman, Mike Kuniavsky,
Andrea Moed
ISBN: 9780123848697

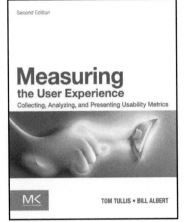

**Measuring the User Experience,
2nd Edition**
*Collecting, Analyzing, and Presenting Usability
Metrics*
Tom Tullis and Bill Albert
ISBN: 9780124157811

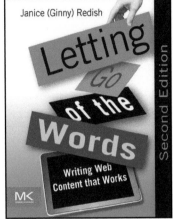

Letting Go of the Words, 2nd Edition
Writing Web Content that Works
Janice (Ginny) Redish
ISBN: 9780123859303

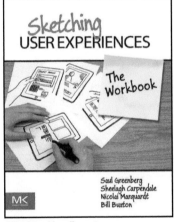

Sketching User Experiences
The Workbook
Saul Greenberg, Sheelagh Carpendale,
Nicolai Marquardt, Bill Buxton
ISBN: 9780123819598

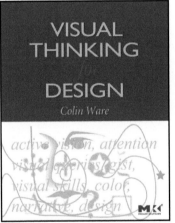

Visual Thinking
for Design
Colin Ware
ISBN: 9780123708960

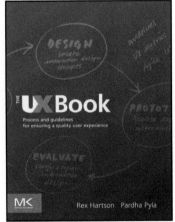

The UX Book
*Process and Guidelines for Ensuring a Quality
User Experience*
Rex Hartson and Partha Pyla
ISBN: 9780123852427

mkp.com

CPI Antony Rowe
Chippenham, UK
2018-12-14 13:06